Money, Distribution Conflict and Capital Accumulation

Also by Eckhard Hein:

Eckhard Hein (*author*)
KONZENTRATION UND PROFITRATENDIFFERENZIERUNG
Theoretische und empirische Aspekte

Andreas Schikora, Angela Fiedler and Eckhard Hein (*editors*)
POLITISCHE ÖKONOMIE IM WANDEL
Festschrift für Klaus Peter Kisker

Eckhard Hein (*author*)
GELD, EFFEKTIVE NACHFRAGE UND KAPITALAKKUMULATION
Eine Betrachtung aus Marxscher, Keynesscher und post-keynesianischer Perspektive

Wolfram von Bülow, Eckhard Hein, Klaus Köster, Winfried Krüger, Hans Peter Litz, Carlos Ossorio Capella and Klaus W. Schüler (*editors*)
GLOBALISIERUNG UND WIRTSCHAFTSPOLITIK

Eckhard Hein and Achim Truger (*editors*)
PERSPEKTIVEN SOZIALDEMOKRATISCHER WIRTSCHAFTSPOLITIK IN EUROPA

Eckhard Hein and Achim Truger (*editors*)
MODERNE WIRTSCHAFTSPOLITIK = KOORDINIERTE MAKROPOLITIK, ARGUMENTE AUS DEN WSI MITTEILUNGEN

Eckhard Hein, Arne Heise and Achim Truger (*editors*)
NEU-KEYNESIANISMUS – DER NEUE WIRTSCHAFTSPOLITISCHE MAINSTREAM?

Eckhard Hein (*author*)
VERTEILUNG UND WACHSTUM
Eine paradigmenorientierte Einführung unter besonderer Berücksichtigung der post-keynesianischen Theorie

Eckhard Hein, Torsten Niechoj, Thorsten Schulten and Achim Truger (*editors*)
EUROPAS WIRTSCHAFT GESTALTEN
Makroökonomische Koordinierung und die Rolle der Gewerkschaften

Eckhard Hein, Arne Heise and Achim Truger (*editors*)
FINANZPOLITIK IN DER KONTROVERSE

Eckhard Hein, Torsten Niechoj, Thorsten Schulten and Achim Truger (*editors*)
MACROECONOMIC POLICY CO-ORDINATION IN EUROPE AND THE ROLE OF THE TRADE UNIONS

Eckhard Hein, Arne Heise and Achim Truger (*editors*)
LÖHNE, BESCHÄFTIGUNG, VERTEILUNG UND WACHSTUM
Makroökonomische Analysen

Eckhard Hein, Arne Heise and Achim Truger (*editors*)
WAGES, EMPLOYMENT, DISTRIBUTION AND GROWTH
International Perspectives

Eckhard Hein, Arne Heise and Achim Truger (*editors*)
EUROPEAN ECONOMIC POLICIES – ALTERNATIVES TO ORTHODOX ANALYSIS AND POLICY CONCEPTS

Eckhard Hein and Achim Truger (*editors*)
MONEY, DISTRIBUTION AND ECONOMIC POLICY
Alternatives to Orthodox Macroeconomics

Philip Arestis, Eckhard Hein and Edwin Le Heron (*editors*)
ASPECTS OF MODERN MONETARY AND MACROECONOMIC POLICIES

Money, Distribution Conflict and Capital Accumulation

Contributions to 'Monetary Analysis'

Eckhard Hein

palgrave
macmillan

First published 2008 by
PALGRAVE MACMILLAN
Houndmills, Basingstoke, Hampshire RG21 6XS and
175 Fifth Avenue, New York, N.Y. 10010
Companies and representatives throughout the world

PALGRAVE MACMILLAN is the global academic imprint of the Palgrave Macmillan division of St. Martin's Press, LLC and of Palgrave Macmillan Ltd. Macmillan®is a registered trademark in the United States, United Kingdom and other countries. Palgrave is a registered trademark in the European Union and other countries.

ISBN-13: 978-0-230-52157-5 hardback
ISBN-10: 0-230-52157-6 hardback

This book is printed on paper suitable for recycling and made from fully managed and sustained forest sources. Logging, pulping and manufacturing processes are expected to conform to the environmental regulations of the country of origin.

A catalogue record for this book is available from the British Library.

Library of Congress Cataloging-in-Publication Data
Hein, Eckhard, 1963–

Money, distribution conflict and capital accumulation: contributions to 'monetary analysis' / Eckhard Hein.
p. cm.
Includes bibliographical references and index.
ISBN 0-230-52157-6 (alk. paper)
1. Monetary policy. 2. Saving and investment. 3. Credit. I. Title.
HG230.3.H443 2007
339.5'3—dc22 2007022294

10 9 8 7 6 5 4 3 2 1
17 16 15 14 13 12 11 10 09 08

Printed and bound in Great Britain by CPI Antony Rowe, Chippenham and Eastbourne

Contents

Foreword

Philip Arestis

This is a really exciting book and one that fully justifies its title: *Money, Distribution Conflict and Capital Accumulation*. There is a great deal on each aspect that the title clearly suggests. The analysis is not only sufficiently rich, but also extremely open-minded. It offers extensive coverage of those approaches that emphasize money, distribution conflict and capital accumulation. These are different from the more standard approaches, such as the 'New Consensus' theories, but the book does a great deal of justice to both sets, and this is commendable. At the same time, however, the book has a focus on those paradigms, which embed in them a number of characteristics highlighted in the title of the book. Most important to the analysis is the full integration of the role of money and credit into the models of distribution and growth, thereby contributing to the research programme of a 'monetary theory of production'. The main characteristic of this programme is the idea that both the volume of credit and the quantity of money are determined endogenously. The driving force of this research programme is the validity of the 'principle of aggregate demand', in the short and in the long run, an important ingredient, which replaces Say's law, the backbone of many of the other paradigms discussed in the book. It is also true, however, that there are important differences amongst the approaches to 'monetary analysis' discussed in the book. These are highlighted and closely examined, along with their theoretical and policy implications. Above all, the book provides its own approach to money, distribution conflict and capital accumulation in a way that avoids a number of problems in the other approaches. Overall, the book presents important contributions to a synthesis of monetary analysis, distribution and growth theory, on the one hand, and to an alternative to modern mainstream New Consensus macroeconomics, on the other hand.

Acknowledgements

I am grateful to the editors and publishers of the journals named below for permissions to draw on my papers published in their journals:

'Money, credit and the interest rate in Marx's economics. On the similarities of Marx's monetary analysis to post-Keynesian economics', *International Papers in Political Economy*, 2004, 11 (2): 1–43 (Chapter 5).

'Money, interest and capital accumulation in Karl Marx's economics: a monetary interpretation and some similarities to post-Keynesian approaches', *European Journal of the History of Economic Thought*, 2006, 13: 113–40 (Chapter 5).

'Interest, debt and capital accumulation – a Kaleckian approach', *International Review of Applied Economics*, 2006, 20: 337–52 (Section 13.2).

'Interest rate, debt, distribution and capital accumulation in a post-Kaleckian model', *Metroeconomica*, 2007, 58: 310–39 (Section 13.3).

'Wage bargaining and monetary policy in a Kaleckian monetary distribution and growth model: trying to make sense of the NAIRU', *Intervention: Journal of Economics*, 2006, 3: 305–29 (Chapter 16).

'On the (in-)stability and the endogeneity of the "normal" rate of capacity utilisation in a post-Keynesian/Kaleckian "monetary" distribution and growth model', *Indian Development Review*, 2006, 4: 129–50 (Chapter 17).

I am indebted to the referees of these journals for helpful comments on the papers I had submitted. Above all, I am most grateful to Philip Arestis for reading the whole manuscript, for extremely helpful comments and for his kind readiness to contribute a foreword. For comments and suggestions concerning different parts of the book, I would also like to thank Amit Bhaduri, Amitava Dutt, Giuseppe Fontana, Geoff Harcourt, Gustav Horn, Costas Lapavitsas, Marc Lavoie, Özlem Onaran, Sergio Rossi, Claudio Sardoni, Malcolm Sawyer, Klaus Schüler, Engelbert Stockhammer, Andranik Tangian, Hans-Michael Trautwein, Andrew Trigg and Achim Truger. I have also benefited from the discussion of some of the material contained in this book at conferences and seminars in

Berlin, Bilbao, Bremen, Cambridge, Dijon, Graz, Kansas City, London, New York, Oldenburg, Rethymnon, and Salt Lake City during recent years, and I would also like to thank the participants in these events. Many thanks also go to Jan-Oliver Menz, Barbara Schnieders, Till van Treeck, and Lena Vogel, who read the manuscript, compiled the lists of variables, figures and tables, and checked the references and quotations. Furthermore, I am grateful to Amanda Hamilton and her staff at Palgrave Macmillan for support throughout this project. It goes without saying that the people mentioned above are not responsible for any remaining errors in the book. For these I am alone responsible.

ECKHARD HEIN
DUESSELDORF, FEBRUARY 2007

List of Tables and Figures

Tables

Figures

List of Variables

a	capitalists' propensity to accumulate out of profits
B	stock of long-term credit
BK	banking sector
C	commodities
C_w	consumption out of wages
C_z	consumption out of rentiers' income
C_Π	consumption out of profits
c_z	propensity to consume out of rentiers' income
D	deposits
E	employment
E^N	employment with consistent target real wage rates of workers and firms
e	employment rate
e^N	employment rate with consistent target real wage rates of workers and firms
F	firm sector
g	accumulation rate, growth rate of the real capital stock
HH	household sector
HH_w	workers' households
HH_z	rentiers' households
h	profit share in nominal income
h^i	interest share in nominal income
h^n	share of profits of enterprise in nominal income
I	investment
I^g	gross investment
I^n	net investment
i	('real') long-term interest rate
i_b	rate of interest set by commercial banks
i_{cb}	base rate of interest set by the central bank
K	capital stock
K_c	capital costs expended in production
L	loans
LF	labour force
l	labour–output ratio
M	money
M_c	money in circulation
m	mark-up
m_B	interest rate mark-up of commercial banks

P	production process
p	commodity price (level)
q	velocity of circulation of a unit of money
r	rate of profit
r^n	rate of profit of enterprise
S	saving
S_z	saving out of rentiers' income
s_c	retention ratio
s_z	propensity to save out of rentiers' income
s_Π	propensity to save out of profits
u	rate of capacity utilization
u^N	rate of capacity utilization with consistent target real wage rates of workers and firms
v	capital–potential output ratio
W	wages
w	nominal wage rate
w^r	real wage rate
w^r_b	labour unions' or workers' target real wage rate
w^r_p	firms' target real wage rate
Y	output
Y^v	potential output determined by the capital stock
y	labour productivity
Z	interest or rentiers' income
α	coefficient in the accumulation function
β	coefficient in the accumulation function
γ	coefficient in the accumulation function
ε	coefficient in the labour unions' target real wage rate function
ϕ	coefficient in the labour unions' target real wage rate function
θ	coefficient in the accumulation function
λ	debt–capital ratio
Π	profits
Π^n	profits of enterprise
ρ	coefficient in the accumulation function
σ	saving rate
τ	coefficient in the accumulation function
ψ	unemployment rate
ψ^N	Non-Accelerating Inflation Rate of Unemployment (NAIRU)
Δx	change in the variable x
$\hat{x}$	growth rate of variable x
x^*	equilibrium value of variable x
x^D	demand for variable x
x^S	supply of variable x

1
Introduction: Money, Distribution Conflict and Capital Accumulation

The role of money and the question of its neutrality – or non-neutrality – have been a contested area of research in political economy, and later on in economics, from the very beginning, with no consensus established until the present. Relating to this issue, Schumpeter (1954) introduced the fundamental distinction between 'real analysis' and 'monetary analysis'. In 'real analysis', the equilibrium values of the economic system – that is, output, employment, distribution and growth – can be determined without any reference to monetary variables. In 'monetary analysis', however, monetary variables are not considered to be merely an inessential veil, but enter into economic theory at the very beginning, and the real equilibrium cannot be determined without reference to monetary variables.

Although important elements of 'monetary analysis' can also be found in Classical and Marx's economics, and have been developed by their modern proponents, 'monetary analysis' gained momentum in particular through Keynes's (1933) research programme of a 'monetary theory of production' and by the work of the Post-Keynesians thereafter. On the one hand, Post-Keynesian research further developed Keynes's monetary theory and removed or clarified some ambiguities therein. On the other hand, Post-Keynesians generated distribution and growth theories carrying Keynes's 'principle of effective demand', based on his view of a monetary production economy, from the short period, in the sense of a given capital stock, to the long period.

However, the explicit introduction of monetary variables into Post-Keynesian distribution and growth models started rather later, in the 1980s/early 1990s, is still incomplete and has to be developed further.

The present book contributes to this line of research and hence to the research programme of a 'monetary theory of production'. The focus is on the short-run and, in particular, on the long-run effects of monetary policies applying the interest rate tool in modern credit money economies, which are characterized by the autonomy of investment from saving also in the long run, the latent long-run underutilization of productive capacities, and by conflict over distribution of the social product. In particular, we will attempt to contribute to a synthesis of Post-Keynesian monetary theory and Post-Keynesian models of distribution and growth, on the one hand, and to a Post-Keynesian alternative to modern mainstream New Consensus macroeconomics, on the other hand.

In the first part of this book we will survey the different paradigms in economics applying Schumpeter's distinction between 'real analysis' and 'monetary analysis', and we will derive some implications for the relationship between monetary policy, distribution and capital accumulation. In chapter 2 we will start with a brief overview of Classical, Neoclassical, Neoclassical Synthesis, Monetarist, New Classical, New Keynesian, and New Consensus theories, which can all be considered as 'real analysis' in Schumpeter's terms. In chapters 4–6 this will be followed by a more detailed treatment of 'monetary analysis' which can be found in Classical theory and its modern proponents, that is the Neo-Ricardian monetary theory of distribution, in Marx's monetary economics and, in particular, in Keynes's approach of a 'monetary theory of production' and its Post-Keynesian developments. The common elements of these approaches to 'monetary analysis' and the major differences between them will be analysed, and they will be summarized in chapter 7. Whereas the views of modern capitalist economies as credit money economies also driven by effective demand in the long run are quite similar in these theories, there are some differences with respect to the views on the distribution effects of changes in the monetary interest rate.

The analysis in the first part of the book will provide the basis for a deeper investigation into the effects of changes in the monetary interest rate on distribution and capital accumulation in the second part. There, we will introduce the monetary interest rate, mainly determined by central bank policies, into Post-Keynesian demand-driven models of distribution and growth in the tradition of Nicholas Kaldor, Joan Robinson and Michal Kalecki. Having briefly reviewed the contributions of the three founding mother and fathers of Post-Keynesian distribution and growth theory to monetary analysis in chapter 9, we will start with the outline of a simple model economy, including a full description of a monetary circuit in chapter 10. Then, this model will be used to analyse and to compare the effects of changes in the interest rate induced by monetary policies in the different variants of Post-Keynesian distribution and growth theory, the Kaldor–Robinson model in chapter 11 and different types of Kaleckian models in chapter 12. As the Kaldor–Robinson model suffers from some serious limitations, in particular the neglect of distribution struggle and the assumption of full utilization of the capital stock in long-period equilibrium, the Kaleckian models will be extended in chapter 13. The extended models will cover the different approaches to the distributive effects of monetary policies contained in the schools of 'monetary analysis', and long-run debt dynamics will also be discussed. Chapter 14 will summarize our main results.

In the models discussed in the second part of the book, the inflationary impact of distribution conflict is excluded from the analysis. Distribution conflict and the use of monetary policies in setting the interest rate are assumed to affect the mark-up in firms' pricing, and hence distribution between firms, rentiers' and workers' households, but not the inflation rate. In the third part of the book we will then take into account the inflationary consequences of distribution conflict and monetary policy reactions fighting accelerating or decelerating inflation. We will make use of those monetary Kaleckian distribution and growth models developed in chapter 13. Doing this, we will address two important problems in Kaleckian models: in chapter 16, the role of an 'inflation barrier' or a 'Non-Accelerating-Inflation-Rate-of-Unemployment' (NAIRU) in this kind of model is analysed and there is also a discussion of the relationship to modern mainstream macroeconomic New Consensus models, building on the idea of a NAIRU as long-run equilibrium unemployment. In chapter 17, the problem of a persistent deviation of the long-run equilibrium rate of capacity utilization from the 'normal rate' of utilization conceived by firms when planning new investment in capital stock will be assessed. Addressing this problem, the sustainability of the main results of the Kaleckian models, the 'paradox of thrift' and at least the possibility of a 'paradox of costs', will be evaluated.

In the concluding chapter 18 the main achievements of this book, in particular its contributions to a synthesis of Post-Keynesian monetary theory and Post-Keynesian models of distribution and growth, on the one hand, and to an alternative to New Consensus macroeconomics, on the other, will be summarized and some implications for future research will be outlined.

Part I
Real and Monetary Analysis in Economic Paradigms

2
Real and Monetary Analysis in Economic Paradigms: Introduction to Part I

In political economy and in economics the neutrality, or non-neutrality, of money has been a contested area of research right from the beginning of this academic discipline, with no consensus established until present. Relating to this fundamental issue, Schumpeter (1954) made the important distinction between 'real analysis' and 'monetary analysis'.[1] In 'real analysis' the equilibrium values of the economic system, that is output, employment, distribution and growth, can be determined without any reference to monetary variables:

> Real Analysis proceeds from the principle that all essential phenomena of economic life are capable of being described in terms of goods and services, of decisions about them, and of relations between them. Money enters the picture only in the modest role of a technical device that has been adopted in order to facilitate transactions. This device can no doubt get out of order, and if it does it will indeed produce phenomena that are specifically attributable to its *modus operandi*. But so long as it functions normally, it does not affect the economic process, which behaves in the same way as it would in a barter economy: this is essentially what the concept of Neutral Money implies. (Schumpeter 1954, p. 277)

In 'monetary analysis', however, monetary variables are not considered to be only an inessential veil, but enter into economic theory at the very beginning and the real equilibrium cannot be determined without reference to money or monetary interest rates:

> Monetary Analysis introduces the element of money on the very ground floor of our analytical structure and abandons the idea that all essential features of economic life can be represented by a barter-economy model. Money prices, money incomes, and saving and

> investment decisions bearing upon these money incomes, no longer appear as expressions – sometimes convenient, sometimes misleading, but always nonessential – of quantities of commodities and services and of exchange ratios between them: they acquire a life and an importance of their own, and it has to be recognized that essential features of the capitalist process may depend upon the 'veil' and that the 'face behind it' is incomplete without it. (Schumpeter 1954, p. 278)

In the first part of the book we will survey the different paradigms in economics applying Schumpeter's distinction and exploring the implications for the analysis of the relationship between monetary variables and real variables – that is, output, employment, distribution and capital accumulation. We will start in chapter 3 with a brief overview of 'real analysis' in Classical, Neoclassical, Neoclassical Synthesis, Monetarist, New Classical, New Keynesian, and New Consensus theory. This will be followed by a more detailed treatment of 'monetary analysis'. 'Monetary analysis' can already be found in Classical theory and its modern proponents, in Marx's economics and, in particular, in Keynes's approach of a 'monetary theory of production' and its Post-Keynesian developments. In chapters 4–6 we will deal with these schools of thought in greater depth, and in chapter 7 we will summarize the implications for the further analysis of monetary policy, distribution and capital accumulation.

3

Real Analysis in Classical, Neoclassical, Neoclassical Synthesis, Monetarist, New Classical, New Keynesian, and New Consensus Theories

Classical orthodoxy since David Ricardo, Lord Overstone and Robert Torrens has assumed the long-run neutrality of money applying the quantity theory of money as proposed by David Hume. In the long run, when prices have adjusted to their equilibrium values, there is a proportional relationship between the quantity of money supplied and the level of prices, assuming that money does not consist of commodity money but of token (paper) money.[2] In the short run, however, with fixed prices and given expectations, a change in the quantity of money supply affects output and employment. Therefore, the classical dichotomy between the real and the monetary sphere is a phenomenon of the long run. The neutrality hypothesis with respect to the effects of monetary policy is further on only related to real *quantities*. The existence and the use of money as a means of circulation are generally assumed to *qualitatively* improve the allocation efficiency of a market system by means of reducing transaction and information costs.

Even the allocation-improving aspect of money as a means of circulation and transaction is neglected by general equilibrium theory in the tradition of Walras, Arrow and Debreu, in its a-temporal and its inter-temporal variant.[3] In a frictionless model in which every imaginable activity and contract ranging into the future can be regulated today, there is no use of worthless token money. Each commodity can be the 'numeraire' which is required to calculate relative temporal and inter-temporal prices. But money as a means of actual circulation or transaction has no place in this kind of models. Money as a means of circulation and Walrasian markets even exclude each other, according to Laidler (1988). And Frank Hahn argues:

> The most serious challenge that the existence of money poses to the theorist is this: the best developed model of the economy cannot find room for it. The best developed model is, of course, the Arrrow-Debreu version of a Walrasian general equilibrium. A world in which all conceivable contingent future contracts are possible neither needs nor wants intrinsically worthless money. (Hahn 1982, p. 1)

The Classical hypothesis of long-run neutrality of money was not seriously questioned by the developments in economics following the publication of Keynes's *General Theory* (1936): In the emerging Neoclassical Synthesis there is an inherent long-run tendency towards full-employment equilibrium, and only rigidities in the market system can prevent the economy from reaching this equilibrium: the liquidity trap, the investment trap, and rigid nominal wages.[4] Only in these cases, do economic policies have real effects and may be required to bring the economy back to its long-run equilibrium determined by production technologies and preferences. Monetary policy has only a minor role to play when it comes to pushing the economy back to full employment equilibrium, because it is only effective in the case of rigid nominal wages. Fiscal policies are generally considered to be superior, because they are also effective in the liquidity and the investment trap.

From a methodological point of view, Milton Friedman's Monetarism, which had become dominant since the late 1960s/early 1970s, differs little from the Neoclassical Synthesis:[5] Money and monetary policies have short-run real effects, but are neutral in the long run when 'adaptive expectations' have adjusted to monetary shocks. The Phillips curve allows for a short-run trade-off between inflation and unemployment. In the long run, however, the Phillips curve is vertical, and changes in the quantity of money supply only affect inflation. Monetarism differs from the Neoclassical Synthesis only with respect to the firmer belief in the stability of the real economic sector and in the stability of the money demand function in a capitalist market economy.

Whereas in Monetarism, assuming 'adaptive expectations', money and monetary policies have at least short-run real effects, in the New Classical economics of the 1970s, applying 'rational expectations', even these short-run real effects are excluded.[6] In contrast to moneyless general equilibrium theory with universal future markets, New Classical models take money and expectations into account, but the way expectations formation is conceived excludes real effects: All economic agents have access to information about the future course of events, they all apply the New Classical model in order to interpret these information, and they act accordingly. This assumption is therefore identical with assuming the existence of universal future markets. Money does exist, but it is inessential in every real respect; money is 'super-neutral'. This conviction also dominates the Real Business Cycle School of the 1980s/1990s.[7]

Since the 1990s this complete exclusion of monetary variables from macroeconomics has been overcome by New Keynesian economics and by the recently proposed New Consensus models.[8] The New Consensus models are characterized essentially by three equations: 1. an aggregate demand function derived from households' and firms' optimization behaviour, which relates the output gap inversely to the real interest rate, 2. an expectations-augmented Phillips curve which makes the rate of inflation positively dependent on the output gap in the short run, and 3. a central bank reaction function in which the nominal interest rate set by the central bank is determined by the equilibrium real interest rate, by the output gap, and by the deviation of actual inflation from the inflation target (Taylor rule). These models generate results similar to the Neoclassical Synthesis and to Monetarism, but they are different in two aspects.

First, rigidities are no longer introduced 'ad hoc', but are the results of rational behaviour in imperfect markets with imperfect contracts and asymmetric information, which means that these models rely on 'microfoundation'. In the short run, a downward-sloping Phillips curve and a trade-off between inflation and unemployment, rejected by New Classicals and Real Business Cycle proponents, is derived again. Similar to the old Neoclassical Synthesis and the Monetarist model, monetary policies have short-run real effects on output and employment, because prices and nominal wages are less flexible than quantities supplied and demanded. Therefore, monetary policy intervention can speed up the process towards equilibrium.

Secondly, in particular in the New Consensus models, the instrument variable of the central bank is no longer the money supply but the short-term interest rate. New Consensus models have accepted that in modern credit money economies the quantities of credit and money are endogenous to the macroeconomic process. Commercial banks supply credit to creditworthy borrowers and the central bank accommodates the required amount of central bank money. All that monetary policy can do is to determine the price of central bank money, the short-term interest rate. In the long run, when inflation has adjusted to the central bank's target rate and unemployment is equal to the NAIRU (Non-Accelerating-Inflation-Rate-of-Unemployment) determined by structural characteristics of the labour market, the wage bargaining and the social benefit system, the real interest rate controlled by the central bank has to be equal to the equilibrium real rate of interest, the 'natural rate'.

The New Keynesian and New Consensus models are therefore quite similar to Wicksell's (1898) model of a pure credit economy.[9] In this model the equilibrium rate of interest is given by real factors, but the monetary interest rate determined by monetary policies may deviate from this rate causing cumulative disequilibrium processes. However, Wicksell remains cautious with respect to identifying the real rate of interest with the marginal productivity of capital. Capital as a value magnitude depends on the distribution of income and the former varies with the latter. In order to determine the marginal productivity of capital, therefore, the rate of interest has to be known and cannot be determined by marginal productivity (Kurz 1987a).

Although they have reintroduced monetary variables, mainstream New Keynesian approaches and New Consensus models pursue 'real analysis' in Schumpeter's definition. The long-run equilibrium is exclusively determined by real variables. Monetary variables only matter during short-run deviations from long-run equilibrium. This verdict, however, may not be true for the whole range of New Keynesian theories.

New Keynesian models, which focus on asymmetric information, moral hazard and adverse selection in financial markets, may generate multiple equilibria, path dependence or cumulative instabilities (Greenwald/Stiglitz 2003). Monetary policies may therefore have long-run real effects (Trautwein 2000). The same is true for New Keynesian labour market models in which short-run unemployment determined by the goods market affects the NAIRU through the phenomenon of 'hysteresis' (Ball 1999; Blanchard/Summers 1987, 1988). We will come back to the implications of these developments in chapter 16 below.

4
Monetary Analysis in Classical Economics: Banking School and Neo-Ricardian Monetary Theory of Distribution

Whereas Classical orthodoxy relied on the quantity theory of money, in the Banking-Currency-Controversy the proponents of the Banking School (Tooke, Fullarton) rejected the determination of the level of prices by the quantity of money.[10] On the one hand, it was argued that money also serves as a store of value so that changes in the quantity of money supply need not necessarily enter circulation and affect the level of prices. On the other hand, a distinction was made between 'paper money' issued by the state and 'paper credit' consisting of bank notes issued by commercial banks, and hence between a money circuit and a credit circuit. Whereas 'paper money' issued by the state can exceed the amount required for circulation and hence affect the price level, for bank notes the 'law of reflux' applies: Bank notes return to the issuing bank and are therefore withdrawn from circulation. The quantity of credit money becomes an endogenous variable which is not under the control of the monetary authorities.[11] It is, rather, determined by the demand for credit and adjusts to the requirements of circulation.

According to the Banking School theorists, the general price level is not determined by monetary aggregates but by production costs, and in particular by interest costs. It is supposed that in the long run, there is a positive relationship between the interest rate and the general level of prices. Monetary policy may therefore affect the price level, but in another way and with opposite results compared to those derived from the quantity theory of money.

The implications of the Banking School view for the relationship between interest rates, distribution and accumulation have been explored by some Neo-Ricardian authors applying Classical long-period analysis.[12] Whereas the degree of freedom of Sraffa's (1960) production price model was closed traditionally by assuming a given subsistence real wage rate, the Neo-Ricardian 'monetary theory of distribution' rather proposes a closure by a given rate of profit determined by the rate of interest. This closure was already suggested by Sraffa himself:

> The rate of profits, as a ratio, has a significance which is independent of any prices, and can well be 'given' before the prices are fixed. It is accordingly susceptible of being determined from outside the system of production, in particular by the level of the money rates of interest. (Sraffa 1960, p. 33)

In these Neo-Ricardian models, the long-term rate of interest determined by the central bank and/or financial markets is part of firms' normal costs which have to be covered by production prices. The rate of profit of enterprise (r^n) is taken as given and is determined by the 'risks and troubles' of real investment. The rate of interest (i) and the rate of profit of enterprise are therefore independently determined variables and add up to the general rate of profit (r): $r = r^n + i$. With a given nominal wage rate, long-run changes in the rate of interest affect firms' normal costs and hence production prices. The real wage rate becomes a residual variable which is adversely affected by the rate of interest. Labour unions and wage bargaining have no longer any direct effect on functional income distribution. There will only be an effect on income shares, if distribution struggle influences monetary policy, because monetary authorities set the short-term interest rate and have a major impact on long-term rates. However, the determination of the rate of profit of enterprise in this view and the following constancy of this rate in the face of changing interest rates have been questioned, because it precludes that profits of enterprise may be compressed when interest rates rise (Mongiovi/Rühl 1993; Nell 1988; Wray 1988a).

The quantity of money in this Neo-Ricardian view is determined endogenously by the level of economic activity. The general level of prices depends on the nominal wage rate when the production technology, the 'risks and troubles' of real investment determining the rate of profit of enterprise, and the rate of interest are given.

Assessing the effects on capital accumulation and growth, temporary changes in the rate of interest have to be distinguished from permanent changes (Pivetti 1991, pp. 41–51). Temporary changes in the rate of interest do not affect normal costs and leave the price level and the general rate of profit unchanged. Investment, output and employment are adversely affected. Rising interest rates may trigger falling prices, if increasing unemployment weakens the labour unions' bargaining position and nominal wages and unit labour costs start to fall.

With permanent changes in the rate of interest, there will be no direct effects on investment, because the general rate of profit changes in the same direction. However, the concomitant change in functional income shares may have indirect effects. Two countervailing forces have to be taken into account: On the one hand, an increasing general rate of profit, *ceteris paribus,* means falling real wages and real unit labour costs which will stimulate investment. On the other hand, there is a redistribution from wage incomes to rentiers' incomes which dampens consumption demand, because the propensity to consume of the latter will be lower than the former. This will restrict investment. The net effect of a change in interest rates on capital accumulation is therefore theoretically indeterminate. It follows that there is no general 'a priori' relationship between the level of interest rates and capital accumulation comparing long-run positions of the economic system.

5
Monetary Analysis in Marx's Economics[13]

Marx's theory of capital accumulation and growth has usually been characterized as 'real analysis' in Schumpeter's (1954) categories. In Marxian theories of accumulation and crisis, focusing on 'underconsumption', 'profit squeeze' or 'falling rate of profit' arguments, money and a monetary interest rate only enter the stage, when general tendencies have already been derived from 'real analysis'.[14] Under these conditions, it comes as no surprise that in modern discussions of distribution and growth Marx's theory is considered to be more similar to Classical 'real analysis' than to Keynes's or to Post-Keynesian 'monetary analysis' (Amadeo 1986a; Marglin 1984a), which will be surveyed below.

Since the publication of Keynes's *General Theory* (1936), however, there has been a range of papers which have attempted to show the similarities between Marx's and Keynes's analysis in the fields of money, effective demand and interest rates.[15] From this perspective, Marx's economics should rather be considered as 'monetary analysis'. Recently, renewed attention has been drawn to the monetary dimension of Marx's economics and its relation to Post-Keynesian economics.[16] From this perspective, Marx's economics can be seen as one of the sources of a broader Post-Keynesian research programme, not only because his theory of capitalist reproduction has had a major impact on Kalecki's theory of effective demand, but also because his monetary economics fit quite well into the Post-Keynesian research programme of a 'monetary theory of production'.

5.1 Marx's 'monetary theory of value'

The interpretation of Marx's theory of value as a 'monetary theory of value' follows the early work by Rubin (1973) and the more recent publications by Heinrich (1991), Matthews (1996), Reuten (1988, 1995), and Williams (2000), among others. There it is shown that the category of value in Marx's theory necessarily includes the category of money and that the theory of value has to contain a theory of money as well. From this it follows that Marx's theory of value cannot be seen as a 'labour embodied theory of value' and his theory of money need not be interpreted as a 'commodity theory of money'. Instead, Marx's theory of value can be interpreted as a 'monetary theory of value', and his theory of money as a 'token' or 'credit theory of money'.

As is well known, Marx's analysis of capitalist reproduction in *Capital*, Vol. I, starts with the analysis of the commodity as the elementary form of wealth in bourgeois society (Marx 1867, pp. 43–75). The products of individual labour in capitalist market economies, characterized by the social division of labour, assume the form of commodities. The co-ordination of the social division of labour through the exchange of commodities takes place in the single social sphere of capitalist economies, in the market sphere. In this sphere, private individual labour expended has to prove that it is a necessary part of the social expenditure of labour, i.e. private labour has to prove to be 'socially necessary labour'.

According to Marx, 'socially necessary labour' is defined as follows: First, it is labour performed under the average technical conditions of production and with average skills and intensity (Marx 1867, p. 47). Second, it requires that the product can be sold in the market sphere (Marx 1867, p. 109). From this it follows that 'socially necessary labour' can neither directly be expended in a specific production process nor be measured by the expenditure of concrete labour. For the substance of value in Marx's economics, we rather get 'abstract labour' which is constituted by exchange and which does not exist prior to the circulation of commodities (Reuten 1988, p. 127). The magnitude of value can therefore only be expressed in a social category in which the product of individual labour is allotted a certain portion of social labour. The socialization of private labour in a capitalist market economy requires the existence of a universal equivalent as representative of abstract labour and social value to which individual labour can be related. This universal equivalent may be termed 'money'.

In the development of the 'money form' from the succession of the 'elementary or accidental form of value', the 'total or expanded form of value' and the 'general form of value' in *Capital*, Vol. I, Marx (1867, pp. 54–75) demonstrates the necessity of a universal equivalent for capitalist reproduction. Money as the result of the development of the value form is not considered to be a device facilitating the exchange of commodities in a barter economy, as in orthodox Classical economics, but is an indispensable condition for commodity production and exchange in capitalist economies (Williams 2000).

Marx's claim that only a commodity ('gold') which incorporates value itself can assume the money form and hence become the universal equivalent (Marx 1867, p. 75), however, cannot be sustained within the 'monetary theory of value' sketched above, as Heinrich (1991), Lipietz (1982), Matthews (1996), Reuten (1988, 1995) and Williams (1992, 2000) have convincingly made clear. Since money has to represent 'abstract labour', its value cannot be determined by the amount of 'concrete labour' expended in the production of a certain money commodity. From this it follows that there is no theoretical metallism in Marx's theory of money (Matthews 1996).[17] Money rather is a socially accepted representative of the universal equivalent which has to be guaranteed by social institutions.

This understanding of money is perfectly compatible with the modern credit money system which can be described as a hierarchy of promises to pay with increasing social validity and liquidity from the bottom to the top (Evans 1997). Graziani (1997) even argues that in Marx's theory the capital–labour relation requires credit money because the purchase of labour power is logically prior to the production of commodities and hence also to the production of a money commodity. In a credit money system, payment between two parties takes place by means of a promise to pay of a third party with higher social validity and liquidity (Foley 1987; Smithin 2003a, pp. 28–35). The ultimate means of payment on the national level is the promise to pay of the social institution 'central bank', central bank money. On the international level, it is central bank money issued by the central bank of the key currency country.[18]

5.2 The level of prices, the rejection of Say's law and the endogeneity of money

According to Marx (1867, pp. 97–106), the first function of money is that of a measure of value and a standard of price. In Marx's commodity theory of money the level of prices is given by the ratio of the weighted average labour value of the commodities in circulation to the labour value of a unit of the money commodity. If the necessity of a money commodity is rejected, however, the level of prices will have to be determined in a different way. As Foley (1983) proposed, the level of prices and the value of money can be seen as given by entrepreneurial pricing which itself depends on the trend of accumulation and on the distribution struggle between capital and labour. The money wage rate therefore assumes a prominent role in the determination of the price level (Matthews 1996). It follows that the level of prices has nothing to do with the supply of money, as supposed by the quantity theory of money.[19]

The second function of money is that of a means of circulation (Marx 1867, pp. 106–30). Commodities (C) have to be traded for money (M) in a capitalist economy. The use of money may hence interrupt the succession of sales (C – M) and purchases (M – C) in the circuit C – M – C. This function of money provides Marx with the first argument to reject Ricardo's version of Say's law in his *Theories of Surplus Value* and constitutes his 'possibility theory of crisis' (Marx 1861–63, pp. 499–508).[20] In Marx's 'possibility theory of crisis' the existence and the use of money is the condition why a general crisis of overproduction *may* occur; it is not yet an explanation why an actual crisis *will* occur.[21] Since money also has the potential to function as a store of value (hoarding), a role of money subsumed under the third function of 'money as money' by Marx (1867, pp. 130–4) in *Capital*, Vol. I, an increase in the willingness to hoard causes a lack of aggregate demand for the economy as a whole and may therefore trigger a general crisis.

A 'general glut'[22] can, however, only occur if the demand for money as a store of value does not constitute a demand for production. If money is a reproducible commodity, an increase in demand for that commodity may cause a partial crisis due to a disturbance of the proportions of demand, which, however, is conceded by the proponents of Say's law, but it will not cause a general crisis due to insufficient aggregate demand. A lack of aggregate demand may only arise if there are no resources devoted to the production of money. Therefore, money has to be non-commodity money to sustain the critique of Say's law in Marx's 'possibility theory of crisis' and to pose the problem of effective demand to capitalist economies. Marx, however, does not seem to have been aware of this problem and of the contradiction that arises between the rejection of Say's law, on the one hand, and the simultaneous acceptance of a commodity theory of money, on the other hand.

For Marx, a second argument against Say's law derives from the function of money as a means of payment in capitalist production (Marx 1861–63, p. 511), a function Marx subsumes under 'money as money' in *Capital*, Vol. I (Marx 1867, pp. 134–41). Money functions as a means of payment when the sale of a commodity and the realization of its price are separated. The seller becomes a creditor, the buyer a debtor, and money is the standard and the subject of a creditor–debtor contract.

Money as a means of payment, therefore, implies a modern credit money system. In such a system, on the one hand, the demand for commodities is no longer limited by income created in production. The crucial nexus of income with expenditure and saving with investment in Ricardo's version of Say's law is hence relaxed. On the other hand, money as a means of payment increases the vulnerability and fragility of the system. Capitalists do not only have to find appropriate demand for their produced commodities, but they have to find it within a certain period of time in order to be able to meet their payment commitments. If there are unanticipated changes in market prices for final products between the purchase of a commodity as an input for production and the sale of the final product, capitalists may be unable to meet their payment commitments. Default of individual capitals may interrupt credit chains and cause a general crisis.[23]

In the discussion of the role of money as a means of circulation in *Capital*, Vol. I, Marx (1867, pp. 116–24) also shows that the quantity of money necessary for circulation (M_c) is given by the volume of traded commodities (Y), the average price of these commodities (p), which is independent of the quantity of money as shown above, and the velocity of circulation of a unit of money (q): $M_c = pY/q$. For capitalist reproduction to proceed smoothly, the quantity of money or the velocity of circulation have to adjust passively to the needs of circulation.

The rejection of Say's law and its necessary replacement by a theory of effective demand as well as the need for endogenous money for the expansion of capitalist economies also become clear in Marx's discussion of simple and expanded reproduction in *Capital*, Vol. II (Marx 1885, pp. 396–527). In the schemes of reproduction Marx analyses the conditions for capitalist reproduction in a two-sector model without foreign trade and economic activity by the state. Sector 1 produces means of production and sector 2 produces means of consumption.[24] Commodities enter circulation with a given price to be realised, consistent with the arguments given above.

The supply price of each sector is given by constant capital costs expended in production (K_c), wage costs (W) and profits (Π). The demand for output of sector 1 consists of gross investment (I^g) in constant capital of both sectors, the demand for output of sector 2 consists of consumption demand out of profits (C_Π) and out of wages (C_w). Assuming that 'workers spend what they get', we obtain from the demand-supply equilibrium $K_{c1} + W_1 + \Pi_1 = I_1^g + I_2^g$ in sector 1 and $K_{c2} + W_2 + \Pi_2 = C_{w1} + C_{\Pi 1} + C_{w2} + C_{\Pi 2}$ in sector 2 the familiar proportionality condition for simple reproduction in which there is no net investment: $I_2^g = C_{w1} + C_{\Pi 1}$. Sector 1's supply of investment goods for sector 2 must be equal to sector 2's supply of consumption goods for sector 1. Marx also shows that expanded reproduction and therefore balanced growth in capitalist economies is generally possible, and he derives the proportionality conditions as an extension of the condition presented above for simple reproduction. Here, however, is not the place to discuss the related details.[25]

Besides this familiar proportionality condition, the schemes of reproduction also contain a treatment of the effective demand problem and contribute to the 'possibility theory of crisis'. From the equality of aggregate demand and aggregate supply and the assumption that workers do not save, we get: $\Pi_1 + \Pi_2 = I_1^n + I_2^n + C_{\Pi 1} + C_{\Pi 2}$, where $I^n = I^g - K_c$ denotes net investment. From this, Kalecki's (1968) interpretation of Marx's schemes of reproduction arises: As capitalists cannot determine their sales and their profits but can only decide about their expenditures on net investment and consumption goods, these expenditures have to ensure that *produced* profits will become *realized* profits. Therefore, net investment determines saving in Marx's schemes of reproduction. A realisation failure, the inability to sell commodities at predetermined prices, may occur if there is insufficient investment or consumption demand by capitalists. Aggregate supply will then exceed aggregate demand and the economy will suffer from unused productive capacity and unemployment. So far Marx's 'possibility theory of crisis' takes us.

In order to come closer to an 'actual theory of crisis', it is necessary to analyse the determinants of the major components of effective demand. It has been argued, however, that there is no theory of investment demand in Marx's schemes of reproduction and hence no determination of the level of output or the rate of growth of the economy (Kalecki 1968; Sebastiani 1991). We hold, however, that such a theory is implicit in production and investment finance also present in the schemes of reproduction. Capitalists' expenditures as the causal force of income and profits require that these expenditures can be financed independently of current income. Capitalists need access to money in order to get the process of reproduction started. In the schemes of reproduction a detailed treatment of related monetary flows can be found. Marx (1885, pp. 329–54, 415–26) shows that already for simple reproduction the circulation of commodities requires money advances by capitalists. After a given period of production capitalists enter circulation with the produced commodities and with an amount of money necessary for circulation.

> He advances to himself (immaterial whether out of his own pocket or by means of credit from the pocket of somebody else) money in

> anticipation of surplus value still to be snatched by him; but in doing so he also advances a circulating medium for the realisation of surplus value to be realised later. ... So far as the entire capitalist class is concerned, the proposition that it must itself throw into circulation the money required for the realization of its surplus-value (correspondingly also for the circulation of its capital, constant and variable) not only fails to appear paradoxical, but stands forth as a necessary condition of the entire mechanism. For there are only two classes: the working class disposing only of its labour-power, and the capitalist class, which has a monopoly of the social means of production and money. (Marx 1885, pp. 424–5)

The necessary amount of money to be advanced by capitalists is determined by the volume of commodities to be traded, the average price of the commodities and the velocity of circulation of a unit of money. With the prices of commodities given and not being affected by the quantity of money, in a growing economy the money advanced by capitalists has to increase from period to period. As potential sources for additional money advances and hence for the endogeneity of money, Marx (1885, pp. 349–50) discusses the transfer of money from hoards and an increasing velocity of money in circulation (Sardoni 1997b). But these sources can only temporarily facilitate an ongoing process of economic expansion, because hoards have a finite amount and the velocity of circulation of money has an upper bound due to payment conventions and institutional factors. In the long run, therefore, the money stock has to increase by means of increasing the production of the money commodity, according to Marx (1885, p. 350, pp. 494–5).[26] As there is no necessity of a money commodity in Marx's monetary economics, we can conceive of the adjustment of the quantity of money to the rate of expansion of the capitalist economy by means of creation and destruction of credit money. In his presentation of Marx's theory, Foley puts it as follows:

> The sustainable rate of growth of the system obviously depends on the level of such new borrowing: the higher the total borrowing, the faster the rate of expanded reproduction that can be achieved by the system. (Foley 1986b, p. 89)

As capitalist expansion presupposes the expansion of credit, the conditions of credit are crucial for capital accumulation and economic growth (Sardoni 1997b). The availability and the price of credit may have an important impact on effective demand, especially on capitalist investment. This is already clear in the circuit of capital discussed by Marx (1867, pp. 145–53) in *Capital*, Vol. I. Capitalists advance money (M) in order to buy commodities (C), means of production and labour power, which are combined in the production process (P), the result being a bundle of commodities (C′) which has to be sold for a higher amount of money (M′): M – C...P...C′ – M′. The difference between M′ and M is of course money profits (Π).

In a growing economy in which at least parts of money advances have to be financed by means of credit, capitalists will only advance money if they have access to credit and if expected money profits will be sufficient to cover credit costs. As money advances by the capitalist class as a whole are of utmost importance for the realization of produced profits, realized profits will depend on the relation between expected profits and credit costs – that is, on the relation between the expected profit rate and the rate of interest. This relation will therefore be of utmost importance for the formulation of a Marxian theory of effective demand and capital accumulation and is analysed next.

5.3 Credit, rate of interest and rate of profit

In *Capital*, Vol. III, Marx (1894, pp. 400–13) distinguishes between commercial credit and bank credit. Bank credit may increase if commercial banks discount commercial credit (bills of exchange) or if additional credit is granted. In this context, Marx does not suppose that credit supply of commercial banks is limited by private saving but assumes that commercial banks can, in principle, create credit without limits which will then circulate as credit money (De Brunhoff 1976, pp. 93–9; Reuten 1988).[27]

> The credit given by a banker may assume various forms, such as bills of exchange on other banks, cheques on them, credit accounts of the same kind, and finally, if the bank is entitled to issue notes – bank-notes of the bank itself. A bank-note is nothing but a draft upon a banker, payable at any time to the bearer, and given by the banker in place of private drafts. This last form of credit appears particular important and striking to the layman, first, because this form of credit money breaks out of the confines of mere commercial circulation into general circulation, and serves there as money; and because in most countries the principal banks issuing notes, being a particular mixture of national and private banks, actually have the national credit to back them, and their notes are more or less legal tender; because it is

> apparent here that the banker deals in credit itself, a bank-note being merely a circulating token of credit. (Marx 1894, pp. 403–4)

The quantity of credit money is therefore endogenous for capitalist reproduction and is determined by credit demand of capitalists.[28] Analysing the medium of circulation in the credit system, Marx concludes: 'The quantity of circulation notes is regulated by the turnover requirements, and every superfluous note wends its way back immediately to the issuer' (Marx 1894, p. 524). The evolution of the contract and credit system implies the establishing of interest-bearing capital with the interest rate as a claim on a part of surplus value produced by productive labourers. Since the capitalist production process requires monetary advances, each sum of money may assume the role of interest-bearing capital which can be 'sold' for interest (Marx 1894, pp. 338–57). The circuit of capital may, therefore, be framed by a credit relation $M - M'$ and extends to: $M - M - C...P...C' - M'' - M'$, with the difference $M'' - M = \Pi$ as profits and the difference $M' - M = Z$ as interest (Z). Total profits split into profits of enterprise (Π^n) and interest: $\Pi = \Pi^n + Z$ (Marx 1894, pp. 358–90).

According to the different functions in the extended circuit of capital, the capitalist class can be distinguished into money capitalists and functioning capitalists. Functioning capitalists are ready to borrow from money capitalists and to pay interest because money has the potential to generate money profits, if it is used to initiate a process of production in which the expenditure of labour power generates surplus value. Since also own capital advanced for production purposes yields imputed interest, the rate of profit on total capital advanced (r) can always be conceived as a sum of the rate of profit of enterprise (r^n) and the rate of interest (i): $r = r^n + i$. In order to make functioning capitalists advance money for production purposes, the rate of profit has to exceed the rate of interest to allow for a positive rate of profit of enterprise.

Following Marx, there is an inverse relation between interest and profits of enterprise. Variations in interest rates do not affect the value or the price of commodities but only have an effect on the distribution of surplus value or total profits between money capitalists and functioning capitalists. Variations in the rate of interest have no influence on the rate of profit but affect the rate of profit of enterprise inversely:[29]

> ... profit of enterprise is not related as an opposite to wage-labour, but only to interest. ... assuming the average profit to be given, the rate of the profit of enterprise is not determined by wages, but by the rate

of interest. It is high or low in inverse proportion to it. (Marx 1894, p. 379)

From this it follows that Marx's determination of income shares takes place in two stages. In the first stage, Marx considers the rate of profit to be determined by the distribution conflict between capital and labour. With the technical conditions of production given, the rate of profit is determined by the real wage rate. In the second stage, the rate of interest is a result of the distribution conflict between money capitalists and functioning capitalists and makes the rate of profit of enterprise a residual variable. In these two steps the two degrees of freedom of Marx's production price model are closed.

Although the rate of profit of enterprise in Marx's economics can be considered as remuneration for the 'risks and troubles' of real investment, Marx's view must be distinguished from the Classical views of Smith and Ricardo and the Neo-Ricardian view referred to above, which consider the rate of interest and the rate of profit of enterprise to be independent variables which do not affect each other and which therefore can be summed up to derive the general rate of profit (Pivetti 1987a). The recent attempts by Ciccarone (1998), Panico (1985) and Pivetti (1985, 1987a, 1987b, 1991) to close the degree of freedom of Sraffa's (1960) Classical production price model by means of an exogenous rate of interest, mentioned above, can therefore not be applied to Marx's theory.[30] As this procedure has to assume a constant rate of profit of enterprise when the interest rate varies, it ignores the distribution conflict between money capital and industrial capital (Argitis 2001). This conflict is essential for Marx's theory. In Marx's economics the rate of interest can therefore not be taken to determine the rate of profit.

In Marx's two-stage determination of income shares, the rate of interest is assumed to be an exogenous variable for production and growth. The rate of interest is determined in the market for money capital, but there is no 'natural rate' as centre of gravity for actual rates (Marx 1894, pp. 358–69). Instead, the rate of interest is given by concrete historical, institutional and political factors which reflect the relative powers of money capital and industrial capital. There is, however, a long-run upper bound for the rate of interest given by the rate of profit as long as the latter, as in Marx's theory, is assumed to be independent of the former. Increasing interest rates approaching or exceeding the rate of profit will induce industrial capitalists to prefer financial investment instead of real investment. This will increase the supply of money capital, on the one hand, and reduce total profits from which interest can be paid, on the other hand, so that the interest rate will finally have to fall below the rate of profit (Marx 1894, p. 378). Only in the sense of setting a long-run maximum limit can the rate of profit be considered to determine the rate of interest in this view (Marx 1894, p. 360).

Summing up, the interest rate in Marx's system can be seen as a monetary category determined by the relative powers of industrial and money capital.[31] With these power relations given, the rate of interest is an exogenous variable for income determination, accumulation and growth, whereas the quantities of credit and money are endogenous, as shown above. If power relations between money capitalists and functioning capitalists change in the course of accumulation, interest rates and the willingness to supply credit will of course vary as well. This Marxian view on interest and credit is compatible with the main features of Post-Keynesian monetary theory, as will become obvious below when we will deal with the Post-Keynesian research programme.

5.4 Implications of Marx's monetary analysis for the theory of accumulation and crisis

The monetary interpretation of Marx's economics has major implications for a theory of capital accumulation. In its orthodox variants based on 'real analysis', Marxian theories of capital accumulation assume that the course of the technical conditions of production and the development of distribution determine the long-run accumulation path (Shaikh 1978a, 1983a). Realization problems may only occur in the short run but do not exert any influence on the long-run growth trend. The long-run accumulation rate, the rate of growth of the capital stock, $g = \Delta K/K = (\Delta K/\Pi)(\Pi/K) = ar$ is determined by the development of the rate of profit (r), defined as the ratio of annual profits (Π) to the capital stock (K), and capitalists' propensity to accumulate out of profits (a). The causality of the models runs from the determination of distribution in real terms to the determination of capital accumulation. It is assumed that accumulation is funded by capitalist profits and the rate of accumulation is determined by the rate of capitalists' saving.[32]

Money, credit and a monetary interest rate are inessential for the determination of the long-run accumulation path in Marxian 'real analysis' and may only cause fluctuations around this path. Economic crises are caused by those factors which make the rate of profit decline: rising labour income shares, i.e. the real wage rate rising faster than labour productivity, or rising capital–output ratios due to technical change. The first cause for falling profitability and economic crisis has been elaborated in the 'profit squeeze' approach, the second cause in the 'falling-rate-of-profit-due-to-rising-organic-composition-of-capital' theories.[33]

Of course, these approaches have solid foundations in Marx's own work. In *Capital*, Vol. I, especially in chapter 25 'The General Law of Capitalist Accumulation', Marx (1867, pp. 574–82) elaborates on the interaction of distribution and capital accumulation. In *Capital*, Vol. III, part III 'The Law of the Tendency of the Rate of Profit to Fall', Marx (1894, pp. 211–66) analyses the effects of technical change on the rate of profit. In each of these passages he abstracts from monetary elements and assumes Say's law to hold in order to derive the pure effects of income distribution and technical change on the rate of profit and on capital accumulation.

From the preceding analysis of Marx's monetary theory, however, we have to reject the impression that the 'real' variants of Marx's accumulation and crisis theory could be the only possible interpretations. In a Marxian model of accumulation based on 'monetary analysis', neither the determination of distribution can take place in real terms in the labour market nor can capital accumulation be determined by capitalist saving. Contrary to a real exchange economy in which Say's law might hold, we have to analyse a monetary production economy in which capital accumulation is independent of capitalist saving. As we have elaborated above, in an expanding monetary production economy capitalists need to have access to means of finance irrespective of current profits or saving. According to Marx, the credit system has the potential to supply these means of finance in the form of credit at a given rate of interest – provided that capitalists meet the credit standards defined by the banking sector, we should add. The rate of interest is the exogenous variable for production, capital accumulation and growth, the quantities of credit and money are endogenous variables in Marx's monetary theory. Taken together, investment is the causal force which determines income and saving in this Marxian framework of accumulation and growth.

This Marxian framework shows broad similarities to Post-Keynesian theories of growth and distribution in the tradition of Nicholas Kaldor (1955/56, 1957, 1961), Joan Robinson (1962) and Michal Kalecki (1954) which will be dealt with below.[34] Whether variations in investment will generate the adequate saving by means of redistribution, as in the Kaldor/Robinson version of the Post-Keynesian model, or by means of variation in the degree of capacity utilization, as in Kalecki's model, depends on the degree of capacity utilization in the initial equilibrium.

If the equilibrium degree of capacity utilization is allowed to deviate from full capacity utilization, as in the Kaleckian model, variations in the rate of accumulation can be adapted by variations in capacity utilization and will have no effect on distribution. Income shares are then rather given by firms' mark-up pricing on unit labour costs in incomplete goods markets, with the mark-up being determined by the degree of price competition in the goods market and by relative powers of capital and labour in the labour market. If, however, there is full capacity utilization in equilibrium, as in the Kaldor/Robinson version of the Post-Keynesian model,[35] variations in the rate of capital accumulation are supposed to affect income shares in order to establish an investment–saving equilibrium.[36] To achieve appropriate redistribution when accumulation rates change in the long run prices in the goods market have to be more flexible than nominal wages in the labour market. There may, however, be major obstacles for the supposed adjustment processes.

In the case of increasing accumulation rates under the conditions of full utilization of the capital stock and low unemployment or even full employment, workers may resist redistribution in favour of profits. Increasing prices in the goods market might trigger rising nominal wages and cumulative inflation may result, so that the system is characterized by an 'inflation barrier'. In the case of decreasing accumulation rates, some price rigidities in the goods market may prevent the necessary redistribution in favour of wages which then may cause decreasing production and capacity utilization with negative feedbacks on investment.

Although the case of full utilization and the potentials for instability should not be neglected in a theory of effective demand and capital accumulation based on a monetary interpretation of Marx's economics, full capacity utilization should not be considered the normal state of affairs in a capitalist monetary economy. According to Marx (1867, p. 424), advanced capitalism displays a high degree of elasticity of production so that increasing demand can be supplied without major disturbances for prices and distribution caused by capacity constraints (Kurz 1987b).

Following Marx's monetary analysis, investment decisions will be influenced by the expected rate of profit and the exogenously given rate of interest. Since the rate of profit can be decomposed into the profit share (h), capacity utilization (u) and the capital-potential output (Y^v) ratio (v): $r = (\Pi/Y)(Y/Y^v)(Y^v/K) = hu(1/v)$, decisions to accumulate will be influenced positively by the development of the profit share and of capacity utilization and negatively by the development of the capital–potential output ratio. Increasing interest rates will have a direct and negative impact on investment because finance or opportunity costs of real investment are rising. But there are also indirect effects on investment, because interest rate variations will affect distribution and hence consumption demand, if we assume that workers do not save, that monetary wealth owners' saving propensity out of interest income is positive but below unity, and that profits of enterprise are completely retained by firms and therefore saved by definition. If prices, and hence the profit share, remain constant in the face of rising interest rates, profits of enterprise will decline and aggregate consumption demand will increase. Changing consumption demand will finally feed back on investment through the effects on capacity utilization.

In conclusion, monetary interest rates and effective demand will exert a major influence on the long-run accumulation path. We will explore this in greater detail in Part II of the book below. Here we can preliminarily conclude that the effects of changes in the interest rate in a monetary extension of Marx's theory of capital accumulation presumably will not be unique, but will depend on the parameters in the saving and the investment function of the model. It will therefore be difficult to derive unique 'laws of accumulation and crisis' for a capitalist monetary economy from such an approach.

6
Keynes's 'Monetary Theory of Production' and the Post-Keynesian Research Programme

6.1 Keynes's 'monetary theory of production'

In order to overcome Classical and Neoclassical 'real analysis', Keynes proposed the research programme of a 'monetary theory of production'. Whereas in the *Treatise on Money* (Keynes 1930), monetary variables only have disequilibrium real effects, and the equilibrium is determined by real variables only, in particular the drafts preceding the *General Theory* (Keynes 1979), and less the *General Theory* (Keynes 1936) itself, aim at this 'monetary theory of production'. In his 1933 contribution to the Spiethoff-Festschrift, Keynes outlines this research programme, which should contribute to an understanding and solution of real world problems and crises, as follows:

> In my opinion the main reason why the problem of crises is unsolved, or at any rate why this theory is so unsatisfactory, is to be found in the lack of what might be termed a *monetary theory of production*. The distinction which is normally made between a barter economy and a monetary economy depends upon the employment of money as a convenient means of effective exchanges – as an instrument of great convenience, but transitory and neutral in its effects. It is regarded as a mere link between cloth and wheat ... It is not supposed to affect the essential nature of the transaction from being, in the minds of those making it, one between real things, or to modify the motives and decisions of the parties to it. Money, that is to say, is employed, but is treated as being in some sense *neutral*. That, however, is not the distinction which I have in mind when I say that we lack a monetary theory of production. An economy, which uses money but uses it merely as a neutral link between transaction in real things and real

> assets and does not allow it to enter into motives or decisions, might be called – for want of a better name – a *real-exchange economy*. The theory which I desiderate would deal, in contradiction to this, with an economy in which money plays a part of its own and affects motives and decisions and is, in short, one of the operative factors in the situation, so that the course of events cannot be predicted, either in the long period or in the short, without a knowledge of the behaviour of money between the first state and the last. And it is this which we ought to mean when we speak of a *monetary economy*. (Keynes 1933, pp. 408–9; italics in the original)

In the drafts of the *General Theory* Keynes distinguishes a monetary economy from a barter economy, a real-wage or co-operative economy, and a neutral economy (Keynes 1979, pp. 76–101).[37] In the barter economy there cannot be any deviation of aggregate demand from aggregate supply, because in real exchange demand is always equal to supply by definition. In the real-wage or co-operative economy, economic agents make use of money, but only as means of exchange in order to facilitate trade and the allocation of the social product. Economic agents are remunerated in terms of money, but only in order to obtain their part of the social product. Hence, there are no leakages from the monetary circuit and aggregate demand always equals aggregate supply. In the neutral economy, money may be used as a store of value and there may hence be leakages from the monetary circuit. However, these leakages are exactly offset by injections of the same amount by an endogenous economic process, and aggregate demand is therefore always equal to aggregate supply.[38] These three model economies can rely on the validity of Say's law.

In a monetary or entrepreneur economy, however, there may be leakages from the monetary circuit which are not exactly compensated by injections, and aggregate demand may therefore fall short of aggregate supply. Say's law might not hold for two reasons.

First, income may be used by households for other purposes than direct spending on consumption goods. It is the specific nature of money which may then cause leakages from the monetary circuit and may hence be responsible for insufficient aggregate demand: Money can neither be fully substituted nor can it be reproduced by means of employing factors of production.

> Perhaps anything in terms of which the factors of production contract to be remunerated, which is not and cannot be a part of current

> output and is capable of being used otherwise than to purchase current output, is, in a sense, money. If so, but not otherwise, the use of money is a necessary condition for fluctuations in effective demand. (Keynes 1979, p. 86)

Secondly, monetary injections may not automatically offset monetary leakages from the monetary circuit. In a modern credit economy, monetary injections are independent of current income. They may hence be insufficient to make aggregate demand equal to aggregate supply at full employment. In particular, firms' production and investment decisions are geared towards monetary profits, and firms' spending for investment purposes may therefore be insufficient for full employment:

> The distinction between a co-operative and an entrepreneur economy bears some relation to a pregnant observation made by Karl Marx, – though the subsequent use to which he put this observation was highly illogical. He pointed out that the nature of production in the actual world is not, as economists seem often to suppose, a case C-M-C', i.e. of exchanging commodity (or effort) for money in order to obtain another commodity (or effort). That may be the standpoint of the private consumer. But it is not the attitude of *business*, which is a case of M-C-M', i.e. of parting with money for commodity (or effort) in order to obtain more money. . . . An entrepreneur is interested, not in the amount of product, but in the amount of *money* which will fall to his share. (Keynes 1979, pp. 81–82, italics in the original)

From these considerations it follows that the long-run level of output and employment in a monetary economy is not determined by available resources, but by effective demand. And an important part of effective demand, investment, is determined by monetary criteria: Entrepreneurs have to achieve a minimum rate of return on monetary advances. This rate of return is given by the monetary rate of interest. In a monetary economy, Say's law is therefore replaced by the 'principle of effective demand'. Aggregate spending determines output and employment, investment determines saving and is determined by monetary criteria itself.

In the *General Theory* (1936), Keynes then focused on the elaboration of the 'principle of effective demand' and less on the development of a 'monetary theory of production' as a sound basis for the 'principle of effective demand'. This might be a reason why he does not fully succeed in his aim to derive a long-term underemployment equilibrium determined by monetary variables (Keynes 1936, p. 48). In the prevailing orthodox tradition, Keynes's theory has therefore been considered to be only a short-run theory explaining deviations from the Neoclassical long-run equilibrium, but not as an alternative to Neoclassical 'real analysis'.

This interpretation has been lent support by some parts of Keynes's *General Theory* itself.[39] There he has no fundamental problems with Neoclassical microeconomic foundations, but only disputes their aggregate relevance. As soon as the aggregate level of output and employment is given, however, Keynes (1936, pp. 378–9) accepts the validity of Neoclassical value and distribution theory. He also accepts the first Classical postulate with respect to the labour market, which implies an inverse relationship between the real wage rate and employment, due to falling marginal productivity of labour (Keynes 1936, pp. 16–17). But, of course, he rejects and reverses the Neoclassical causality between the real wage rate and employment.

Keynes's (1936, pp. 165–74, 194–209) liquidity preference theory of the interest rate as a theory of money demand has been insufficient to determine a monetary underemployment equilibrium, too. Assuming a given nominal money supply by the monetary authorities, Keynes derives an inverse relationship between the nominal interest rate in the bonds market and money demand for speculative purposes. The interest rate inverse speculative money demand supposes that economic agents have expectations concerning the long-run equilibrium rate of interest without, however, determining this rate of interest in the model (Robertson 1937). Therefore, the liquidity preference theory of the rate of interest might be seen as a short-run theory of the deviation of the market rate of interest from its long-run equilibrium level due to expectations and speculation. So far, this seems to be compatible with the Neoclassical real interest rate theory which can be taken to determine the long-run equilibrium. The 'liquidity trap', in which changes in the (real) money supply do not affect the market rate of interest, can then be considered as a rigidity in the market system, in the same way as interest rate inelastic investment in the 'investment trap' and rigid nominal wages are seen as rigidities, which prevent the real balance effect from being effective and hence the achievement of full employment equilibrium.

This kind of interpretation facilitated the reintegration of Keynes's theory into the orthodoxy, making it a theory of short-run deviations from Neoclassical long-run equilibrium. Hicks's (1937) IS-LM model laid the foundation for this kind of interpretation, and in the Neoclassical Synthesis Keynes's *General Theory* then became a special case theory within a seemingly more general Neoclassical approach.

On the other hand, in chapter 17 of the *General Theory*, Keynes (1936, pp. 222–44) provides the foundation of a long-period equilibrium determined by monetary variables in which the monetary rate of interest determines the rate of return of real assets and the level of economic activity:

> It seems, then, that the *rate of interest on money* plays a peculiar part in setting a limit to the level of employment, since it sets a standard to which the marginal efficiency of a capital-asset must attain if it is to be newly produced. (Keynes 1936, p. 222, italics in the original)
>
> The money-rate of interest, by setting the pace for all the other commodity-rates of interest, holds back investment in these other commodities without being capable of stimulating investment for the production of money, which by hypothesis cannot be produced. (Keynes 1936, p. 235)

In chapter 17, money is considered as an asset the holding of which competes with other assets. Holding wealth in its most liquid form, money, which can be neither reproduced nor substituted,[40] provides a liquidity premium due to fundamental uncertainty in a monetary production economy. The monetary rate of interest can therefore be viewed as a compensation for parting with money and for holding less liquid assets instead. Provided that the rates of return of reproducible real assets are declining when the volume of these assets increases, the monetary rate of interest sets the standard for these real rates of return and restricts the holding and production of real capital assets. A long-period equilibrium is attained in which the rates of return of capital assets adjust to the monetary rate of interest, corrected for carrying costs and differentials in liquidity. Monetary variables do not cause disequilibrium, but the monetary rate of interest determines the long-period equilibrium value of the real rate of profit, the point of effective demand and hence output and employment (Rogers 1989, pp. 201–71).

But in chapter 17 of the *General Theory*, Keynes still assumes a given nominal money supply which is under the control of the monetary authorities. With an exogenous money supply the long-term rate of interest becomes an endogenous variable. In principle, it can be adjusted to its full employment equilibrium level, either by means of expanding nominal money supply or through reductions in nominal wages and prices, and hence by means of increasing real money supply. Therefore, in order to explain unemployment in long-period equilibrium, Keynes (1936, pp. 232–9) has again to rely on the liquidity trap or on the destabilizing effects of falling nominal wages on the marginal efficiency of capital and hence on private investment. These destabilizing effects are rooted in the cumulative effects expectations of falling wages and prices might have on demand and, in particular, in the real debt effects of falling prices which were highlighted already by Fisher (1933). Destabilizing real debt effects, however, require money to be predominantly credit money generated endogenously by creditor-debtor-contracts.

The endogeneity of credit and money was addressed by Keynes in a debate with Ohlin, Hawtrey and Robertson in *The Economic Journal* in 1937/38.[41] In this debate Keynes comes to the conclusion that there is a finance demand for money by investing firms. In order to allow for economic expansion, this finance demand has to be supplied by commercial banks, by means of creating credit at a given rate of interest. Therefore, in a continuously expanding economy commercial banks have to increase credit, otherwise increasing interest rates will abort investment and economic expansion. There has been renewed discussion on the status of the finance demand for money in Keynes's monetary theory, on the relation between finance and saving, and on the required amount of finance to be generated by banks until recently in Post-Keynesian and Monetary Circuit theory. We will discuss this in chapter 10 below, where we will analyse a monetary circuit in detail.[42]

6.2 The development of the Post-Keynesian research programme

The reintegration of Keynes's deviation into the orthodoxy was rejected by Keynes's close collaborators and pupils right from the beginning, in particular by Richard Kahn, Nicholas Kaldor and Joan Robinson. Their research programme since the 1950s has been to develop the revolutionary elements in Keynes's theory against Neoclassical orthodoxy.[43] Major influences on the Post-Keynesian research programme have also been exerted by the works of Michal Kalecki and Piero Sraffa. Kalecki started from Marx's economic theory and discovered the 'principle of effective demand' simultaneously with, and independently of, Keynes.[44] Unlike Keynes, Kalecki and the Kaleckian Post-Keynesians have integrated functional income distribution and distribution conflict into macroeconomic theory right from the beginning. Sraffa's (1960) reformulation of Classical price and distribution theory laid the foundation for the fundamental critique of Neoclassical price and distribution theory. The 'capital controversy' flourished in particular during the 1950s and 1960s.[45]

The Post-Keynesian research programme was initially developed in the field of distribution and growth theory. It started with the work of Harrod, and was further carried on in particular by Kaldor and Robinson. The main task of this endeavour is to extend Keynes's 'principle of effective demand' from the short period – in the sense of a given capital stock – to the long period.[46] Contrary to Keynes's programme of a 'monetary theory of production', however, money and a monetary rate of interest are inessential for the long-run equilibrium in the early distribution and growth models (Kregel 1985). For instance, Kaldor's contributions to distribution and growth theories from the 1950s and 1960s do not contain any reference to money or a monetary rate of interest. This is the more surprising because the extension of the 'principle of effective demand' to the long period and the associated independence of investment from prior saving immediately raises the question of investment finance, a question which Keynes at least addressed in the discussions following the publication of the *General Theory*, as mentioned above. Kaldor's models of steady growth seem to implicitly assume a system of adaptive finance. Also the more recent Post-Keynesian distribution and growth models which build on the work of Kalecki (1954) and Steindl (1952) do not allocate an essential role to the monetary sphere when it comes to equilibrium determination.[47]

Although there are quite a lot of remarks in the early work of Kaldor, Robinson and Kalecki which today can be interpreted as foundations for Post-Keynesian monetary theory,[48] the monetary aspects of the Post-Keynesian research programme were not pushed forward before the 1970s and 1980s. Basic work was again provided by Kaldor who laid the foundation for the Post-Keynesian 'horizontalist' approach in his critique of Monetarism.[49] According to this approach, the rate of interest is an exogenous distribution parameter under the control of monetary policies, and the supply of credit and money adjust endogenously to credit and money demand which are determined by real economic activity and payment conventions. Liquidity preference does affect the structure of interest rates from the supply side in this endogenous money approach, but has no effect on the general level of interest rates.

Post-Keynesian monetary theory was also coined by the work of Paul Davidson. This work focuses on fundamental uncertainty in a non-ergodic world in which future events cannot be deduced from past data (Davidson 1988, 1994, 2002). In such a world liquidity preference becomes a determinant of asset holding, and money is non-neutral. Money is primarily considered as a standard of value for contracts ranging into an uncertain future. This view is similar to the one proposed by the Berlin School of Monetary Keynesianism: The liquidity premium of holding money affects economic agents' portfolio choice and determines therefore the rate of profit of real investment, and hence functional income distribution as well as economic activity (Riese 1983, 1986, 1987; Heine/Herr 1999, pp. 315–447).

Post-Keynesian monetary theory, however, was not integrated into the distribution and growth models of this approach until the late 1980s/early 1990s. An exception was Pasinetti's (1974, pp. 139–41) natural rate of growth model in which the normal rate of profit is positively associated with the rate of interest, as long as the latter is lower than the former.[50] In the 1980s/90s Post-Keynesians have then started to take Keynes's (1933) research programme of a 'monetary theory of production' more and more seriously and have introduced monetary variables into the Kaldorian and Kaleckian variants of the Post-Keynesian distribution and growth models.[51] Nonetheless, this is a field of research which still seems to be underdeveloped and which therefore requires more attention.[52] Before we proceed with this in the Part II of the book, however, we have to discuss some issues in Post-Keynesian monetary theory and derive some implications for the introduction of monetary variables into distribution and growth models.

6.3 Fundamental uncertainty, liquidity premium and the interest rate

Starting points of Post-Keynesian monetary analysis are the following basic characteristics of a capitalist monetary economy: the existence of fundamental uncertainty, the development of economic processes in historical time – from a known but unchangeable past to an unknown future – and the concomitant irreversibility of economic activity. In a world with fundamental uncertainty expectations have a major impact on economic activity. Keynesian or fundamental uncertainty cannot be tamed by probability calculus. It is therefore different from risk, which can be assessed and managed economically by means of allocating probability values to future events. This is impossible with fundamental uncertainty: Future events are not known and there is hence no way to allocate probability values to them. Davidson (1988, 1994, pp. 86–108) terms such a world 'non-ergodic'.

Under the conditions of fundamental uncertainty, however, economic activity does not become irrational and inaccessible to theorizing. Economic activity can rather be assumed to be subjectively rational, but it takes place in a world in which the future is unforeseeable, in principle, and hence uncertain. Therefore, expectations and general sentiments have major impacts on economic development. The causes of fundamental uncertainty, however, remain unclear und there is no general consensus on this in Post-Keynesian theory. Davidson (1988) considers uncertainty to be a major characteristic of human life as such. Arestis (1992, p. 92) attaches it to economic processes taking place in historical time. Riese (1983, 1986), Herr (1988a), and Rousseas (1998, pp. 24–5) argue that fundamental uncertainty is caused by the systemic characteristics of an anarchic capitalist monetary economy.

As a rational reaction, fundamental uncertainty induces economic agents to hold wealth in its most liquid form, money. This allows for responding to unforeseen payment requirements or investment opportunities (Davidson 1988). Money as a means of payment with a close to zero elasticity of reproduction and of substitution is therefore non-neutral with respect to the real economic sphere. Under these conditions, Say's law does no longer hold, because the demand for money is a non-demand for produced goods and also a non-supply of credit finance for investment purposes.

> Thus, the human propensity to use some portion of current wealth to purchase (and maintain) liquidity (idle balances for precautionary and speculative purposes) instead of committing income completely to the purchase of currently producible goods and services, reflects a *sensible* behaviour by decision makers (in a nonergodic world); a behaviour which negates Say's law. (Davidson 1988, p. 333, italics in the original)

The liquidity premium of holding money generates the rate of interest as the price for parting with money. Interest has to be paid in order to make economic agents hold wealth in a less liquid form than money.

Fundamental uncertainty induces economic agents further to enter into contracts denominated in monetary units in order to reduce individual uncertainty associated with consumption and investment decision ranging into an uncertain future. Money and contracts denominated in money units become a bridge between the present and the future. The stability or rigidity of prices and wages expressed in monetary units becomes a precondition for a monetary economy to operate smoothly. The smooth operation of a contract economy further requires a social institution of contract enforcement. The most important contracts are, of course, the wage–labour contract and the credit contract.

Money in Post-Keynesian theory is hence not introduced as a means of circulation, but as a standard of value for creditor-debtor- and wage-labour-contracts and as an ultimate means of payment to fulfil these contracts. Money is therefore 'money-of-account' in the first instance, as Keynes has already made clear in his *Treatise on Money*:

> Money-of-Account, namely that in which Debts and Price and General Purchasing Power are *expressed*, is the primary concept of a Theory of Money.
>
> A Money-of-Account comes into existence along with Debts, which are contracts for deferred payment, and Price-Lists, which are offers of contracts for sale or purchase. Such Debts and Price-Lists, whether they are recorded by word of mouth or by book entry on baked bricks or paper documents, can only be expressed in terms of Money-of-Account.
>
> Money itself, namely that by delivery of which debt-contracts and price-contracts are *discharged*, and in the shape of which a store of General Purchasing Power is *held*, derives its character from its relationship to the Money-of-Account, since the debts and prices must first have been expressed in terms of the latter. (Keynes 1930, p. 1, italics in the original)

Being the unit of account for debt contracts, money also becomes the most liquid form of holding wealth and also assumes the standard of value for goods market transactions. Therefore, at the very basis of a monetary economy we have the creditor–debtor relationship which requires a standard of value and a means of ultimate payment from which the further roles of money can then be derived. Also in Post-Keynesian theory, money is essentially a social relation. This is also true for a monetary economy which uses a money commodity (Smithin 2003a, pp. 25–34).[53]

In this view, the meaning of Keynes's liquidity preference theory from the *General Theory* changes, from a determinant of money demand to a determinant of credit supply. Liquidity preference denotes the unwillingness to part with the ultimate means of payment in exchange with a debtor's promise to pay which is less liquid, but which yields interest.[54] A credit money economy is hence characterized by a hierarchy of promises to pay with increasing validity and liquidity from the bottom to the top and a related inverse hierarchy of interest rates. At the top we have the promise to pay with the highest social validity and liquidity, which can only be exchanged against itself and which is therefore the ultimate means of payment. The holding of this means of payment does not yield interest. In modern monetary economies this is central bank money guaranteed by the state.[55]

6.4 Interest rate, profit rate and investment

In Post-Keynesian monetary theory, the economic process in a capitalist economy is determined by entrepreneurs' investment which precedes income generation and hence saving. Investment and capital accumulation cannot be limited by saving, but investment generates a sufficient amount of saving either through output and quantity effects and/or through price and distribution effects. The independence of investment from saving presupposes that firms have access to credit in order to finance production and investment.[56] Production requires money advances and hence access to credit. Investment decisions are determined by expected profitability compared to finance costs, and hence by the expected rate of profit on real investment and the monetary interest rate.

The rate of interest – in relation to the expected profit rate – has an inverse impact on investment. Different arguments have been presented by Keynes and the Post-Keynesians for such a relationship.[57] The first is the *General Theory* argument of a falling marginal efficiency of capital (Keynes 1936, pp. 135–46), the rate of discount which makes the present value of expected returns from a capital asset just equal to its supply price. A falling marginal efficiency of capital can therefore be interpreted as a falling expected rate of profit on additional capital assets. According to Keynes (1936, p. 136), the schedule of the marginal efficiency is downward sloping, because in the short period the supply price of capital goods increases with demand, due to rising marginal costs in production of capital goods. In the long period, marginal yields of increasing capacity decline because of limitations in demand due to decreasing marginal utility of consumers. With the curve of the marginal efficiency of capital and hence profit expectations given, an increasing rate of interest is associated with a declining 'equilibrium' capital stock intended by entrepreneurs and hence decreasing or even negative net investment.

A second argument for a negative relationship between the rate of interest and investment in capital stock is associated with investment finance. For a firm operating with borrowed capital an increasing rate of interest means an increase in fixed payment obligations relative to uncertain yields from real investment. This implies an increase in borrower's and in lender's risk.[58] For the borrower, the risk of future insolvency and bankruptcy increases, and for the lender, the risk of credit default rises.

> Two types of risk affect the volume of investment which have not commonly been distinguished, but which it is important to distinguish. The first is the entrepreneur's or borrower's risk and arises out of doubts in his own mind as to the probability of his actually earning the prospective yield of which he hopes. If a man is venturing his own money, this is the only risk which is relevant.
>
> But where a system of borrowing and lending exists, by which I mean the granting of loans with a margin or real or personal security, a second type of risk is relevant which we may call lender's risk. This may be due either to moral hazard, i.e. voluntary default or other means of escape, possibly lawful, from the fulfilment of the obligation, or to the possible insufficiency of the margin of security, i.e. involuntary default due to the disappointment of expectations. (Keynes 1936, p. 144)

The effects of interest rate variations on investment will therefore depend not only on the relationship between the rate of interest and the expected rate of profit, but also on the degree of debt finance of the firms' capital stock. On the one hand, the investor's credit demand is affected by the amount of his own capital in order to minimize borrower's risk and hence future insolvency or bankruptcy. On the other hand, the commercial bank's willingness to supply credit will be affected by the collateral and hence the own capital the investor has to offer, or by the share of expected profits which is not yet earmarked for fixed interest payments, in order to minimize lender's risk.

The effects of own capital on investment were highlighted, in particular, in Kalecki's (1937) 'principle of increasing risk'. Also with a constant marginal efficiency of capital, investment of a single firm will be limited because increasing investment is associated with an increasing rate of interest. This is due to increasing risk premia in the face of a given amount of own capital.

> There are two reasons for the increase or marginal risk with the amount invested. The first is the fact that the greater is the investment of an entrepreneur the more is his wealth position endangered in the event of unsuccessful business.

> The second reason making the marginal risk rise with the size of investment is the danger of 'illiquidity'. The sudden sale of so specific a good as a factory is almost always connected with losses. Thus the amount invested k must be considered as a fully illiquid asset in the case of sudden need for 'capital'. In that situation the entrepreneur who has invested in equipment his reserves (cash, deposits, securities) and taken 'too much credit' is obliged to borrow at a rate of interest which is higher than the market one.
>
> If, however, the entrepreneur is not cautious in his investment activity it is the creditor who imposes on his calculation the burden of increasing risk charging the successive portions of credits above a certain amount with a rising rate of interest. (Kalecki 1937, p. 442)

Contrary to the Modigliani/Miller (1958) hypothesis for a perfectly competitive capital market, own capital and borrowed capital are not perfect substitutes with respect to investment finance. Own capital and retained earnings from current profits are further determinants of investment.[59]

> The enterprises started in a given industry at a given moment are not of equal size because the own capital of entrepreneurs is not equal. The 'business democracy' is a fallacy: the own capital is a 'factor of investment'. (Kalecki 1937, p. 443)

The question remains of whether the 'principle of increasing risk', which implies an increasing interest rate with increasing debt financed investment of the single firm assuming a given capital stock and given own capital, is also valid on the macroeconomic level, implying an upward-sloping credit supply curve in interest credit space for the economy as a whole (Sawyer 2001a)?[60] And the question arises whether increasing marginal risk, independently of increasing interest rates, generates a long-run equilibrium at the macroeconomic level. Kalecki (1937) is pretty clear in stressing that his 'principle of increasing risk' results only apply to a single firm but not to the macroeconomic level. His 'principle of increasing risk' defines a planned equilibrium for the single firm at a given point in time, but not a long-run equilibrium taking into account interactions at the macro level: 'We examined the planning of the entrepreneur in a given situation which in general is not the position of the long run equilibrium' (Kalecki 1937, p. 445).

In a period-by-period analysis of investment decisions, the feedback effects of realized investment on profits have to be taken into account, according to Kalecki (1937). Since rising investment spending triggers rising profits for the business sector as a whole, retained earnings and own capital improve. This may improve access to borrowed capital in the succeeding period without increasing marginal risk. Therefore, the result for the economy as a whole may be a cumulative process and not a stable long-run equilibrium. For similar reasons, Kalecki (1936) criticized Keynes's idea of a downward-sloping schedule of the marginal efficiency of capital giving rise to an 'equilibrium' level of investment for the economy as a whole (Lopez 2002; Sardoni 1987, pp. 104–13). Whereas an individual firm at a given moment in time may be faced with a downward-sloping schedule of the marginal efficiency of capital, rising investment in the economy as a whole may shift this schedule upwards and cause a cumulative process. We will discuss this issue in greater detail in chapter 13 where we will develop Kaleckian models of distribution and growth with debt dynamics.

6.5 Exogenous interest rate and endogenous credit and money

External finance for firms' investment and hence economic expansion can be supplied either by those households holding financial wealth or by the banking sector.[61] But it is only the banking sector, consisting of a central bank and commercial banks, which is capable of supplying any creditworthy credit demand by firms at a given rate of interest without limits, in principle. In Post-Keynesian monetary theory, the volume of credit (as a flow) and the quantity of money (as a stock) are therefore endogenous to the income generation and accumulation process.[62]

The volume of credit supply is determined by credit demand which commercial banks consider creditworthy, that is by that part of credit demand which is able to supply securities accepted by the central bank as collateral when providing commercial banks with central bank money in the money market. Loan demand which commercial banks deem creditworthy is granted, deposits are created with commercial banks, and the central bank accommodates the required amount of central bank money. The central bank is the 'lender of last resort' and is responsible for providing liquidity to the monetary system. The central bank determines the price for central bank money, the base rate of interest,[63] and commercial banks mark-up this base rate when supplying credit to investors. Endogenous credit and money are prerequisites for the 'principle of effective demand' to hold. Only the endogenous creation of means of finance allows for the determination of income generation and growth by firms' investment spending independent of previous saving.

There are, however, two major issues in Post-Keynesian monetary economics, which have yet remained unsolved. These are discussed under the labels 'horizontalists' (or 'accommodationists') versus 'structuralists'.[64] The first issue is related to the central bank's supply curve of reserves in base interest rate central bank money space and hence the degree of central bank accommodation of reserves in the face of expanding credit. The second is related to the commercial banks' supply curve in market interest rate credit space and to the relevance and uniqueness of changes in commercial banks' liquidity preference when credit demand expands. We will deal with these issues in what follows.

The horizontalist view

In the horizontalist view, pioneered by Kaldor (1970, 1982, 1985), Lavoie (1984) and Moore (1988, 1989),[65] it is argued that the central bank's monetary policy determines the base rate of interest and that the central bank as 'lender of last resort' is responsible for the liquidity and stability of the whole monetary system. Therefore, the central bank fully accommodates the generation of credit, and hence deposits with commercial banks, with the required amount of central bank money, provided that commercial banks only grant credit to creditworthy borrowers. This implies that there is always some sort of 'rationing' in the sense that the willingness to pay the rate of interest demanded by the central bank is a necessary but not a sufficient condition for commercial banks to get hold of reserves. Within this limit, however, the central banks' money supply curve becomes horizontal. The horizontalist view can therefore be summarized as follows: 'Money is credit-driven; loans make deposits; deposits make reserves. The supply of and the demand for credit money are interdependent. The control instrument of the central bank is not a quantity but a price, the rate of interest' (Lavoie 1992a, p. 170).

Commercial banks determine the interest rate in the credit market by marking up the central bank's base rate, and then supply credit at this rate to those borrowers whom they consider to be creditworthy. Banks are therefore price makers and quantity takers, within the limits given by borrowers' creditworthiness. Again, the willingness of firms and households to pay the rate of interest set by banks in the credit market is a necessary, but not a sufficient condition to obtain credit, and there will always be some sort of 'credit rationing' for those who are unable to provide required collateral.[66] The commercial banks' mark-up on the base rate is determined by their risk and liquidity considerations, and also by the degree of competition in the commercial banking sector. In this approach, liquidity preference determines the structure of interest rates, but not the level this structure is based on. The commercial banks' liquidity preference is a determinant of the mark-up and hence the spread between the base rate and the market rate of interest.

> Briefly put, a generalised liquidity preference theory tells us to what extent the various agents in the economy are ready to become illiquid and to abandon liquid assets ... The central bank determines the base rate, and all other rates are adjusted to that rate, through liquidity preference or other considerations. Liquidity preference does not determine *the* rate of interest, ... Rather liquidity preference determines the *differential* between the base rate and all the other rates. (Lavoie 1996a, p. 293, italics in the original)

The horizontalist view can be presented graphically adopting Palley's (1994, p. 74) approach in Figure I.1.[67] The upper left quadrant shows the central bank's horizontal base money supply curve (M^S) at a given base rate of interest (i_{CB}) set by the central bank. In the upper right

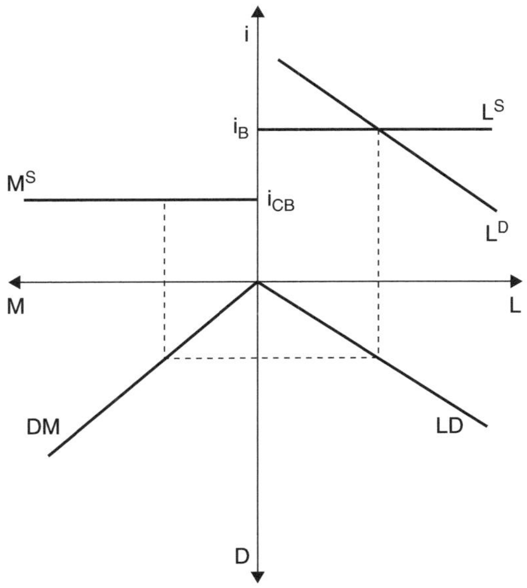

Figure I.1 The horizontalist approach of endogenous money and credit

quadrant we find the interest rate inverse loan demand curve (L^D) and the horizontal loan supply curve (L^S) of commercial banks at a given rate of interest (i_B) calculated by marking up the central bank's base rate [$i_B = (1 + m_B)i_{CB}$]. The mark-up (m_B) is determined by commercial banks' risk and liquidity premia, and by the degree of competition in the banking sector. The lower right quadrant with the loan-deposit curve (LD) shows that 'loans (L) make deposits (D)', and the lower left quadrant with the deposit-reserves curve (DM) displays that 'deposits (D) make reserves (M)'. For the sake of simplicity it is assumed that each 'making' takes place in fixed proportions. The loan-deposit and the deposit-reserves curves will be affected by the deposit–loan ratio, by the required reserve ratios for deposits, and by excess reserves (Palley 1994).

An increase in loan demand, hence an outward shift in the loan demand curve, will increase loan and money supply at given interest rates, provided the loan demand is deemed creditworthy by commercial banks. Higher standards for creditworthiness associated with a more cautious credit supply will be associated with a downward shift in the loan demand curve in Figure I.1.

If liquidity preference and risk considerations of commercial banks and, hence, their mark-ups remain constant, the central bank's interest rate setting in the base money market also determines the market rate of interest in the credit market (Smithin 2003a, pp. 121–7). Under these conditions, changes in the base rate and in the credit market rate of interest are due to changes in the monetary policy stance. Changes in the central bank's base rate will therefore also shift the credit supply curve and affect credit demand and hence real economic activity financed by credit.

However, if commercial banks' liquidity and risk considerations or the degree of competition, and hence their mark-ups, also change in the face of a changing base rate of interest, monetary policy may not be able to determine the credit market rate of interest directly. Here an asymmetry may arise: An increasing base rate of interest will always trigger an increasing credit market rate, because commercial banks have to recover costs of refinancing and have to gain minimum profits. But a decreasing base rate may not be followed immediately by a falling credit market rate, if commercial banks' liquidity and risk premia increase due to rising uncertainty, or if banks' profit aspirations increase. Note, finally, that the horizontalist view does not imply that monetary policy is free to set the rate of interest at whatever level, irrespective of economic conditions. On the contrary, modern central banks use the interest rate tool in order to stabilize inflation – and/or the exchange rate, depending on the exchange rate regime. We will discuss some of the related issues in chapter 16 below.

The structuralist view

Post-Keynesian structuralists share the view that money is endogenous and that the central bank uses the base rate of interest as an economic policy instrument. But they object to the money and credit supply curves being perfectly elastic and argue that also the rate of interest becomes an endogenous variable.[68] First, it is argued, central banks may not always accommodate rising bank loans with the required amount of central bank money at a given rate of interest. Therefore, commercial banks may be forced to attract reserves from the public or to introduce financial innovations; that means commercial banks have to use liability management. The rate of interest in the money market will hence have to rise in order to make economic agents part with central bank money, and the money and credit supply curves become upwards sloping. Households' liquidity preference becomes important again in determining the levels of the money and the loan rates of interest. This is shown in Figure I.2, also adopted from Palley (1994, p. 75).[69]

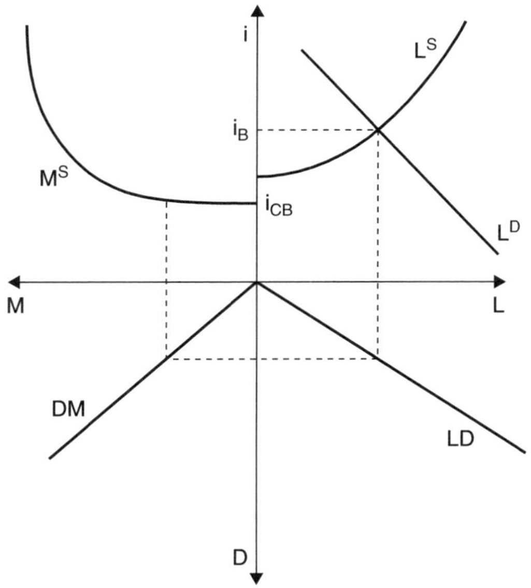

Figure I.2 The structuralist approach with incomplete accommodation of the central bank

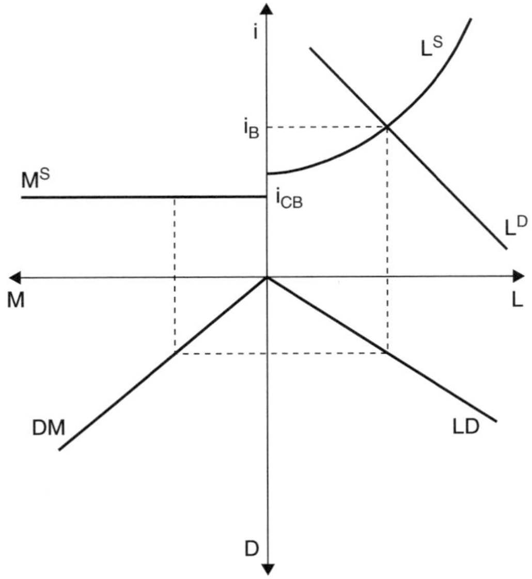

Figure I.3 The structuralist approach with complete accommodation of the central bank

Even if the central bank fully accommodates the commercial banks' demand for money, structuralists put forward arguments in favour of a rising credit supply curve in interest rate credit space. Expanding credit decreases commercial banks' liquidity position and increases firms' degree of indebtedness, it is argued. Increasing credit supply is hence associated with increasing liquidity and risk premia of commercial banks. Liquidity preference and increasing risk induce commercial banks to increase the mark-up on the base rate when credit supply is expanded. Contrary to the horizontalist view, liquidity preference has again a role to play in the determination of the level and the time paths of market rates of interest. This is shown in Figure I.3.[70]

A reconciliation?

Fontana (2003, 2004a, 2004b) has recently tried to reconcile the horizontalist and the structuralist approaches to endogenous money. Following a distinction by Hicks (1982), Fontana argues that horizontalists have put forward a 'single period analysis' with given expectations, and hence given liquidity preferences and risk assessments of commercial banks and the central bank. This allows the horizontalists to derive a model

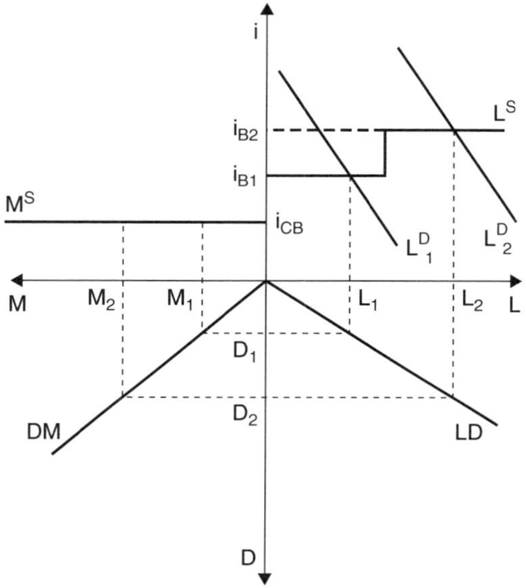

Figure I.4 A time framework explanation of endogenous money with complete accommodation of the central bank

with simple and stable relationships that explains the creation, circulation, and destruction of money, according to Fontana. Structuralists are said to pursue a 'continuation analysis' of money in which expectations, and hence liquidity preference and risk assessments, may change period by period over time. The effects of changing expectations on money and loan rates of interest are therefore integrated into the analysis. Therefore, the difference between the horizontalist and the structuralist approach boils down to different assumptions about the state of expectations, Fontana argues. Since the structuralist approach covers more than a single period, it is considered to encompass the horizontalist view and to be able to generate a richer and more complex explanation of credit and money supply. This is shown in Figure I.4 adopted from Fontana (2004a, p. 374).

Assuming first that the central bank fully accommodates the commercial banks' demand for central bank money, an increase in loan demand from L^D_1 in period 1 to L^D_2 in period 2 is considered. In period 1 firms' loan demand is met by a horizontal credit supply curve at a given interest rate i_{B1} calculated as a mark-up on the base rate i_{CB}. Note that credit supply at this rate is not infinite. An increase in credit demand and hence a shift

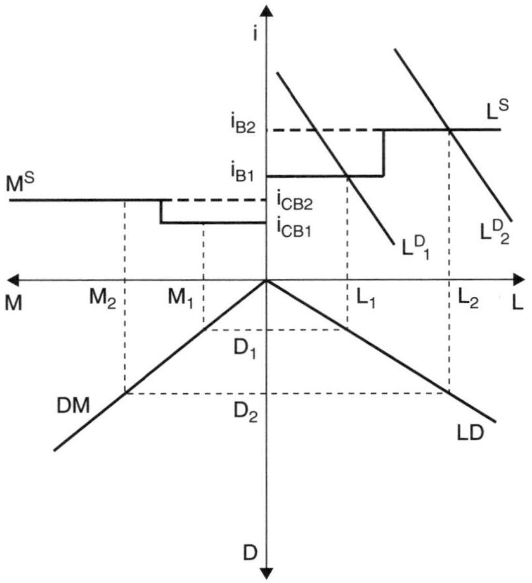

Figure I.5 A time framework explanation of endogenous money with incomplete accommodation of the central bank

in the loan demand curve from L^D_1 to L^D_2 is assumed to be associated with a decrease in the commercial banks' liquidity position and an increase in the degree of indebtedness of firms, following the structuralist view. Liquidity and risk considerations induce commercial banks to increase the mark-up on the central bank's base rate, so that the loan rate moves to i_{B2}. A rise in credit demand is therefore associated with an increase in the loan rate of interest.

A similar exercise can be undertaken with respect to the base interest rate set by the central bank in the face of a rise in the demand for central bank money in Figure I.5. If the central bank decides not to accommodate a rising demand for reserves triggered by an increasing demand for loans, the supply functions of central bank money and of loans both shift upwards. An increasing demand for loans and reserves will only be supplied at increasing interest rates. The central bank's base rate for reserves rises from i_{CB1} to i_{CB2}, and the loan rate increases from i_{B1} to i_{B2}. The increase in the loan rate may even exceed the increase in the base rate due to 'increasing risk', as can be seen in Figure I.5.

Indeed, Fontana's contributions have helped to clarify the issue. However, whereas the effects of central bank's non-accommodation on interest rates is not disputed in the controversy between horizontalists and structuralists, it is by no means clear that commercial banks will necessarily raise loan rates in the face of increasing credit demand when it is supposed that the central bank accommodates. Lavoie (1996a) argues that an increasing interest rate in the face of increasing economic activity and credit demand can only be attributed to central bank's non-accommodation. If central banks decide not to accommodate an increasing demand for reserves, this is tantamount to increasing the base rate of interest with the concomitant effects demonstrated in Figure I.5. It is therefore the central bank's interest rate policy which causes changes in the rate for reserves and in the loan rate.

Of course, it is conceded that the commercial banks' loan rate may also vary when the central bank maintains the base rate at a constant level. Changes in the degree of competition in the banking sector, shifts in expectations and hence in liquidity preference or risk assessments of commercial banks may be a cause for this. What is disputed from a macroeconomic perspective, however, is the necessity of an increase of the loan rate in the face of rising demand for credit, due to decreasing liquidity of commercial banks and increasing indebtedness of credit seeking firms (Lavoie 1996a).

Following Kalecki's (1937) 'principle of increasing risk', increasing demand for credit is associated with increasing indebtedness of the individual firm and hence increasing lender's and borrower's risk which may cause an increase in the loan rate of interest. From a macroeconomic perspective, however, increasing spending of firms financed by means of credit generates increasing realized profits. Therefore, an increasing degree of indebtedness of firms or a rising share of interest payments in total profits is by no means necessary for the economy as a whole. This will be analysed in more detail in a Kaleckian monetary distribution and growth model in chapter 13 below.

A similar argument applies with respect to the liquidity position of commercial banks when credit supply is increased (Lavoie 1996a). An increase in long-term loans relative to short-term deposits does not necessarily cause rising loan rates due to the perceived problem of decreasing liquidity. Rising loans mean rising deposits, the spending of which will remain within the banking sector. Individual banks may face liquidity constraints, but the banking sector as whole will not, as long as the demand for central bank money remains constant. However, increasing credit will be associated with increasing demand for central bank money, too. Commercial banks will face liquidity problems if the central bank is not willing to accommodate increasing demand for reserves at a given rate of interest, and the loan rate of interest will have to rise. This increase in interest rates, however, is caused by central bank policies and not by the commercial bank sector. It is tantamount to an increase in the central bank's base rate, that is an upward shift in the central bank's horizontal supply curve of reserves.

Summing up so far, at every moment in time there are horizontal supply curves of reserves and loans. Considering change in historical time, however, there may be an increase in interest rates when money and credit supply rise. But this is the result of a change in the central bank's base rate, hence a change in the monetary policy regime, which causes shifts in the horizontal supply curves (see also Palley 2002).

Arestis/Howells (1996, 1999) and Howells (1995a), however, have argued that an increase in the volume of credit may affect the whole structure of interest rates, because an increase in the flow of credit may be associated with a rise in the stock of money. In order for this increase in stocks to be held voluntarily by economic agents, changes in interest rate differentials and hence in the whole structure of interest rates may be required. But Lavoie (1999) considers these changes in the structure of interest rates to be of secondary importance. If economic agents dispose of involuntary stocks of money, they will use them to pay back debt or to buy assets which will enable other agents to pay back credit. For the economy as a whole the 'law of reflux' applies and changes in the structure of interest rates are only of temporary nature.

As a first approximation we will therefore follow the arguments put forward by Lavoie: The central bank determines the base rate of interest and, with the degree of competition in the banking sector, expectations, liquidity preference and hence commercial banks' mark-up constant, the central bank also determines the market rate for long-term credit. We concede that expectations and liquidity preferences may change in the process of time. But in our view there is no reason to believe in a necessary increase of liquidity preference when economic activity and the volume of credit expand, and hence there is no reason to necessarily believe in rising credit supply curves in interest rate loan space.

If sudden increases in liquidity preferences occur, they may limit the capacities of the central bank to lower market rates of interest in the short run. And there may be short-run inversions in the yield curves, as is usually witnessed in economic recessions. However, these are temporary phenomena, and in the long run it is monetary policies which determine the short-term rate of interest and also the tendency of development of the long-term rate, if the central bank is ready to lend to commercial banks at the given short-term rate: 'In short, in an endogenous money environment, the central bank should always be able eventually to drive down the general level of interest rates if they so choose, provided they are sufficiently persistent' (Smithin 2003a, p. 126).

We follow Smithin's conclusion, with the qualification that lowering real interest rates, i.e. nominal rates corrected for inflation, requires that there is enough room of manoeuvre for the central bank to lower its instrument variable, the nominal short-term rate. This means that the zero lower bound for nominal rates has not been approached in order for the central bank to be able to drive down real market rates in an environment of low inflation or even deflation. We will come back to this issue in chapter 16 below.

6.6 Summary of Post-Keynesian monetary analysis

We can now summarize the main characteristics of Keynes's and the Post-Keynesian monetary analysis, as we see it. In this approach, the rate of interest is a distribution parameter, in a closed economy mainly under the control of the central bank. The central bank sets the base rate of interest and the commercial banks mark up this base rate according to the degree of competition in the banking sector, liquidity preference, risk assessment and period of validity of loans. Therefore, with the degree of competition, expectations and hence liquidity preference given, the central bank's interest rate policy also determines the long-term market rate of interest. With inflation (expectations) given, the central bank's variation of the nominal interest rate also determines the short- and long-term real rates, which are the nominal rates corrected for inflation (expectations). Liquidity preference affects the structure of interest rates, the spread or the yield curve at every moment in time, but has no systematic effect on the development of short- or long-term rates over time.

The central bank's control of the long-term market rate may be limited in the face of changes in expectations and in liquidity preference – taking the degree of competition in the commercial banking sector as constant. But these changes are not related to economic activity in any systematic way, and hence have to be treated as exogenous. In deep recessions with rising liquidity preference and deterioration of expectations, the central bank may be incapable of bringing down market rates. But this may be only a short-run disequilibrium phenomenon. In the long run, the movement of the whole structure of interest rate is determined by central bank policies, with liquidity preference at each point in time affecting the spread. This is true for a closed economy. In the world economy it is the central bank policy of the key currency country which determines the level on which the interest rate structure is built.

The volume of credit and the quantity of money are endogenous variables with respect to economic activity. The volume of credit supplied by commercial banks is determined by creditworthy credit demand at the given rate of interest. Credit demand derives mainly from that part of investment which is debt-financed. The quantity of money depends on the public's money demand, and it is supplied by the central bank to commercial banks at the base rate of interest set by the central bank.

With uncertainty and expectations given, the long-term real rate of interest determines the rate of profit on real investment, and it also sets a limit to real investment. Since an increase in the volume of investment is supposed to be associated with a decline in the actual or expected rate of profit, investment will be negatively related to the real rate of interest through different channels (opportunity costs, internal finance). Since credit demand mainly derives from investment finance, the endogenously determined volume of credit is also assumed to be inversely related to the rate of interest.

Under the conditions of given expectations, variations in the rate of interest are supposed to have uniquely inverse effects on investment. However, since investment is heavily dependent on profit expectations, changes in these expectations may undermine the effectiveness of monetary policies, in particular when it comes to stimulating the economy in a deep recession. Since there is no upper limit for the rate of interest, monetary policies are always able to choke an investment boom fuelled by rising profit expectations if it generates accelerating inflation. In a deep recession with deteriorating profit expectations, monetary policies, however, may not be able to stimulate investment, even if the central bank manages to bring down market interest rates – which by no means can be taken for granted, as we have argued above. There is hence a potential asymmetry in the effectiveness of monetary policies manipulating the rate of interest and affecting the real economy.

The price level and, hence, inflation is not determined by the quantity of money, which is endogenous, but by the development of unit costs, in particular, unit labour costs. This assumes that the firms' mark-up on unit labour costs remains roughly constant when economic activity varies. Whereas monetary policies setting the interest rate affect investment, output, employment and distribution, nominal wage setting in the labour market determines the price level and hence inflation. Unemployment as a condition of price stability may therefore be required to be a permanent feature of a monetary economy, if there is no other way to limit upwards pressure on nominal wages in the face of high or full employment. Monetary policies manipulating the rate of interest may therefore affect the price level and inflation, but only via its effects on investment demand, output and finally employment.

With the level of uncertainty and expectations taken as given, the Post-Keynesian approach derives a fragile long-period equilibrium determined by monetary forces. Due to uncertainty and changing expectations, however, this equilibrium will hardly be reached by economic processes taking place in historical time. In equilibrium, the real long-term rate of interest – that is, the nominal rate corrected for inflation (expectations) – determines the profit rate on real investment, income distribution and relative prices. The real wage rate becomes a residual variable and the nominal wage rate determines the price level. The volume of credit and the quantity of money are endogenous variables. The real rate of interest sets a limit to the investment in real capital and therefore determines output, employment and also capital accumulation in a unique way – always assuming that there are no sudden shifts in expectations. In Post-Keynesian theory, however, it is not yet clear how distribution effects of interest rate variations interact with the direct effects on investment and capital accumulation. This issue has therefore to be explored analytically in part II of the book applying more formal models.

7
Real and Monetary Analysis in Economic Paradigms: Summary of Part I

In the first part of the book we have surveyed the relationship between the monetary and the real sphere in different economic paradigms applying Schumpeter's distinction between 'real analysis' and 'monetary analysis', and we have derived some implications for the relationship between monetary policy, distribution and capital accumulation. We have argued that Classical orthodoxy, Neoclassical economics, Neoclassical Synthesis, Monetarist, New Classical, but also today's mainstream New Keynesian and New Consensus theories are dedicated to 'real analysis'. In the long run – in New Classical theory also in the short run – the economic equilibrium is determined by real forces only. Relative prices, income distribution, output, employment and growth are determined by 'real analysis'. Monetary variables, the quantity of base money or the base rate of interest controlled by the central bank, have real effects in the short run when nominal rigidities prevail. These real effects are therefore confined to short-run disequilibria, and in the long run monetary variables are neutral with respect to real outcomes. In long-run equilibrium, monetary policies only affect the price level or inflation. Therefore, in long-run equilibrium the Classical dichotomy between the monetary and the real sphere and Say's law are assumed to hold. The real rate of profit, or the 'natural rate of interest', determines the monetary rate of interest. Money is neutral with respect to output, employment, distribution and growth.

Classical heterodoxy (Banking School, Neo-Ricardian monetary theory of distribution), Marx's, Keynes's and Post-Keynesian theories pursue 'monetary analysis' in Schumpeter's terms. Monetary and real forces are not treated separately in the determination of long-run equilibrium. On the contrary, monetary variables are integral and indispensable elements of the total model and hence also in the determination of long-run equilibrium. In this sense, money is fundamentally non-neutral. Although there are significant differences between Classical heterodoxy, Marx's, Keynes's and Post-Keynesian approaches, these theories share the view that modern capitalist economies should be considered as credit money economies. In such an economy the rate of interest is an exogenous variable for the processes of income generation and capital accumulation, and it is not automatically and uniquely affected by these processes. The volume of credit and the quantity of money are endogenous variables determined by the creditworthy demand for credit and by historically and institutionally given payment conventions. The demand for credit is mainly affected by firms' production and investment decisions and the associated requirements of external finance.

Firms' investment is the driving force of the economic process and is mainly determined by the expected profit rate and the interest rate. It might also be affected by the financial position of the firm (own capital, retained earnings) which may influence firms' access to external finance. From a macroeconomic point of view, investment is not limited by saving, but generates the adequate amount of saving via changes in prices and distribution and/or via effects on output and capacity utilization. Say's law is therefore rejected by all the proponents of 'monetary analysis' and it is replaced by the 'principle of effective demand', to use Keynes's terminology. The level of employment is determined by monetary policies, the asset market and the goods market. From the perspective of the labour market it is a 'given' variable which is not determined in this market. The labour market rather sets the nominal wage rate which is a crucial variable for the price level and inflation.

In each of the schools of 'monetary analysis', the monetary variable 'interest rate' has a decisive impact on long-run equilibrium and hence on the real variables output, employment, distribution and growth. However, the schools of 'monetary analysis' differ when it comes to the explicit and concrete analysis of the effects of monetary policy on distribution and economic activity. In order to highlight these differences we assume the technical conditions of production and the degree of competition in the macroeconomic markets (money, credit, goods, labour) to be constant, and we take economic agents' expectations to be given.

In Post-Keynesian monetary theory the exogenous monetary interest rate determines functional income distribution and economic activity in a unique way in long-run equilibrium, which, of course, may never be reached in an economy developing in historical time. The rate of profit on real investment adjusts to the real long-term monetary interest rate, and the real wage rate becomes a residual. Simultaneously, the rate of interest determines the volume of reproducible capital goods and hence output and capital accumulation adversely. In Post-Keynesian theory, however, it has not yet been made convincingly clear how distribution effects of interest rate variations interact with the direct effects on investment and capital accumulation.

In Classical heterodoxy, in particular in the Neo-Ricardian monetary theory of distribution, the monetary rate of interest also determines a unique distribution equilibrium in the long run. However, the rate of interest is not equal to the real rate of profit, but the latter is derived by summing up the rate of interest and the rate of profit of enterprise which is assumed to be given. Therefore, variations in the rate of interest have an unambiguous effect on the rate of profit. The effects of variations in the rate of interest on output and capital accumulation, however, are not unique in long-period equilibrium, because the rate of interest is not associated with a unique volume of investment. The distribution effects of changes in the interest rate rather exert contradicting cost and demand effects on investment and capital accumulation. The total effect on investment then depends on the relative strength of these effects.

In the monetary interpretation of Marx's economics we also get an indeterminate effect of interest rate variations on economic activity for similar reasons as in Neo-Ricardian monetary theory. But we obtain a different effect on functional income distribution in this approach. Since the rate of profit of enterprise is considered to be a variable which is affected by distribution conflict, Marx deals with a three-party conflict between rentiers or financial capital, firms or industrial capital, and wage labour. He assumes that changes in the rate of interest affect industrial profits and therefore leave real wages unaffected.

In the following part of the book we will investigate deeper into the effects of changes in the monetary rate of interest on distribution and capital accumulation and try to resolve some of the problems raised above. For this purpose, we will take into account the main elements of 'monetary analysis' in the three approaches outlined so far, the Post-Keynesian monetary theory, the Neo-Ricardian monetary theory of distribution and the monetary interpretation of Marx's economics.

Part II
Interest Rate, Distribution and Capital Accumulation – Post-Keynesian Models

8

Interest Rate, Distribution and Capital Accumulation – Post-Keynesian Models: Introduction to Part II

In the second part of the book we will analyse the relationship between the monetary interest rate, functional income distribution and capital accumulation in more detail. The analysis will be based on Post-Keynesian approaches to distribution and growth. We will develop a basic model in which the long-run distribution and accumulation effects of monetary policies can be analysed and different variants of Post-Keynesian models can be compared. Following Post-Keynesian monetary theory, but also the Neo-Ricardian monetary theory of distribution and Marx's monetary analysis, all of them outlined in the first part of the book, we will consider the interest rate as an exogenous variable for the processes of income generation and accumulation which is mainly controlled by the policies of the central bank. The volume of credit and the quantity of money are endogenous with respect to production, capital accumulation and growth. Money and credit are generated by the interaction of the central bank, commercial banks, firms and private households.

The basic model developed in this part follows the Post-Keynesian distribution and growth theory in the tradition of Joan Robinson, Nicholas Kaldor and Michal Kalecki.[1] These theories attempt to extend Keynes's (1936) 'principle of effective demand' from the short period, in the sense of a given capital stock, to long-period capital accumulation and growth:

> The Keynesian models (including our own) are designed to project into the long period the central thesis of the *General Theory*, that firms are free, within wide limits, to accumulate as they please, and that the rate of saving of the economy as a whole accommodates itself to the rate of investment that they decree. (Robinson 1962, pp. 82–3, italics in the original)

Although the long-period independence of investment from saving immediately raises the problem of investment finance and finance costs, the introduction of monetary variables and an explicit analysis of the effects of a monetary rate of interest on distribution and growth were missing in the older Post-Keynesian growth and distribution models in the tradition of Kaldor and Robinson, and until recently also in the models based on the work of Kalecki. Money and a monetary rate of interest do not have a role to play in the determination of the long-period accumulation 'equilibrium' in both variants (Kregel 1985), in contrast to what Keynes (1933) demanded for a 'monetary theory of production'. This is the more surprising since it is now well known that the three founding figures also developed the Post-Keynesian monetary theory outlined in chapter 6 above, or at least shared the main propositions of this monetary approach.

In what follows, we will start in chapter 9 with an outline of the development of Post-Keynesian monetary theory in the work of Joan Robinson, Nicholas Kaldor and Michal Kalecki, on the one hand, and the Post-Keynesian models of distribution and growth pioneered by these authors, on the other hand. In the following chapters we will attempt to systematically introduce the rate of interest, finance and credit into Post-Keynesian distribution and growth theory. The procedure we pursue is inspired by Lavoie's (1995a) approach, although our way differs in many aspects from Lavoie's. Having developed the basic model economy in chapter 10, we shall introduce the rate of interest, mainly determined by central bank policies, into the accumulation function of the Kaldor–Robinson model and into the different variants of the Kaleckian model in chapters 11 and 12. As the Kaldor–Robinson model suffers from serious limitations – in particular the neglect of distribution struggle and the assumption of full utilization of the capital stock in long-period equilibrium – we will focus on monetary extensions of the Kaleckian models in chapter 13. There, firms' indebtedness will be addressed explicitly, but we will also consider interest-rate effects on distribution between capital and labour, and the effects of redistribution on consumption and saving triggered by variations in the interest rate. In chapter 14 we will summarize our main results.

9
Post-Keynesian Monetary Theory and the Models of Distribution and Growth

As early as the 1950s, Joan Robinson developed major elements of Post-Keynesian monetary theory (Lavoie 1999; Rochon 2001b; Vernengo/Rochon 2001). In her analysis of a monetary circuit Robinson (1956, pp. 225–44) shows that money supply of banks adjusts flexibly to money demand, mainly determined by production and investment decisions of firms and payment conventions, by means of credit generation and repayment. The banking sector does not directly control the quantities of credit or money, but has control only over the interest rate and can use this rate to influence credit and money demand. The rate of interest is determined by production costs in the banking sector and by the degree of competition in this sector. The rate of interest is hence treated as an exogenous variable for production and accumulation, whereas the volume of credit and the quantity of money are endogenous variables. Investment is not limited by previous saving, but investment can be financed by means of credit creation at a given rate of interest. Firms' investment decisions are affected by expected profits, and banks' decisions to finance depend on creditworthiness of prospective debtors. The latter is affected by the degree of indebtedness, because liabilities – together with the rate of interest – determine the part of profits which is to be distributed to existing creditors and which is therefore not available to pay for further credit.

These monetary considerations, however, do not matter much in Robinson's theory of capital accumulation and growth. Robinson (1962, pp. 42–4), for example, briefly discusses the role of rentiers, finance and interest rates, but the assumptions for her growth theory are chosen such that monetary policies only matter as a 'stopper to inflation' (Robinson 1962, p. 44) in case the 'inflation barrier' (Robinson 1962, p. 59) is reached. Finance constraints on capital accumulation are subsumed under 'animal spirits' in the investment function. It is assumed that investment is mainly financed out of profits and that external finance by means of bank credit at a given rate of interest is available without limits, in principle. The effects of changes in the interest rate on saving and investment which are exerted via changes in income distribution or changes in firms' internal funds are not explicitly discussed and hence do not affect long-period capital accumulation.

Nicholas Kaldor's contributions to distribution and growth theory in the 1950s and 1960s also do not contain any explicit considerations of the influence of monetary variables on distribution and long-run growth (Kaldor 1955/56, 1957, 1961). Kaldor's models of steady growth with full employment and full utilization of the capital stock implicitly assume an accommodating financial system supplying the means of finance for the growth process. At roughly the same time, however, Kaldor (1958) presented a critique of the causal relationship between the quantity of money and the level of prices as implied by the quantity theory in his report for the Radcliffe Committee. In this report he focuses on financial innovations and an increasing velocity of circulation of money in the face of rising money demand which question a stable money demand function (Bertocco 2001; Rochon 1999, pp. 99–117, 2000; Vernengo/Rochon 2001). A reversal of the Monetarist causality between the quantity of money and the price level in Kaldor's work only appeared in the 1970s and 1980s and became the foundations of the Post-Keynesian horizontalist approach discussed in chapter 6 (Kaldor 1970, 1982, 1985). But Kaldor did not relate these monetary considerations, in particular the distribution effects of monetary policies setting the interest rate, to his earlier distribution and growth models.

Michal Kalecki did not deal with the monetary and financial system in any systematic way (Sawyer 2001a). But his 'laconic' (Sawyer 2001a, p. 487) writings on the subject are perfectly compatible with Post-Keynesian monetary theory and can be integrated into this approach (Arestis 1996b; Dymski 1996; Lopez 2002; Sawyer 1985, pp. 88–107, 2001a, 2001b). In an early paper, Kalecki (1932) supposes that economic expansion requires the simultaneous expansion of the volume of credit as a precondition to allow for financing of increasing production and investment. The volume of credit is determined by credit demand, and the banking sector is capable of supplying the required amount of credit at a given rate of interest. Therefore, Kalecki follows the Post-Keynesian causality in monetary theory: Credit demand determines credit supply, generating deposits with the commercial banks and making credit money an endogenous variable which is determined by credit creation and repayment. Money is mainly credit money.

However, Kalecki's view is not truly horizontalist. In his theory of the rate of interest, Kalecki (1954, pp. 73–88) assumes a given quantity of money, but a variable velocity of money circulation. For this reason, the rate of interest is a monetary phenomenon, which has nothing to do with productivity or thrift, or with the demand for and the supply of loanable funds. But the rate of interest is not a completely exogenous variable for production and capital accumulation, as in the Post-Keynesian horizontalist view. Therefore, Sawyer (2001a) argues that Kalecki's monetary work is closer to the Post-Keynesian structuralist approach, outlined in chapter 6. According to Kalecki, the short-term rate of interest is determined by money supply and money demand for transaction purposes, with the velocity of circulation being a positive function of the short-term rate of interest. The long-term interest rate is determined by expectations about the future short-term rate.[2]

A direct impact of the long-term interest rate on investment and growth is denied by Kalecki (1954, pp. 88, 99). He argues that the long-term interest rate is rather stable in the course of the trade cycle and cannot therefore be a causal force of cyclical fluctuations. But in Kalecki's models, investment finance has a prominent role to play in the investment function. With a given amount of own capital, creditor's and borrower's risks rise with increasing investment financed by means of credit. Therefore an increasing risk premium and hence rising finance costs finally set a limit to investment of the individual firm. This 'principle of increasing risk' and its macroeconomic validity, already alluded to in chapter 6 above, will therefore have to be considered in more detail when discussing monetary extensions of Kaleckian distribution and growth models in chapter 13.

In the non-monetary Post-Keynesian distribution and growth models of Kaldor (1955/56, 1957, 1961) and Robinson (1956, 1962), investment decisions by firms, determined by 'animal spirits' and expected profits, affect functional income distribution in the long period. With the propensity to save out of wages falling short of the propensity to save out of profits, variations in income shares allow for the adjustment of saving to investment. In this way a long-period equilibrium determined by investment is established, although full utilization of the capital stock is supposed – Kaldor also assumes full employment.

In the Post-Keynesian models in the tradition of Kalecki (1954, 1971) and Steindl (1952), pioneered by Rowthorn (1981), Dutt (1984, 1987, 1990) and Amadeo (1986a, 1986b, 1987), the assumption that the capital stock is always fully utilized in the long period is abandoned. The degree of capacity utilization rather becomes an endogenous variable of the accumulation process which is determined by investment, taking the propensities to save out of profit and out of wages again as given, with the former exceeding the latter. Investment is mainly determined by expected sales and expected profits. Functional income distribution is not directly affected by spending decisions of firms and households, but it is determined by firms' pricing decisions in incompletely competitive goods markets. It is supposed that firms mark up unit variable costs, which are assumed to be roughly constant up to full capacity output. The mark up can be seen as an indicator for firms' capacity to attain a certain claim on profits against competitors and labourers. Therefore, the mark-up is determined by the degree of competition in the goods market and by relative powers of capital and labour in the labour market.

In the Rowthorn–Dutt–Amadeo variant of the Kaleckian model changes in functional income distribution have unique effects on the growth equilibrium: A rising wage share causes higher capacity utilization, capital accumulation and also a higher profit rate. In contrast to this 'stagnationist' view, Bhaduri/Marglin (1990) have shown that in a Kaleckian framework different regimes of accumulation are possible. If the profit rate as the main determinant of investment is decomposed into the profit share and capacity utilization – taking the technical conditions of production as given and constant – and if the effects of redistribution on these components of the profit rate are taken into account, equilibrium growth may be either 'wage-led' or 'profit-led', depending on the parameter values in the saving and the investment functions of the model. Therefore, the identification of an accumulation regime in a certain country in a certain period of time becomes a question of concrete historical and empirical analysis.[3] But this theoretically open variant of the Kaleckian model also suffers from the absence of monetary variables, as do the other variants of Post-Keynesian distribution and growth models treated so far.

As we have already argued in chapter 6, it was not before the late 1980s/early 1990s that Post-Keynesians started to take Keynes's (1933) research programme of a 'monetary theory of production' more and more seriously and have introduced monetary variables into the Kaldorian-Robinsonian and the Kaleckian variants of the distribution and growth models.[4] Pasinetti's (1974, pp. 139–41) natural rate of growth model, in which the normal rate of profit is positively associated with the rate of interest as long as the latter is lower than the former, has been an early exception from this general tendency of neglecting the relevance of monetary variables. In the following chapters we will not review the recent attempts to introduce monetary variables into Post-Keynesian distribution and growth models in any detail, but we shall rather attempt to systematically introduce a monetary interest rate, credit and debt finance step by step into the basic non-monetary models, with a focus on the Kaleckian approaches for reasons to be exposed below.

10
The Model Economy

10.1 Production, prices, interest, and credit

In our model we assume a closed economy with no economic activity on the part of the state. Technical change is not considered explicitly and technical conditions of production are taken as constant. There is just one type of commodity produced which can be used for consumption and investment purposes. It is assumed that there is a constant relation between the employed volume of labour (E) and real output (Y), i.e. there is no overhead labour. The productivity of labour is constant up to full capacity output and we get a constant labour–output ratio (l). The capital–potential output ratio (v) which relates the real capital stock (K) to potential real output (Y^v) is also supposed to be constant. The capital stock is assumed not to depreciate. The rate of capacity utilization (u) is given by the relation between actual real output and potential real output determined by the capital stock. Full utilization of the capital stock is not necessarily associated with full employment of labour. If output is limited by supply, it is the capital stock, rather than the labour force, which is the limiting factor. In the long period, labour supply can be assumed to adjust passively to labour demand as soon as full employment is approached, through rising participation rates or immigration.[5]

The profit rate (r) relates the annual flow of profits (Π) to the nominal capital stock (pK). Writing w^r for the real wage rate and h for the profit share, the rate of profit can be decomposed in the following ways:

$$r = \frac{\Pi}{pK} = \frac{Y - w^r L}{Y} \frac{Y}{Y^v} \frac{Y^v}{K} = (1 - w^r l) u \frac{1}{v}, \tag{II.1a}$$

$$r = \frac{\Pi}{pK} = \frac{\Pi}{pY} \frac{Y}{Y^v} \frac{Y^v}{K} = h u \frac{1}{v}. \tag{II.1b}$$

Equation (II.1a) displays the relationship between the profit rate, the real wage rate and capacity utilization. Equation (II.1b) shows that the profit rate depends on the profit share, the rate of capacity utilization and the capital–potential output ratio.

Functional income distribution, and hence the profit share is related to firms' pricing (p) in the following way:

$$p = (1 + m)wl, \quad m > 0. \tag{II.2}$$

$$h = \frac{\Pi}{pY} = 1 - \frac{1}{1+m}, \tag{II.3}$$

Writing w for the nominal wage rate, we assume that firms set prices (p) according to a mark-up (m) on constant unit labour costs up to full capacity output. The mark-up can be determined by different factors: In the Kaldor–Robinson model it is affected by effective demand in competitive goods market, in Kaleckian models it is determined by the degree of monopoly in incompletely competitive goods markets, and applying the Neo-Ricardian monetary theory of distribution it is the interest rate which determines the mark-up. Generally, we can apply the pricing equation (II.2). From this we get the profit share in equation (II.3).

Introducing monetary variables into the model, we follow the Post-Keynesian 'horizontalist' monetary view developed by Kaldor (1970, 1982, 1985), Lavoie (1984, 1992a, pp. 149–216, 1996a) and Moore (1988, 1989), which we have already outlined in chapter 6. We assume that the monetary interest rate is an exogenous variable for the accumulation process whereas the quantities of credit and money are determined endogenously by economic activity. In this view, the central bank controls the base rate of interest. Commercial banks set the market rate of interest by marking up the base rate and then supply the credit demand of consumers and investors they consider creditworthy at this interest rate. The central bank accommodates the necessary amount of cash.

For the sake of simplicity, in what follows we suppose that the central bank's interest rate policy controls the real long-term interest rate, i.e. the nominal long-term interest rate corrected by the inflation rate. The pace of capital accumulation has no direct feedback effects on the interest rate. The position taken here differs from the Post-Keynesian 'structuralist' view, also outlined in chapter 6, which assumes that a decreasing liquidity position of commercial banks and rising lenders' and borrowers' risk will finally lead to rising interest rates when the volume of credit is expanding in the accumulation process (Minsky 1986, Palley 1996b, Rousseas 1998, Wray 1990). We therefore follow Pasinetti's recommendation for the treatment of the rate of interest in the theory of effective demand:

> However important a role liquidity preference may play in Keynes' monetary theory, it is entirely immaterial to his theory of effective demand. What this theory requires, as far as the rate of interest is concerned, is not that the rate of interest is determined by liquidity preference, but that it is determined *exogenously* with respect to the income generation process. Whether, in particular, liquidity preference, or anything else determines it, is entirely immaterial. (Pasinetti 1974, p. 47, italics in the original)

In what follows, the rate of interest is considered as a purely monetary and conventional phenomenon mainly determined by the central bank. Changes in the interest rate are due to changes in the central bank's monetary regime.

In the following models the pace of accumulation and growth is determined by firms' investment. The 'principle of effective demand' also applies to the long period. Since investment determines the income generating process and hence saving, investment cannot be limited by saving. But investment, and more generally production, has to be financed independently of saving. This requires that firms have access to credit. In a growing economy, firms have to advance increasing amounts of money in order to realize production and produced profits, and this requires that the banking sector is able to generate increasing credit on demand. The volume of credit and the quantity of money are therefore endogenous to the accumulation process.

10.2 Endogenous money, credit and finance in a monetary circuit

The endogeneity of credit and money will now be analysed in more detail using a monetary circuit framework. Monetary circuit models were developed in the Monetary Circuit School, but have recently been used more frequently in Post-Keynesian work.[6] Whereas Post-Keynesian theory has focused on money as an asset which is part of the stock of wealth, Monetary Circuit theory has concentrated on money as a means of payment and therefore on money as a flow. Theses two views, however, can be synthesised in a monetary circuit model as outlined here.

The starting point of our analysis is the Post-Keynesian conviction that economic processes should be analysed as taking place in historical time and that they can therefore be treated sequentially, as in the Monetary Circuit School. Since production in a monetary economy requires monetary advances in order to obtain the required factors of production, monetary circuit models focus on the creation of money via creation of credit, the circulation of money and credit and finally the dissolution of the credit relationship and the related effects on the quantity of money (Graziani 1994). As soon as this framework is established, further assumptions about commercial banks' credit supply, about firms' credit demand deriving from their production and investment decisions, about functional income distribution, and about consumption and portfolio decisions of private households allow for the analysis of the effects of monetary policies on income shares, investment and growth.

Analysing a monetary circuit, we distinguish three sectors of the economy: the firm sector (F), the banking sector (BK) and the private household sector (HH). The firm sector produces investment and consumption goods. The banking sector consists of a central bank and commercial banks. Whereas commercial banks supply credit to the firm sector, the central bank supplies central bank money to commercial banks. The private household sector consists of workers' households (HH_W) and rentiers' households (HH_Z). Whereas workers' households sell their labour power to firms, receive wages and spend these wages on consumption goods produced and supplied by the firm sector, rentiers' households receive capital income (interest, dividends, distributed profits) from their holdings of capital assets. Rentiers' income is only partly consumed.

The agents of our model economy interact in the following macroeconomic markets: the money market, the market for short-term credit (which we will simply call the credit market) the market for long-term credit, bonds, stocks and shares (which will simply be labelled the financial market), the labour market, and the investment and consumption goods market.

On the money market, the central bank supplies central bank money to commercial banks at a base rate of interest (i_{CB}) determined by central bank policies. Commercial banks will obtain central bank money if they are willing to pay this base rate and if they are able to supply securities which meet the quality criteria determined by the central bank.

On the credit market, commercial banks grant short-term credit to those private agents who are willing to pay the rate of interest determined by commercial banks and who are considered to be creditworthy by commercial banks. We shall assume that only firms will demand short-term credit in order to initiate production. Creditworthiness mainly requires that the firms' promises to pay meet the standards defined by the central bank for the securities it is willing to accept in exchange for central bank money. Provided that firms are considered creditworthy, commercial banks are ready to supply firms' credit demand at a given rate of interest (i_B). In a credit economy, therefore, the main task of commercial banks is to collect and process information about creditworthiness and to supervise and control borrowers.[7] The rate of interest for short-term credit is determined by a mark-up on the central bank's base rate. This mark-up is affected by the degree of competition in the private banking sector and by private banks' liquidity and risk considerations.

Commercial banks also offer private agents, households and firms, the opportunity to hold deposits with them. For the sake of simplicity, we shall assume that banks do not pay interest on deposits. Net income of the private banking sector is given by the difference between interest receipts from granting credit and interest costs for obtaining central bank money, if the latter is required. This income is assumed to be distributed completely to those rentiers' households who own the private banks.

For the interest receipts the central bank receives for supplying central bank money to commercial banks, it may be assumed that this seignorage derived from monopoly supply of central bank money is distributed completely to the owner of the central bank, the state. The state may then be assumed to use these receipts for the employment of public servants and, therefore, the central bank's interest receipts would finally go to wage earners' households.[8] The net income of the banking sector as a whole will therefore flow to workers' and rentiers' households. However, in what follows, we shall assume that economic agents do not actually make use of central bank money, and hence that there are no costs for commercial banks to get hold of central bank money. Net income received by the banking sector only consists of interest on credit granted to firms, which is then assumed to be completely distributed to rentiers' households.

In order to transform short-term credit granted by commercial banks into long-term finance, either through issuing stocks and shares or through issuing bonds, firms make use of the financial market. Whereas the money and the credit markets are characterized by the creation of money and credit as preconditions for initiating a production and income-generating process, the financial market is characterized by the allocation of already existing income and wealth. We assume a uniform long-term interest rate (i) in the financial market which is affected by the central bank's base rate, commercial banks' mark-up on the base rate and by liquidity preference of rentiers' households.

In our simple monetary circuit model we have therefore three interest rates: the central bank's base rate (i_{CB}), the interest rate for short-term credit (i_B), and the long-term interest rate in the financial market (i). As long as the degree of competition in the commercial banking sector as well as liquidity preference of commercial banks and private households do not change, the interest rate structure remains constant. Under these conditions, the central bank's monetary policy applying the base rate as an instrument has unique effects on the interest rates in the credit and in the financial market. A rising base rate will shift all the other rates upwards, a falling base rate makes all the other rates decline.[9]

For this simple model economy we are now able to discuss the four phases of a monetary circuit shown in Figure II.1.[10] We do not explicitly consider the interaction between the central bank and the commercial banks, which derives from the supply of central bank money in exchange with securities or from commercial banks' holdings of compulsory minimum reserves of central bank money.[11] For the sake of simplicity we assume that payments between economic agents only take place through transfers between accounts in commercial banks, without any actual flows of central bank money. Our model economy can therefore be seen as a pure credit economy. Liquidity is held in checking accounts with commercial banks. In order to trace the monetary flows, we start with a given level of economic activity which may be considered to be compatible with goods market equilibrium: Firms' output is determined by effective demand in the goods market.

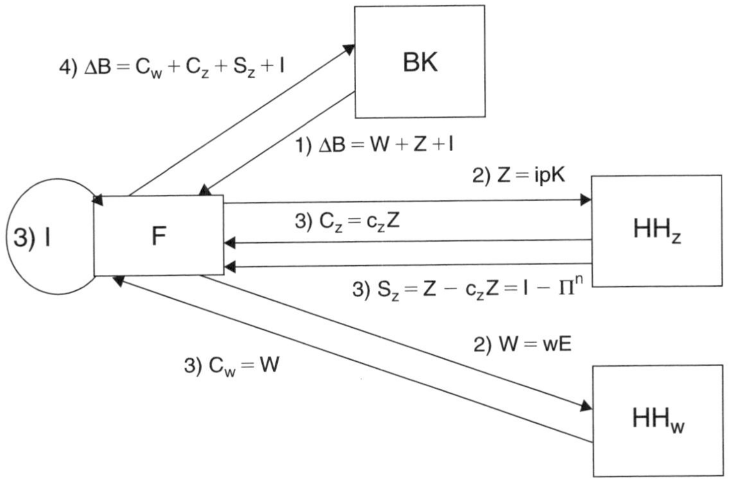

Figure II.1 Monetary circuit

In the first phase, the 'efflux phase' (Seccareccia 2003), firms demand short-term credit in the credit market. We assume that at the start of the circuit neither firms nor households dispose of liquid funds, that initiating production only requires the purchase of labour power, and that wages have to be paid in advance for the whole period of production and circulation. Therefore, in order to initiate production, firms need short-term credit (ΔB) equal to the wage bill (W) to be paid. The wage bill is determined by the nominal wage rate (w) set in the labour market and by the amount of labour (E) required for planned production ($W = wE$), with the labour–output-ratio given by the technical conditions of production. Furthermore, at the start of the circuit, firms need short-term credit in order to fulfil their payment commitments to creditors, shareholders and owners (Z), which are given from the past. At this stage of the analysis, we do not distinguish between own capital (shares) and borrowed capital (bonds, long-term credit), but assume that payment commitments to rentiers' households are determined by the long-term rate of interest (i) on the value of the capital stock (pK) at the beginning of the circuit ($Z = ipK$). If firms intend to invest in the capital stock, they will also need short-term credit for the purchase of investment goods ($I = \Delta(pK)$).[12] Therefore, 'initial finance' (Graziani 1989, p. 7) to be supplied by commercial banks' credit has to cover the wage bill, payment commitments of firms to rentiers' households, and intra-sectoral payments for investment goods in the firm sector: $\Delta B = W + Z + I = wE + ipK + I$. The 'ex nihilo' creation of credit ΔB implies that deposits with commercial banks and hence credit money (M) is created 'uno actu' by the amount $\Delta M = \Delta B$.

There has been a debate among and between authors from the Monetary Circuit School and Post-Keynesians about the necessary amount of credit creation at the start of a monetary circuit (Rochon 2005). In our view, this debate has two aspects which are usually not treated separately:

First, there is the question for which purposes firms demand 'initial finance'. Graziani (1989) assumes that firms only need short-term credit for the wage bill. According to Lavoie (1992a, pp. 152–7), 'initial finance' is not only required for the wage bill but also for payment commitments to rentiers' households. Parguez/Seccareccia (2000) and Seccareccia (1996, 2003), however, hold that 'initial finance' also has to cover firms' purchases of investment goods. We follow this approach, because in this view there is no problem of profit realization, as will be seen below. For the other approaches, however, it remains unclear how produced profits are completely realized as money profits.

Secondly, the quantitative amount of 'initial finance' has to be determined. This amount depends crucially on the velocity of circulation of credit money created by commercial banks. In a rejoinder to Renaud (2000), for instance, Nell (2002) in a two-sector framework shows that 'initial finance' only has to cover a fraction of value added, if each unit of credit money is used for several goods market transactions within a circuit, before it is paid back to the issuing bank and hence destroyed.[13] In order to avoid the associated complications, in what follows we will assume that each unit of credit money is only used for one goods or financial market transaction. This assumption is only made for convenience and does not change anything of substance in our analysis.

In the second phase of the circuit, firms use 'initial finance' in order to initiate production. They buy labour power, and workers' households receive wages (W), and firms pay capital income deriving from the holding of the stock of equity capital, bonds and credit to rentiers' households (Z). The flow of credit money created in the first phase has now partly been received as income by workers' and rentiers' households. But short-term credit bound for the purchase of investment goods (I) is still held in the firm sector. At the end of the second phase of the circuit, firms are in a position to produce the planned amount of consumption and investment goods.

In the third phase, the 'reflux-phase' (Seccareccia 2003), workers' households make use of their wage income to purchase consumption goods ($C_W = W$). This part of credit created in the first phase, therefore, flows back to the firm sector and stands ready for repayment to the banking sector. Rentiers' households use a part of their capital income, according to their average propensity to consume ($c_Z < 1$), for the purchase of consumption goods, too ($C_Z = c_Z Z$). Therefore, this part of 'initial finance' also flows back to the firm sector. Simultaneously, firms use short-term credit granted for investment purposes in order to purchase produced capital goods. Therefore, this part of credit money remains within the firm sector. The consumption expenditures of the household sector and the investment expenditures of the firm sector constitute effective demand in the goods market, and we have assumed above that firms' supply of goods just meets this effective demand. Consumption and investment expenditures also help to realize firms' gross profits as the difference between sales and wage costs. Since 'workers spend what they get', the sum of realised gross profits at the macroeconomic level is determined by firms' investment expenditures and rentiers' households' consumption expenditures: $\Pi = I + C_Z + C_W - W = I + C_Z$.

So far, the firm sector has received credit money flows amounting to $W + c_Z Z + I$, which falls short of initial credit granted to firms amounting to $W + Z + I$. Firms are therefore not yet able to repay the whole amount of short-term credit to the banking sector. Therefore, rentiers' saving $S_Z = (1 - c_Z)Z$ has to be considered next. If rentiers use the whole amount of saving for the purchase of equity capital or bonds issued by firms in the financial market, rentiers' saving will also flow back to the firm sector and will be available for the repayment of credit. Firms will transform short-term investment finance into long-term finance of their capital stock extensions. Of course, this will increase their payments commitments to rentiers' households at the start of the next circuit. It can also be seen that saving is not a precondition for the creation of credit and investment. It is just an endogenously generated source of long-term investment finance. Long-term finance of net investment, 'final finance' (Graziani 1989, p. 7), does not only draw on rentiers' saving but also on the difference between realized gross profits and capital income distributed to rentiers' households at the start of the circuit, the retained profits of enterprise: $\Pi^n = \Pi - Z$. As will be made clear in the following chapters, we assume profits of enterprise to be positive in order for production to take place. This further implies that prices set by firms in the goods market do not only have to cover wage and capital costs but also a positive contribution to profits of enterprise.

If rentiers have used their saving entirely for the purchase of shares and bonds issued by firms, in the fourth phase of the circuit firms will be in a position to pay back the whole amount of initial credit to commercial banks: $\Delta B = C_W + C_Z + S_Z + I$. The monetary circuit will therefore be closed. Credit will be repaid and the liquidity initially created will be destroyed. In order for production to continue at the same level, the same amount of credit will have to be created at the start of the next circuit. If production is to be expanded in the next round, the creation of credit will have to expand, too.

Even if each circuit is closed and there are no disturbances by changes in liquidity preference and hence money holdings, the 'initial finance' decisions by commercial banks, together with the production and investment decisions by firms, determine the level of economic activity and its increase over time. This has already been made clear by Keynes in a debate with Ohlin, Hawtrey and Robertson in the *Economic Journal* which followed the publication of the *General Theory*.[14] Whereas firms' production and investment decisions depend on sales and profit expectations, which will be dealt with in more detail below, banks' finance decisions will depend on expectations about firms' ability and willingness to pay back credit. This means that creditworthiness and the perspectives of the production and investment projects of firms will matter. Summing up, firms' production decisions and commercial banks' finance decisions will jointly determine the level of economic activity and hence employment.

If rentiers decide to hold parts of their saving as a liquid store of wealth in their checking accounts with commercial banks, firms will not be able to pay back the whole amount of initial short-term credit to banks. Rentiers' liquidity holding will constitute a stock of credit money which is equal to firms' indebtedness to the commercial banks. Holding liquidity makes the quantity of credit money increase, and also the indebtedness of the firm sector to the banking sector. If rentiers decide to hold liquidity, 'final finance' of net investment will have to be covered not only by retained earnings of firms and equity or bond purchases of rentiers' households, but also by the commercial banks' substitution of short-term credit with long-term credit granted to firms. Therefore, rentiers' portfolio decisions affect the indebtedness of firms to commercial banks. Whereas the amount of rentiers' saving has an inverse effect on firms' profits, the use of saving affects firms' indebtedness.

If commercial banks are not ready to accept increasing firms' debts in the face of rentiers' liquidity holdings, credit creation at the beginning of the following circuit will decrease and the level of economic activity will decline. The commercial banks' unwillingness to increase credit will prevent the level of economic activity from being sustained. The reason for this may be declining creditworthiness of firms associated with increasing indebtedness.[15] At a given loan rate of interest fewer firms will obtain credit. If firms attempt to reduce outstanding loans from the commercial banks at the end of the circuit in order to sustain the level of production, an increasing rate of interest in the financial market will be required in order to induce rentiers to reduce liquidity holdings in favour of the purchase of shares or bonds. Therefore, rising liquidity preference of rentiers' households may cause a reduction of banks' loan supply at a given rate of interest for short-term credit, on the one hand, and an increasing spread between the long-term and the short-term rate of interest, on the other hand. Both effects may contribute to lower production and less investment in the following circuit. Note that the introduction of liquidity preference does not cause a rising credit supply curve in interest rate loan space, as in the Post-Keynesian structuralist view outlined in chapter 6. It rather implies changes in the interest rate structure and in the number of debtors considered to be creditworthy by commercial banks. This result is perfectly compatible with the Post-Keynesian horizontalist view discussed in chapter 6.

So far, we have examined the conditions under which firms able to repay initial credit to commercial banks. We have not yet taken into account that commercial banks will demand interest on short-term credit: Initial credit ΔB will hence be associated with firms' repayment commitment amounting to $(1 + i_B)\Delta B$. Firms will only be able to comply with this commitment if they receive additional money flows of the amount $i_B \Delta B$. Since we have assumed that neither firms nor households dispose of liquid wealth at the beginning of the circuit, only commercial banks are able to inject this amount into the circuit.

In order to enable firms to repay credit plus interest in the final phase of the circuit, commercial banks have to inject an amount equal to firms' short-term interest payment obligations, either by means of buying firms' shares or bonds in the financial market (Bossone 2001), or by means of distributing this amount to bank owners (rentiers) who will then have to spend it in the financial or in the goods market. We may as well assume that interest payments on short-term initial credit of the present circuit will take place at the start of the next circuit – or during future circuits, as assumed by Rochon (2005). But it remains true that the means to pay interest have to be injected into the circuit by the commercial banks. If commercial banks refrain from injecting an amount equal to firms' short-term interest obligations into the circuit, *ceteris paribus*, the firm sector will become increasingly indebted to the banking sector, with the debt in each circuit rising by the amount of interest on short-term credit (Seccareccia 1996).

If firms' interest payments on short-term bank loans are taken into account and if it is assumed that commercial banks inject an amount equal to these obligations into the circuit, the prices for investment and consumption goods set by firms will not only have to cover wage costs, long-term capital costs and retained profits, but also interest costs for short-term bank loans, the 'initial finance' costs. With rigid nominal wages, rising interest rates will therefore, at least when retained profits have been compressed to zero, trigger increasing prices. A central bank policy of high interest rates may hence accelerate inflation. We will analyse this in more detail in chapter 16 below.

Having so far outlined the basic characteristics of a monetary circuit and explained the endogeneity of money and credit within this framework, in the following analysis we will make some simplifying assumptions. We shall assume that the monetary circuit is closed in each period and that there are hence no disturbances coming from variations in liquidity holdings of rentiers' households. Therefore, we can also do without a distinction between short-term finance of production ('initial finance') and long-term finance of investment ('final finance'), and deal only with the latter.

Under these conditions we do not have to distinguish between an interest rate for short-term credit and a long-term rate in the financial market. We can rather proceed with a single interest rate which is the interest rate in the financial market. It will be assumed that central banks' policies have a major impact on this rate. This interest rate can be considered as a 'real' interest rate, that is the nominal rate corrected for inflation, because in a model with endogenous money central banks cannot directly control inflation (by means of varying money supply, for instance) and have to take inflation as given, at least in the short run. The variation in the central bank's instrument variable, the nominal interest rate, therefore also affects the real interest rate. The role and the effectiveness of monetary policy in a Post-Keynesian/Kaleckian model of conflict inflation will be discussed in more detail in chapter 16.

10.3 Interest rate and functional income distribution

Introducing the interest rate and interest payments to rentiers' households into our model, total profits (Π) split into profit of enterprise (Π^n) and rentiers' interest income (Z). At this stage, 'interest' is generally conceived as income deriving from capital ownership. 'Interest' as a part of total profits, therefore, includes interest on credit, dividends on shares, and imputed interest on own capital. 'Interest' includes all rentiers' incomes which derive from 'pure' ownership of wealth. It does not include profit of enterprise which is associated with entrepreneurs' activity. In this sense we follow Robinson (1956, p. 247, italics in the original):

> We use the term *rentier* in an extended sense, to represent capitalists in their aspect as owners of wealth, as opposed to their aspect as entrepreneurs. We include in the incomes of rentiers dividends as well as payments of interest and we include the sums handed over to their households by entrepreneurs who own their own businesses.

Further on, we assume that rentiers' income as defined above is distributed completely to rentiers' households. Therefore, with respect to distributed profits we do not distinguish between capital stock financed by means of own capital or by means of debt. Distributed capital income to rentiers' households is given by the long-term rate of interest related to the capital stock. Therefore, the rate of interest determines 'pure' capital income distributed to rentiers. The firms' debt-capital ratio is not yet important, but will be introduced and considered in detail in chapter 13. From our assumptions so far, it follows:

$$\Pi = \Pi^n + Z = \Pi^n + ipK. \tag{II.4}$$

For the relationship between the rate of profit (r), the rate of profit of enterprise (r^n) and the interest rate (i) we get:

$$r = \frac{\Pi}{pK} = \frac{\Pi^n + Z}{pK} = r^n + i. \tag{II.5}$$

Retained profits contribute to 'final finance' of net investment in capital stock, together with issued equity capital, bonds and long-term bank credit. Retained profits in the period under consideration, therefore, contribute to an increasing value of the capital stock and hence to increasing rentiers' income in the following period, provided that there is no relevant decline in the rate of interest as a co-determinant of rentiers' income. In the real world, however, long-term investment finance by means of retained earnings will only affect the value of equity capital, but not of debt. This is another reason why we will have to consider firms' debt–capital ratio explicitly below. Being aware of this, however, we will first keep the model as simple as possible in order to analyse some basic relationships.

In order for production to take place, there has to be a positive difference between the rate of profit and the interest rate, and hence a positive rate of profit of enterprise. There have been put forward different arguments for a positive equilibrium rate of profit of enterprise and its determinants: higher uncertainty of real investment compared to financial investment, 'risks and troubles' of real investment, effective demand in the goods market, the degree of competition in the goods market, and power relations in the distribution conflict between rentiers, firms and wage earners. As we have outlined in chapter 7, there is no general agreement in the schools of thought following 'monetary analysis' concerning the relationship between the rate of profit and the rate of interest, and the constancy of the rate of profit in the face of persistent changes in the rate of interest. Therefore, we do not impose the assumption that the rate of interest determines the rate of profit, but rather keep the model more flexible.

From equations (II.1) and (II.5) we get for the profit share:

$$h = \frac{\Pi}{pY} = \frac{\Pi^n}{pY} + \frac{Z}{pY} = r^n\frac{v}{u} + i\frac{v}{u} = h^n + h^i. \tag{II.6}$$

The profit share can also be decomposed in the profit of enterprise share (h^n) and the interest share (h^i) in nominal income. The same is true for the mark-up, which can be decomposed in a part covering profits of enterprise and a part covering interest income to be distributed to rentiers.

If the mark-up remains constant in the face of interest rate changes, the real wage rate and the labour income share will not be affected. A change in the interest rate will hence not affect distribution between wages and gross profit income, but will rather influence the distribution of gross profits between firms and rentiers.

If changes in the rate of interest cause changes in the mark-up in the same direction, real wages and the labour income share will immediately be affected: Rising (falling) interest rates and rising (falling) mark-ups mean rising (falling) prices and cause falling (rising) real wages. A change in the rate of interest causes changes in the gross profit share in the same direction.

In what follows, the terms 'profit', 'profit share' and 'profit rate' will be related to gross profits as the sum of profit of enterprise and interest.

11

The Rate of Interest in the Kaldor–Robinson Model of Distribution and Growth

11.1 The model

In the Kaldor–Robinson model the attempt is made to integrate major elements of the early Post-Keynesian distribution and growth theory pioneered by Joan Robinson (1956, 1962) and Nicholas Kaldor (1955/56, 1957, 1961) into a simple model, without being able to do justice to the rich flavour of their theories.[16] The main characteristics of these theories, and hence of the Kaldor–Robinson model, are as follows: First, full or normal utilization of the capital stock in long-period growth equilibrium is assumed.[17] Secondly, it is assumed that firms' investment decisions determine capital accumulation and growth and are themselves mainly affected by the expected profit rate. Third, a flexible mark-up is supposed, which means that in goods market disequilibrium, goods market prices change faster than nominal wages. Under the conditions of full utilization of the capital stock, this allows for the adjustment of saving to investment through redistribution of income, provided that the propensity to save out of wages is lower than the propensity to save out of profits. The goods market equilibrium, therefore, also establishes equilibrium income shares in this model. The Kaldor–Robinson model shall now be extended by means of introducing an exogenously determined interest rate into the accumulation function. We get the following model:

$$r = (1 - w^r l)u\frac{1}{v} = hu\frac{1}{v}, \tag{II.1}$$

$$u = 1, \tag{II.7}$$

$$\sigma = \frac{S}{pK} = \frac{s_\Pi \Pi}{pK} = s_\Pi r, \quad 0 < s_\Pi \leq 1, \tag{II.8}$$

$$g = \frac{I}{pK} = \alpha + \gamma r - \theta i, \quad \alpha, \gamma, \theta > 0, \quad g > 0 \text{ only if } r - i > 0, \tag{II.9}$$

$$g = \sigma, \tag{II.10}$$

$$\frac{\partial \sigma}{\partial r} - \frac{\partial g}{\partial r} > 0 \Rightarrow s_\Pi - \gamma > 0. \tag{II.11}$$

Equation (II.1) describes the structure of production and the relationship between the profit rate, the rate of capacity utilization, and the real wage rate, or the profit share. The assumption from equation (II.7), full or 'normal' utilization of the capital stock in long-period growth equilibrium, implies a strictly inverse relationship between the rate of profit and the real wage rate.[18] In equation (II.8) a classical saving function is supposed, which means that wages are completely spent on consumption goods and that saving only derives from profits. The saving rate (σ), which relates saving (S) to the nominal capital stock (pK), is determined by the rate of profit and by the propensity to save out of profits (s_Π). A potential dependence of the propensity to save out of profits on the distribution of profits between retained earnings and rentiers' income is not taken into account.

The model is driven by firms' investment (I). Firms' decisions to invest depend positively on the expected rate of profit, which in equilibrium is equal to the actual rate, and in our monetary extension of the Kaldor–Robinson model also negatively on the rate of interest. The accumulation function in equation (II.9) describes the growth rate of the capital stock (g) as a linear function of the rate of profit and the interest rate. The positive effect of the rate of profit on investment decisions does not rely only on a supposed positive relation between actual and expected profits. It also takes into account that profits have a positive effect on internal means of long-term investment finance, as well as on firms' access to external means of finance from banks or financial markets.

> Profit influences investment not only by providing the motive for it but also through providing the means. An important part of the gross investment of firms is financed by gross retained profits. Moreover, the amount that a firm puts up of its own finance influences the amount that it can borrow from outside. (Robinson 1962, p. 86)

Therefore, a negative impact of the interest rate on capital accumulation is given, because prospective interest payments have a negative influence on expected profits of enterprise, on the one hand, and actual interest payments reduce internal means of investment finance and also access to external finance, on the other hand. Investment is also affected by animal spirits (α) and a positive rate of capital accumulation requires a positive difference between the rate of profit and the interest rate, and hence a positive rate of profit of enterprise.

Equation (II.10) contains the equilibrium condition: The goods market equilibrium requires the equality of the accumulation rate and the saving rate. The equilibrium will be stable, if saving responds more elastically to the endogenous variable of the model, the rate of profit, than investment, and hence if the stability condition in equation (II.11) is valid.

Inserting equations (II.8) and (II.9) into the equilibrium condition in equation (II.10) yields the equilibrium rate of profit (r^*):

$$r^* = \frac{\alpha - \theta i}{s_\Pi - \gamma}. \tag{II.12}$$

From this and from equations (II.8) and (II.9) it follows for the equilibrium rates of capital accumulation and saving:

$$g^* = \sigma^* = \frac{s_\Pi(\alpha - \theta i)}{s_\Pi - \gamma}. \tag{II.13}$$

A change in the rate of interest has a uniquely negative effect on the equilibrium rates of profit and capital accumulation:

$$\frac{\partial r}{\partial i} = \frac{-\theta}{s_\Pi - \gamma} < 0, \tag{II.14}$$

$$\frac{\partial g}{\partial i} = \frac{-s_\Pi \theta}{s_\Pi - \gamma} < 0. \tag{II.15}$$

A rising (falling) interest rate reduces (increases) the accumulation rate and hence the profit rate in long-period growth equilibrium. Increasing interest rates reduce firms' investment, and hence effective demand. Goods prices decrease, and with constant nominal wages, real wages will rise. In this model, rising interest rates are linked, through falling capital accumulation, with falling mark-ups and a falling profit share.[19] A direct and positive relationship between the rate of interest and the rate of profit does not exist. Robinson (1956, p. 242) notes:

> The level of interest rates is therefore not closely tethered to the level of profits and enjoys, so to say, a life of its own. …In so far as high interest rates are discouraging to investment they tend to retard

accumulation, and the slower is the rate of accumulation the lower is the level of profits and the more discouraging any given level of interest rate becomes.

11.2 Limitations of the model

The simple monetary extension of the Kaldor–Robinson model suffers from some serious limitations which are already contained in the basic non-monetary model.

First, the Kaldor–Robinson model has only little space for distribution conflict between capital and labour and its potential effects on real wages and income shares. The real wage rate remains a residual variable which adjusts passively to decisions about consumption and investment demand and hence to goods market processes. Only the 'inflation barrier' (Robinson 1962, pp. 58–9) at which labourers refuse real wage cuts sets a limit to this adjustment and causes cumulative inflation processes.

Secondly, the determination of income shares by investment and saving supposes symmetrical reactions in case of goods market disequilibria. With excess demand, prices will have to rise and the real wage rate will have to fall. With excess supply, prices will have to fall and real wages will have to rise. This supposes the goods market to be highly competitive and prices to adjust flexibly to variations in demand, whereas nominal wages in the labour market have to be rather rigid. Only under these conditions will demand always be equal to full capacity output and supply. However, if goods markets deviate only slightly from perfect competition, the outcome might be completely different. If there are some price rigidities in the goods market, output adjustment may be faster than price adjustments in the face of falling demand, and the economy may get to rest at a level below full utilization of productive capacity. Therefore, the assumption of full utilization of productive capacity given by the capital stock in long-period growth equilibrium may be overly rigid. This assumption implies a strictly inverse relationship between the real wage rate and the profit rate, and also between the real wage rate and the rate of capital accumulation. It precludes the possibility that the economic system adjusts to changes in consumption and investment demand through variations in the degree of capacity utilization.

Thirdly, the accumulation function in the Kaldor–Robinson model is not wholly convincing. For a monetary production economy relying on expected monetary returns as a precondition for monetary advances which are necessary to initiate production, the expected profit rate and the rate of interest should be important determinants for investment.

However, it should also be considered that the rate of profit is affected by different forces. With the technical conditions of production given, these include changes in costs and changes in demand. Therefore, these forces should be made visible in the accumulation function of the model, and its effects on investment should be analysed in more detail.

12
The Rate of Interest in Kaleckian Models of Distribution and Growth

12.1 The basic structure: endogenous rate of capacity utilization, mark-up pricing, and classical saving hypothesis

The Kaleckian models of distribution and growth which build on the foundations of Kalecki (1954, 1971) and Steindl (1952) show the following characteristics:[20] First, unlike the Kaldor–Robinson model, it is supposed that productive capacities in the industrial sector of the economy may not be fully utilized also in the long period. Unemployment and underutilization of capacity given by the capital stock are not only short-period but, rather, permanent features of capitalist economies. Secondly, with the technical conditions of production given and constant unit variable costs up to full capacity output, functional income distribution is determined by firms' mark-up pricing in incompletely competitive goods markets. Thirdly, in complete agreement with the Kaldor–Robinson model, investment is viewed to be independent of saving also in the long period. But, contrary to the Kaldor–Robinson model, the adjustment of saving to investment is supposed to take place through output and growth, and not through redistribution between wages and profits.

In the basic Kaleckian model, investment decisions also depend on the expected profit rate. However, it is taken into account that the profit rate itself depends on different forces. This has given rise to different accumulation functions in the Kaleckian framework with different implications for the behaviour of the model economy. Below, we shall distinguish two variants of the Kaleckian model, the Rowthorn–Dutt–Amadeo model and the Bhaduri/Marglin model,[21] and we shall extend these models by an exogenously given rate of interest. Before doing this, however, we shall consider in more detail two major characteristics of the Kaleckian model alluded to above, which the two variants have in common: the long-run variable rate of capacity utilization and the determination of functional income distribution by mark-up pricing.

There have been given several reasons for the treatment of the degree of capacity utilization as an endogenous variable of the accumulation process and hence for a potential deviation of capacity utilization from full utilization in long-period accumulation equilibrium. Kalecki (1971, pp. 135–7) argued that the long-run accumulation path is nothing more than the average of past cyclical fluctuation in capital accumulation. Only in the boom phase of the cycle, productive capacities are fully utilized. The average degree of utilization over the cycle, however, is well below full utilization:

> Even on the average the degree of utilisation throughout the business cycle will be substantially below the maximum reached during the boom. Fluctuations in the utilisation of available labour parallel those in the utilisation of equipment. Not only is there mass unemployment in the slump, but average employment throughout the cycle is considerably below the peak reached in the boom. The reserve of capital equipment and the reserve army of unemployed are typical features of capitalist economy at least throughout a considerable part of the cycle. (Kalecki 1971, p. 137)

Steindl (1952, pp. 9–14) made the argument that in oligopolistic markets firms deliberately hold excess capacity in order to meet unforeseen fluctuations in demand and to prevent potential competitors from market entry. Sylos-Labini (1969) also focussed on the entry-preventing effect of excess capacity. Indivisibilities of the capital stock and firms' strategic considerations in imperfect goods markets hence prevent a continuous adjustment of productive capacity to varying demand. Planned excess capacity does not imply that the whole capital stock is used inefficiently, contradicting cost minimization. We may rather suppose that with excess capacity a part of the capital stock, i.e. some plants of a firm, is not used at all whereas the other part, i.e. the other plants, is used in an economically efficient way (Lavoie 1992a, pp. 327–8).

The Kaleckian view on the endogenous determination of capacity utilization, however, has been criticized by some neo-Marxian and neo-Ricardian authors (Auerbach/Skott 1988; Committeri 1986). It is argued that the endogenously determined equilibrium rate of capacity utilization in Kaleckian models may deviate permanently from firms' target rate of utilization, the long-period 'normal rate', without any tendency of adjustment.[22] This is seen to be inconsistent with the requirement that firms' investment decisions should be based on expectations of some 'normal rate' of utilization of new productive equipment. Therefore, firms are supposed to adjust productive capacity to demand in the long period, and it is argued that capacity utilization should be equal to firms' target rate of utilization in a 'fully adjusted long-period position'. We shall deal with this and associated problems, and with Kaleckian solutions in more detail in chapter 17 below.

With an endogenous rate of capacity utilization in Kaleckian models, the strictly inverse relationship between the real wage rate, or the wage share, and the profit rate prevalent in the Kaldor–Robinson model is abandoned. From equation (II.1) it can be seen that an increasing real wage rate and hence a decreasing profit share need not be associated with a falling profit rate, if the degree of capacity utilization rises simultaneously.

$$r = (1 - w^r l)u\frac{1}{v} = hu\frac{1}{v}. \tag{II.1}$$

Income shares in our simple Kaleckian models are determined by mark-up pricing.[23] According to Kalecki (1954, pp. 11–41), the industrial sector of developed capitalist economies is characterized by imperfect competition and excess capacity. Firms adjust output and capacity utilization when they are facing variations in demand. Prices are actively set by firms marking up unit variable costs. The mark-up is determined by the 'degree of monopoly' (Kalecki 1954, p. 13). It is assumed that marginal and average variable costs are roughly constant up to full capacity output.

According to Kalecki (1954, pp. 17–18), the degree of monopoly is mainly determined by economic concentration. The higher the share of output of the leading firms in total output of an industry, the less intense price competition and the higher the degree of monopoly will be. The degree of monopoly is further affected by the relative importance of price competition compared to non-price competition through advertising, product differentiation, and so on. The less important price competition, the higher will be the degree of monopoly. Further on, the degree of monopoly is affected by the development of overheads relative to prime costs and by the power of trade unions. If overhead costs rise for most of the firms, a tacit agreement will be likely to increase prices relative to prime costs. This implies an increase in the degree of monopoly. However, the relationship between overhead costs and the degree of monopoly is not very strict and clear-cut: 'The degree of monopoly *may*, but need not necessarily, increase as result of a rise in overheads in relation to prime costs' (Kalecki 1954, p. 18, italics in the original).

The power of trade unions affects the degree of monopoly and hence the mark-up inversely. According to Kalecki, a high degree of monopoly will induce trade unions to demand higher wages. Increasing costs, however, will then endanger the competitive position of the firm or the industry in question. Therefore, the more powerful trade unions are to push for higher wages, the lower will be the degree of monopoly and hence the mark-up firms are able to sustain. It has to be noted that trade unions and distribution conflict will only be able to increase the wage share if the degree of monopoly and hence the mark-up is affected. Raising nominal wages in the labour market is therefore not a sufficient condition for an increasing wage share in our simple one good, constant technology, and closed economy framework.[24]

> Kalecki considered the impact of trade unions through their effect on the degree of monopoly. Trade unions are seen as only able to raise real wages and wage share in so far as they are able to modify the degree of monopoly. Thus power in the labour market is seen as of little use without some corresponding power in the product market or some constraint on firms in that market to offset power in the labour market. (Sawyer 1985, p. 113)

Summing up so far, the mark-up and hence the profit share in equations (II.2) and (II.3) are determined by economic concentration and the relative importance and intensity of price competition in the goods market, and by the strength and power of the trade unions:

$$p = (1 + m)wl, \quad m > 0, \tag{II.2}$$

$$h = 1 - \frac{1}{1+m}. \tag{II.3}$$

Changes in the interest rate may, but need not, affect distribution between wages and gross profits. Rising interest rates imply rising overheads and may, therefore, increase the degree of monopoly, the mark-up and hence the profit share. However, we have seen that Kalecki does not strictly advocate this view. Therefore, rising interest rates may, but need not, be associated with a rising profit share and a falling wage share. They may also cause a falling share of profits of enterprise. In Kaleckian and Post-Keynesian models of cost-plus pricing there is also no direct relationship between the interest rate and the firms' mark-up in the goods market.[25] In this chapter we shall, therefore, assume that the mark-up in the Kaleckian distribution and growth models is interest-inelastic. Changes in the rate of interest cause a redistribution of profits between firms and rentiers but do not affect the distribution between wages and gross profits. As we have outlined in chapter 5, this view can also be found in Marx's analysis of the relationship between the interest rate and the rate of profit. Equations (II.2) and (II.3) can now be specified as follows:

$$p = (1 + m)wl, \quad m > 0, \ \frac{\partial m}{\partial i} = 0, \qquad \text{(II.16)}$$

$$h = 1 - \frac{1}{1+m}, \quad \frac{\partial h}{\partial i} = 0. \qquad \text{(II.17)}$$

The implications and consequences of interest-elastic mark-ups and profit shares, which are also compatible with Kalecki's view, shall be discussed in chapter 13.

Finally, in the Kaleckian distribution and growth models we shall again assume a classical saving hypothesis, which means that there is no saving out of wages. Potential effects of redistribution between profits of enterprise and rentiers' income on the average propensity to save out of profits are not yet taken into account, but will also be considered in chapter 13. Therefore, we can apply again the saving function which has already been used in the Kaldor–Robinson model above:

$$\sigma = \frac{S}{pK} = \frac{s_\Pi \Pi}{pK} = s_\Pi r = s_\Pi h u \frac{1}{v}, \quad 0 < s_\Pi \leq 1. \qquad \text{(II.8)}$$

So far, we have outlined the common elements of the different variants of Kaleckian distribution and growth theory. As already noted, there are major differences among Kaleckian models with respect to the accumulation function. These shall be discussed next.

12.2 The choice of the investment function

The choice of an investment function for a Kaleckian model of distribution and growth raises major problems. In Kalecki's work there can be found different investment functions, and in his latest publications, he still was looking for an adequate modelling of firms' investment decisions.[26] In his early work, published in 1933 in Poland, Kalecki (1933) supposed that the rate of capital accumulation depends positively on the expected gross rate of profit and negatively on the rate of interest. Firms' investment decisions are therefore determined by the rate of profit of enterprise – the difference between the rate of profit and the rate of interest. Since the long-term rate of interest varies little over the cycle, according to Kalecki, the investment function is then simplified and the rate of capital accumulation is supposed to depend positively on the rate of profit (Kalecki 1969, pp. 7–10). And since profits under the conditions of a classical saving hypothesis are determined by capitalists' consumption and investment expenditures, and since the rate of profit also depends on the capital stock, investment decisions are positively affected by past investment and negatively by the volume of the present capital stock. The positive demand effects of investment stimulate further investment, on the one hand, but the capacity effect of investment dampens further investment, on the other hand. These contradicting effects of investment may hence generate a trade cycle.

In Kalecki's later work, in particular in Kalecki (1954, pp. 96–108), investment decisions are affected by firms' financial resources, and by changes in profits and in the capital stock which together determine the rate of profit. Following his 'principle of increasing risk', already published in Kalecki (1937), the effect of internal means of finance on investment is caused by the dominance of imperfect capital markets which restrict access to external means of finance (Kalecki 1954, pp. 91–5).[27] Therefore, retained profits have an immediately positive effect on investment financed by internal means. Further on, own capital and retained earnings improve access to external finance in financial markets, because firms can offer more collateral: 'The access of a firm to the capital market, or in other words the amount of rentier capital it may hope to obtain, is determined to a large extent by the amount of its entrepreneurial capital' (Kalecki 1954, p. 91).

A compensation of a lack of entrepreneurial capital or retained earnings by the firm's willingness to pay higher interest rates is explicitly denied by Kalecki (1954, pp. 91–2). For the creditor, the firm's willingness to pay higher interest rates in the face of uncertain proceeds rather reinforces scepticism with respect to the firm's future solvency and its creditworthiness. With own capital of the single firm given, the possibility of a positive relationship between investment and the rate of interest, as conceded in Kalecki (1937), is therefore abandoned, even for the single firm.

Also for the firm as debtor, the willingness to go into debt increases with the amount of own capital. Because of the uncertainty of prospective proceeds, firms tend to minimize the share of fixed payment obligations in uncertain future profits in order to avoid illiquidity or loss of entrepreneurial capital in the case of unsuccessful business.

> A firm considering expansion must face the fact that, given the amount of the entrepreneurial capital, the risk increases with the

amount invested. The greater the investment in relation to the entrepreneurial capital, the greater is the reduction of the entrepreneur's income in the event of an unsuccessful business venture. (Kalecki 1954, p. 92)

Entrepreneurial capital as a limit to investment finance for the single firm due to the 'principle of increasing risk' is also valid for joint-stock companies' access to the market of equity. Kalecki (1954, pp. 93–4) argues that new share issues in order to finance investment may endanger the position of the dominant share holders, decrease dividend payments on existing shares, if investment does not increase profits proportionally, or may reduce share prices if the market is too limited. From this it follows that investment of joint-stock companies is also limited by retained profits.

The profit rate, as the second determinant of investment, is affected positively by a change in firms' current profits, and negatively by a change in the capital stock. Therefore, the profit rate also enters into Kalecki's (1954) determinants of investment.

Finally, Kalecki (1954, p. 98) gets an investment function in which investment decisions are affected positively by retained profits and by changes in current profits, and negatively by changes in the capital stock.[28] An impact of the rate of interest on investment is denied again, because Kalecki (1954, p. 99) holds that the long-term rate of interest is rather stable in the course of the trade cycle and therefore cannot explain cyclical fluctuations in investment. The Kaleckian models of distribution and growth discussed in the present book, however, do not focus on short-run cyclical fluctuations but rather deal with medium- to long-term developments. And in this perspective the rate of interest has shown considerable changes in OECD countries over the recent decades (Hein/Ochsen 2003).

In the Kaleckian models to be discussed, a generally positive effect of the profit rate on capital accumulation is not controversial, for the reasons given by Kalecki. The concrete impact of profits on capital accumulation, however, is modelled differently. As mentioned above, we can distinguish two variants of the Kaleckian model: the Rowthorn–Dutt–Amadeo model, pioneered by the work of Rowthorn (1981), Dutt (1984, 1987) and Amadeo (1986a, 1986b), and the Bhaduri/Marglin model, first published in Bhaduri/Marglin (1990).

Rowthorn (1981) and Dutt (1987) assume that firms' decisions to accumulate are determined by the degree of capacity utilization and by the realized rate of profit. Amadeo (1986a, 1986b, 1987) omits the realized rate of profit and only includes the rate of capacity utilization into his models. The results, however, are essentially the same as those in Rowthorn (1981) and Dutt (1987), because in these models it is implicitly assumed that increasing capacity utilization is always associated with an increasing rate of profit. A constant profit rate in the face of increasing capacity utilization would imply a falling profit share. The profit share or the real wage rate, however, does not explicitly enter into the accumulation function. Therefore, a dominant effect of capacity utilization and a negligible impact of wage costs on investment seem to be supposed. The non-monetary Rowthorn–Dutt–Amadeo model displays clear-cut stagnationist or wage-led features: A reduction of the mark-up and hence the profit share causes increasing equilibrium rates of capacity utilization, capital accumulation and profit.

These unique results cannot be sustained in the Bhaduri/Marglin (1990) approach, in which capital accumulation also depends on the profit rate. Their model, however, takes into account the contradicting effects of redistribution on the profit rate and, hence, on capital accumulation. Redistribution at the expense of profits pushes consumption demand, and hence capacity utilization and the profit rate. But it also increases firms' unit labour costs and reduces unit profits and the profit rate. With constant technical conditions of production, as in our model, the decomposition of the profit rate makes investment decisions of firms depend on capacity utilization and on the profit share. Taking these contradictory effects of redistribution into account, Bhaduri/Marglin (1990) derive different accumulation regimes in a model which is otherwise identical with the Rowthorn–Dutt–Amadeo model. Depending on the values of the coefficients in the saving and in the accumulation function, 'wage-led' or 'profit-led' regimes may emerge.

The introduction of a monetary rate of interest into these models can make use of Kalecki's 'principle of increasing risk' outlined above. Firms have to finance their investment over the long term. This can take place through retained earnings, but firms will also need external long-term finance, which can be raised either by means of issuing shares and bonds or by looking for long-term bank credit. Access to external finance in imperfect financial markets is positively affected by firms' own capital and by retained profits. This is particularly true for access to bank credit, but retained earnings also affect investment of joint stock companies' access to equity capital in financial markets. Therefore, the higher the amount of retained profits, the more external finance will be available for investment purposes.

In our model economy, the firms' retention ratio (s_C) depends on the relationship between the rate of interest and the rate of profit, because so far the rate of interest determines distributed profits. Taking into account equations (II.4) and (II.5) we get:

$$s_C = \frac{\Pi - Z}{\Pi} = 1 - \frac{i}{r}. \tag{II.18}$$

Since retained profits depend negatively on the rate of interest, the latter becomes a determinant of investment through this channel. On the one hand, the lower the actual rate of interest relative to the actual rate of profit, the more internal means of finance for investment are available and the more external means can be raised without approaching the maximum degree of indebtedness tolerated by creditors or financial investors, and by firms themselves. On the other hand, the lower the expected rate of interest in relation to the expected rate of profit, the lower are creditor's and debtor's risks and the higher the maximum degree of indebtedness which will be tolerated by creditors and debtors. An increasing rate of interest will therefore negatively affect firms' investment.

Note that the effect of the interest rate on investment does not so much depend on direct financing costs or opportunity costs of real investment, as in Keynes (1936), but more on the effect of the interest rate on internal funds and the related access to external finance in imperfect financial markets. These basic insights, going back to Kalecki (1937), have recently been rediscovered by New Keynesian economists focussing on asymmetric information, adverse selection and moral hazard in financial markets, without acknowledging Kalecki's work, however.[29] Empirical papers on the determinants of firms' investment have also convincingly confirmed this channel of influence.[30] In the next sections we will therefore introduce this effect of the interest rate into the two variants of the Kaleckian distribution and growth model.

12.3 The rate of interest in the Rowthorn–Dutt–Amadeo model

Introducing the effect of an exogenous rate of interest on investment into the stagnationist or 'wage-led' variant of Kaleckian distribution and growth theory yields the following model:

$$r = hu\frac{1}{v}. \tag{II.1b}$$

$$p = (1+m)wl, \quad m > 0, \ \frac{\partial m}{\partial i} = 0, \tag{II.16}$$

$$h = 1 - \frac{1}{1+m}, \quad \frac{\partial h}{\partial i} = 0, \tag{II.17}$$

$$\sigma = s_{\Pi} h u \frac{1}{v}, \quad 0 < s_{\Pi} \leq 1, \tag{II.8}$$

$$g = \alpha + \beta u - \theta i, \quad \alpha, \beta, \theta > 0, \quad g > 0 \text{ for } r - i > 0, \tag{II.19}$$

$$g = \sigma, \tag{II.10}$$

$$\frac{\partial \sigma}{\partial u} - \frac{\partial g}{\partial u} > 0 \Rightarrow s_{\Pi}\frac{h}{v} - \beta > 0. \tag{II.20}$$

Equation (II.1) defines the profit rate, the equilibrium value of which now also depends on endogenously determined equilibrium capacity utilization which may diverge from full or 'normal' utilization. Functional income distribution in equation (II.17) is determined by mark-up pricing in equation (II.16), assuming an interest-inelastic mark-up at this stage. The saving rate in equation (II.8) supposes a classical saving hypothesis. Extending the accumulation function of the Rowthorn–Dutt–Amadeo model by an exogenous interest rate gives equation (II.19). Capital accumulation is positively affected by the degree of capacity utilization and negatively by the rate of interest. For capital accumulation to be positive, the rate of profit has to exceed the rate of interest, and hence the rate of profit of enterprise has to be positive. Equation (II.10) is the equilibrium condition and equation (II.20) the stability condition for the goods market equilibrium. Since in Kaleckian models the rate of capacity utilization is the endogenous variable, stability of the goods market equilibrium requires that the rate of capital accumulation responds less elastically to a variation in this rate than does the saving rate.

The equilibrium values of the rates of capacity utilization, capital accumulation and profit are given as follows:

$$u^* = \frac{\alpha - \theta i}{s_{\Pi}\frac{h}{v} - \beta}, \tag{II.21}$$

$$g^* = \sigma^* = \frac{s_{\Pi}\frac{h}{v}(\alpha - \theta i)}{s_{\Pi}\frac{h}{v} - \beta}, \tag{II.22}$$

$$r^* = \frac{\frac{h}{v}(\alpha - \theta i)}{s_{\Pi}\frac{h}{v} - \beta}. \tag{II.23}$$

Changes in the monetary interest rate have uniquely inverse effects on the real equilibrium values of the model: An increase in the rate of interest causes a reduction in the rates of capacity utilization, capital accumulation and profit:

$$\frac{\partial u}{\partial i} = \frac{-\theta}{s_\Pi \frac{h}{v} - \beta} < 0, \tag{II.24}$$

$$\frac{\partial g}{\partial i} = \frac{-s_\Pi \frac{h}{v}\theta}{s_\Pi \frac{h}{v} - \beta} < 0, \tag{II.25}$$

$$\frac{\partial r}{\partial i} = \frac{-\frac{h}{v}\theta}{s_\Pi \frac{h}{v} - \beta} < 0. \tag{II.26}$$

Following our assumption with respect to the mark-up made above, functional income distribution, and hence the profit share, is not affected by changes in the interest rate.

12.4 The rate of interest in the Bhaduri/Marglin model

The Bhaduri/Marglin model differs from the Rowthorn–Dutt–Amadeo model only with respect to the accumulation function (equation (II.27) below). For the reasons mentioned above, it is assumed that investment in capital stock is affected positively by the rate of profit and negatively by the rate of interest. With the technical conditions of production given and constant, the rate of profit depends on the profit share and the rate of capacity utilization. An increasing profit share caused by an increasing mark-up stimulates investment, *ceteris paribus*, because unit profits increase and internal means of finance for investment purposes are raised. A rising rate of capacity utilization is also associated with increasing internal means of finance and it indicates an improved relationship between demand and productive capacity. Therefore, increasing capacity utilization also stimulates investment. The separate effects of the profit share and capacity utilization are explicitly introduced into the investment function and supplemented by the negative impact of the rate of interest. Again, we assume that the rate of capital accumulation will only be positive, if the rate of profit exceeds the rate of interest and the rate of profit of enterprise is positive. Therefore, we obtain the following model:

$$r = hu\frac{1}{v}, \tag{II.1}$$

$$p = (1 + m)wl, \qquad m > 0, \ \frac{\partial m}{\partial i} = 0, \tag{II.16}$$

$$h = 1 - \frac{1}{1 + m}, \qquad \frac{\partial h}{\partial i} = 0, \tag{II.17}$$

$$\sigma = s_{\Pi}hu\frac{1}{v}, \qquad 0 < s_{\Pi} \leq 1, \tag{II.8}$$

$$g = \alpha + \beta u + \tau h - \theta i, \qquad \alpha, \beta, \tau, \theta > 0, \quad g > 0 \text{ for } r - i > 0, \tag{II.27}$$

$$g = \sigma, \tag{II.10}$$

$$\frac{\partial \sigma}{\partial u} - \frac{\partial g}{\partial u} > 0 \Rightarrow s_{\Pi}\frac{h}{v} - \beta > 0. \tag{II.20}$$

The equilibrium values for the endogenously determined rates of capacity utilization, capital accumulation and profit are as follows:

$$u^* = \frac{\alpha + \tau h - \theta i}{s_{\Pi}\frac{h}{v} - \beta}, \tag{II.28}$$

$$g^* = \sigma^* = \frac{s_{\Pi}\frac{h}{v}(\alpha + \tau h - \theta i)}{s_{\Pi}\frac{h}{v} - \beta}, \tag{II.29}$$

$$r^* = \frac{\frac{h}{v}(\alpha + \tau h - \theta i)}{s_{\Pi}\frac{h}{v} - \beta}. \tag{II.30}$$

Also in the Bhaduri/Marglin model, the effects of a change in the exogenous monetary interest rate on the real equilibrium values of the model are uniquely inverse. With the assumed constancy of the profit share, an increasing rate of interest causes falling equilibrium rates of capacity utilization, capital accumulation and profit:

$$\frac{\partial u}{\partial i} = \frac{-\theta}{s_{\Pi}\frac{h}{v} - \beta} < 0, \tag{II.31}$$

$$\frac{\partial g}{\partial i} = \frac{-s_\Pi \frac{h}{v}\theta}{s_\Pi \frac{h}{v} - \beta} < 0, \tag{II.32}$$

$$\frac{\partial r}{\partial i} = \frac{-\frac{h}{v}\theta}{s_\Pi \frac{h}{v} - \beta} < 0. \tag{II.33}$$

Although changes in functional income distribution may have different effects in the Bhaduri/Marglin model than in the Rowthorn–Dutt–Amadeo model, both simple monetary extensions of these Kaleckian models display similar results with respect to the effects of changes in the rate of interest. However, the monetary extensions discussed in this chapter are far too simple, because they only consider a negative impact of the interest rate in the investment functions of the models. Therefore, we have to extend these models in the following chapter.

13
Kaleckian Models Extended

13.1 Extensions

Further monetary extensions of the Kaleckian models are related to three important aspects. First, we shall distinguish between own capital and debt capital and we shall hence introduce the debt–capital ratio into the investment functions of the models. The long-run dynamics of this ratio will be studied in both variants of the Kaleckian model. Secondly, we shall explicitly consider the effects of changes in the rate of interest and in the debt–capital ratio also in the saving functions of the models. In the simple models discussed so far, we have implicitly assumed that changes in the rate of interest and hence in distribution between profits of enterprise and rentiers' income do not affect the aggregate propensity to save out of profits. Since the propensity to save out of retained earnings is unity by definition, we have therefore implicitly assumed that the rentiers' propensity is also unity. This is a serious restriction which has to be removed. Third, we shall also consider the possibility of an interest-elastic mark-up. Changes in the rate of interest may hence affect distribution between gross profits and wages.

The debt–capital ratio

In the models discussed so far, we have distinguished between profits of enterprise, or retained earnings, on the one hand, and 'pure' capital income, interest or rentiers' income, on the other hand. We have assumed that rentiers' income is determined by the rate of interest on the whole capital stock. This has been the easiest way to introduce distribution conflict between firms and rentiers into Post-Keynesian distribution and growth models. However, to do without a distinction between own capital and debt has some major disadvantages. First, it is unrealistically implied that an increase in the capital stock financed by retained earnings, *ceteris paribus*, will increase future income distributed to rentiers, being determined by the rate of interest and the increased capital stock. Secondly, firms' indebtedness as a determinant of investment is only insufficiently taken into account. So far, we have only been able to integrate the negative effects of interest payments on retained earnings and hence on firms' willingness to invest and creditors' willingness to finance. The stock of debt as a determinant of investment (and saving) has not been considered at all. In order to remedy these omissions, we shall augment the Rowthorn–Dutt–Amadeo as well as the Bhaduri/Marglin model by the explicit introduction of the firms' debt–capital ratio into the saving and the investment functions of the models.

In the extended models we shall assume that long-term investment finance is supplied by retained earnings or by long-term credit of rentiers' households (directly or through banks). Only the stock of long-term credit gives rise to interest payments and hence distributed profits. We do not consider long-term finance by shares or bonds. By means of this simplification we do not have to distinguish between creditor households receiving interest income, on the one hand, and shareholder households receiving dividend income, on the other hand, and their different saving propensities, in contrast to what was done, for example, in Lavoie (1995a).[31] Under these conditions, profit splits again into profit of enterprise (Π^n), which is retained and used for long-term investment finance, and rentiers' income (Z) which is distributed to rentiers' households and either consumed or saved by them. Rentiers' income is now determined by the stock of long-term credit (B) granted to firms and the exogenously given rate of interest (i).

$$\Pi = \Pi^n + Z = \Pi^n + iB. \tag{II.34}$$

The debt–capital ratio (λ) relates the stock of debt to the nominal capital stock:

$$\lambda = \frac{B}{pK}. \tag{II.35}$$

In what follows in this chapter, we shall assume that the debt–capital ratio is given in the short run. In the long run, however, the debt–capital ratio will vary and we shall briefly study its dynamics within the Kaleckian models.

Interest rate and the mark-up

Following Kalecki's (1954, p. 18) idea that a change in overhead costs, and hence in the interest rate, may but need not increase the mark-up, we shall now allow for an interest-elastic mark-up when considering the distribution effects of interest rate variations:

$$p = [1 + m(i)]wl, \quad m > 0, \frac{\partial m}{\partial i} \geq 0, \tag{II.36}$$

$$h = h(i), \quad \frac{\partial h}{\partial i} \geq 0. \tag{II.37}$$

If an interest-elastic mark-up dominates, changing interest rates will directly affect the real wage. Rising (falling) interest rates will cause rising (falling) mark-ups, rising (falling) prices, and falling (rising) real wages at constant nominal wages. Under these conditions, changing interest rates affect the distribution of income between profits and wages. This position, which considers interest a part of firms' costs of production, can be found in the Neo-Ricardian work discussed in chapter 4. There it is assumed that the exogenously given interest rate determines the rate of profit and closes the degree of freedom of the production price model by Sraffa (1960). Since there have been put forward some objections to this view, in particular with respect to the assumed constancy of the rate of profit of enterprise in the face of changing interest rates, we shall consider an interest elastic mark-up only as a possibility, not as a necessity.

As the successful shifting of variations in the interest rate to prices means a change in the mark-up, the ability to enforce a permanent and stable redistribution of income at the expense of labour income by means of shifting interest rate changes to prices depends on those factors that determine the mark-up, i.e. the intensity of price competition in the goods market and the relative strength of labour unions in the labour market. We expect that a high intensity of competition and powerful unions prevent rising interest rates from being shifted to higher prices permanently, but enforce falling interest rates to be transferred to falling prices. If the intensity of competition is rather low and labour unions are rather weak, rising interest rates will probably be accompanied by rising prices, whereas falling interest rates will not lead to falling prices. Changing interest rates may therefore affect the income share of firms as well as the share of labourers, depending on the circumstances in the goods and in the labour market. If there is an effect on the mark-up and the profit share in the models below, it will be a change in the interest rate and not in the actual interest payments which is relevant, because we assume that firms are well aware of imputed interest costs on own capital – that is, on accumulated retained earnings.

Interest rate and saving

Finally, we have to introduce the effects of changes in the interest rate on consumption and saving into the extended models. In order to keep the argument simple, we shall maintain a classical saving hypothesis, i.e. labourers do not save. The part of profits retained is completely saved by definition. The part of profits distributed to rentiers' households, i.e. the interest payment, however, is used by those households according to their propensity to save (s_Z). Therefore, total saving (S) comprises retained profits (Π-Z) and saving out of interest income (S_Z). Taking equations (II.1b), (II.34) and (II.35) into account, we get for the saving rate (σ) which relates total saving to the nominal capital stock:[32]

$$\sigma = \frac{S}{pK} = \frac{\Pi - Z + S_Z}{pK} = h\frac{u}{v} - i\lambda(1 - s_Z), \quad 0 < s_Z < 1. \qquad \text{(II.38)}$$

The higher the interest rate at a given rate of profit, a given debt–capital ratio and a given propensity to save of rentiers' households, the lower will be the saving rate, because more income is transferred from firms which do not consume to rentiers who consume at least a part of their income. An increasing debt–capital ratio reduces the saving rate, *ceteris paribus*, for the same reason. However, if a higher interest rate is associated with an interest-elastic mark-up and hence a rising profit share, the redistribution at the expense of labour income may cause a rising saving rate for the economy as a whole.

13.2 The Rowthorn–Dutt–Amadeo model extended[33]

The basic model

Introducing the extensions outlined above into the Rowthorn–Dutt–Amadeo variant of the Kaleckian distribution and growth theory yields the following model. This model is also supplemented by a modified investment function with stagnationist features:

$$r = hu\frac{1}{v}, \qquad \text{(II.1b)}$$

$$\lambda = \frac{B}{pK}, \qquad \text{(II.35)}$$

$$p = [1 + m(i)]wl, \qquad m > 0, \frac{\partial m}{\partial i} \geq 0, \tag{II.36}$$

$$h = 1 - \frac{1}{1 + m(i)}, \qquad \frac{\partial h}{\partial i} \geq 0, \tag{II.37}$$

$$\sigma = h\frac{u}{v} - i\lambda(1 - s_Z), \qquad 0 < s_Z < 1, \tag{II.38}$$

$$g = \alpha + \beta u + \rho\left(h\frac{u}{v} - i\lambda\right), \qquad \alpha, \beta, \rho > 0, \quad \rho < 1, \tag{II.39}$$

$$g = \sigma, \tag{II.10}$$

$$\frac{\partial \sigma}{\partial u} - \frac{\partial g}{\partial u} > 0 \quad \Rightarrow \quad (1 - \rho)\frac{h}{v} - \beta > 0. \tag{II.40}$$

Equation (II.1b) defines the profit rate, and equation (II.35) the debt–capital ratio, which is assumed to be given in the short run, but which is an endogenously determined variable in the long run. The mark-up in the price equation (II.36) and hence the profit share in equation (II.37) may be interest-elastic. Equation (II.38) is our new saving function containing the effects of the interest rate and the stock of debt on the macroeconomic saving rate.

Equation (II.39) describes an augmented investment function. The accumulation rate relating net investment to the capital stock closely follows the arguments in Kalecki (1954, pp. 91–108) and assumes that investment decisions are positively affected both by expected sales and by retained earnings. Expected sales are determined by the rate of capacity utilization. Retained earnings, in relation to the capital stock, are given by the difference between the rate of profit and the rate of interest times the debt–capital ratio. Therefore, the rate of interest and the debt–capital ratio both have a negative impact on investment because they adversely affect internal funds. This also limits the access to external funds on imperfect capital markets according to Kalecki's (1937) 'principle of increasing risk'. It is therefore important to explicitly consider the debt–capital ratio as a determinant of investment and not only the rate of interest, as in Dutt (1992), Dutt/Amadeo (1993), Lavoie (1992a, pp. 362–371, 1995a, pp. 148–52), or Lima/Meirelles (2006), because both variables determine internal funds for investment. In the face of rising interest rates firms may try to maintain internal funds by increasing the mark-up and hence the profit share. The success of such a reaction, however, depends on the effects on the rate of capacity utilization, as can be seen in equation (II.39).

Equation (II.10) defines the goods market equilibrium and equation (II.40) the stability condition. Note that the necessary condition for a stable equilibrium requires: $\rho < 1$, which means that the effects of internal funds on investment have to be restricted in order to achieve a stable goods market equilibrium.

Short-run equilibrium

Following Lavoie (1995a, pp. 164–73), we take the debt–capital ratio as a constant in the short run which, however, becomes a variable to be endogenously determined in the long run. The equilibrium values (*) for capacity utilization, capital accumulation and the rate of profit in the short run are as follows:

$$u^* = \frac{i\lambda(1 - s_Z - \rho) + \alpha}{\frac{h}{v}(1 - \rho) - \beta}, \tag{II.41}$$

$$g^* = \frac{i\lambda\left[\beta(1 - s_Z) - \rho\frac{h}{v}s_Z\right] + \alpha\frac{h}{v}}{\frac{h}{v}(1 - \rho) - \beta}, \tag{II.42}$$

$$r^* = \frac{\frac{h}{v}[i\lambda(1 - s_Z - \rho) + \alpha]}{\frac{h}{v}(1 - \rho) - \beta}. \tag{II.43}$$

With a given debt–capital ratio in the short run, we get the following reactions of the equilibrium values in the face of changing interest rates:

$$\frac{\partial u}{\partial i} = \frac{\lambda(1 - s_Z - \rho) - \frac{\partial h}{\partial i}(1 - \rho)\frac{u}{v}}{\frac{h}{v}(1 - \rho) - \beta}, \tag{II.44}$$

$$\frac{\partial g}{\partial i} = \frac{\lambda\left[\beta(1 - s_Z) - \rho\frac{h}{v}s_Z\right] - \frac{\partial h}{\partial i}\beta\frac{u}{v}}{\frac{h}{v}(1 - \rho) - \beta}, \tag{II.45}$$

$$\frac{\partial r}{\partial i} = \frac{\frac{h}{v}\lambda(1 - s_Z - \rho) - \frac{\partial h}{\partial i}\beta\frac{u}{v}}{\frac{h}{v}(1 - \rho) - \beta}. \tag{II.46}$$

If only stable short-run equilibria are considered, then also in this model with a more 'wage-led' investment function, the short-run effects of interest rate variations are not unique.[34] They depend on the interest elasticity of the mark-up (and hence the profit share), on the parameters in the saving and investment functions, i.e. the rentiers' saving propensity and the elasticities of investment with respect to capacity utilization and internal funds, and may as well be affected by the debt–capital ratio (Table II.1).

In the case of a rigid mark-up, the reaction of the short-run equilibrium values to changes in the interest rate is determined mainly by the rentiers' propensity to save and by the investment elasticity with respect to internal funds (and by the elasticity with respect to capacity utilization for the equilibrium rate of capital accumulation). If the rentiers' saving propensity is rather high and the internal funds elasticity of investment is also high (and capacity utilization does hardly affect investment), rising interest rates will cause falling rates of capacity utilization, profit and capital accumulation. This is the 'normal case' usually expected in Post-Keynesian models.

If, however, the propensity to save out of interest income is relatively low and investment is hardly affected by internal funds (and capacity utilization has a major impact on investment decisions), regimes of accumulation with positive responses throughout the endogenously determined short-run equilibrium values may arise. This is what Lavoie (1995a, pp. 164–73) in his 'Minsky–Steindl model' calls the 'puzzling case'. With a rigid mark-up, the debt–capital ratio does not affect the direction of change of the equilibrium values, but only affects the extent

Table II.1 Responses of the profit share, the rate of capacity utilization, the rate of accumulation and the rate of profit to a variation in the interest rate in the extended Rowthorn–Dutt–Amadeo model: stable short-run equilibria

	$\frac{\partial u}{\partial i}$	$\frac{\partial g}{\partial i}$	$\frac{\partial r}{\partial i}$
$\frac{\partial h}{\partial i}=0$	$\frac{\partial u}{\partial i}>0$, if	$\frac{\partial g}{\partial i}>0$, if	$\frac{\partial r}{\partial i}>0$, if
	$\lambda(1-s_Z-\rho)>0$	$\lambda\left[\beta(1-s_Z)-\rho\frac{h}{v}s_Z\right]>0$	$\frac{h}{v}\lambda(1-s_Z-\rho)>0$
$\frac{\partial h}{\partial i}>0$	$\frac{\partial u}{\partial i}>0$, if	$\frac{\partial g}{\partial i}>0$, if	$\frac{\partial r}{\partial i}>0$, if
	$\lambda(1-s_Z-\rho)$	$\lambda\left[\beta(1-s_Z)-\rho\frac{h}{v}s_Z\right]$	$\frac{h}{v}\lambda(1-s_Z-\rho)$
	$-\frac{\partial h}{\partial i}(1-\rho)\frac{u}{v}>0$	$-\frac{\partial h}{\partial i}\beta\frac{u}{v}>0$	$-\frac{\partial h}{\partial i}\beta\frac{u}{v}>0$

of change: The lower the debt–capital ratio, the smaller will be the real effects of interest rate variations.

In the case of an interest-elastic mark-up we get an additional effect on the short-run equilibrium values which is negative for each variable. This result is due to the 'wage-led' characteristics of the present model. Raising the mark-up and the profit share when interest rates increase will have a positive impact on internal funds but will simultaneously reduce consumption demand, sales and hence capacity utilization which will negatively feed back on internal funds. Furthermore, lower capacity utilization will also have a negative impact on investment decisions. That is why, with a flexible mark-up, the probability of a 'normal case' for interest rate effects on the short-run equilibrium position will increase. And a 'puzzling case' will become less likely if firms manage to shift varying interest costs to prices.[35] The extent to which the negative impact of a flexible mark-up will be able to (over-)compensate a direct positive effect of interest rate variations will now depend on the given debt–capital ratio. The higher the debt–capital ratio, the stronger will be the (probably positive) direct effects of changing interest rates. The initial debt–capital ratio may, therefore, under certain circumstances affect the direction of change of the equilibrium position caused by an interest rate variation in the case of an interest-elastic mark-up.

Long-run equilibrium

In the long run, the debt–capital ratio becomes an endogenous variable which then also has some feedback effects on the other variables of the system. In order to analyse this, we follow the procedure in Lavoie's (1995a, pp. 164–73) 'Minsky–Steindl model'. We start with equation (II.35) and assume away inflation – that is, the mark-up may change, but not the price level. This implies – somewhat unrealistically – that nominal wages fall when mark-ups rise. If prices would rise in the face of rising mark-ups we might have an effect on the debt–capital ratio, depending on what is assumed with respect to the stock of debt. If debt is not indexed to the price level, rising mark-ups and prices imply a falling debt–capital ratio which then has further effects on saving and investment. If debt is indexed to changes in the price level, there will be no such effects. Since we do not want to deal with these complications here, we assume constant prices.[36] For the growth rates of the variables it therefore follows from equation (II.35):

$$\hat{\lambda} = \hat{B} - \hat{K} = \hat{B} - g. \qquad \text{(II.47)}$$

Given our assumptions above, the additional long-term credit granted in each period (ΔB) is equal to rentiers' saving in the period under consideration.[37]

$$\Delta B = S_Z = s_Z iB. \tag{II.48}$$

For the growth rate of debt it follows:

$$\hat{B} = \frac{\Delta B}{B} = s_Z i. \tag{II.49}$$

In long-run equilibrium the endogenously determined debt–capital ratio has to be constant, i.e. $\hat{\lambda} = 0$. Integrating this condition into equation (II.47) and making use of equations (II.42) and (II.49) we get for the long-run equilibrium debt–capital ratio:

$$\lambda^* = \frac{s_Z i\left[\frac{h}{v}(1-\rho) - \beta\right] - \alpha\frac{h}{v}}{i\left[\beta(1-s_Z) - \rho\frac{h}{v}s_Z\right]}. \tag{II.50}$$

This equilibrium will be stable, if $\frac{\partial\hat{\lambda}}{\partial\lambda} < 0$. Making use of equation (II.47) and applying equations (II.42) and (II.49) yields:

$$\frac{\partial\hat{\lambda}}{\partial\lambda} = \frac{-i\left[\beta(1-s_Z) - \rho\frac{h}{v}s_Z\right]}{\frac{h}{v}(1-\rho) - \beta}. \tag{II.51}$$

From this it follows for the stability condition:[38]

$$\frac{\partial\hat{\lambda}}{\partial\lambda} < 0, \text{ if } \beta(1-s_Z) - \rho\frac{h}{v}s_Z > 0. \tag{II.52}$$

The long-run equilibrium will tend to be stable, if the rentiers' saving propensity is low and investment decisions are very elastic with respect to changes in capacity utilization, but very inelastic with respect to changes in internal funds. This is the same parameter constellation which favours a 'puzzling' positive effect of interest rate variations on capacity utilization, capital accumulation and the profit rate in the short run. The intuition behind this is quite straightforward and follows from equations (II.42) and (II.51): Long-run stability of the debt–capital ratio requires that a rise in this ratio is accompanied by a rise in the rate of capital accumulation, because long-run stability from equation (II.52) is tantamount to $\frac{\partial g}{\partial \lambda} = \frac{i\left[\beta(1-s_Z) - \rho\frac{h}{v}s_Z\right]}{\frac{h}{v}(1-\rho) - \beta} > 0$ derived from equation (II.42), assuming the interest rate to be positive and given. And if $\frac{\partial g}{\partial \lambda} > 0$, this also implies $\frac{\partial g}{\partial i} > 0$ in equation (II.45) (also derived from equation (II.42)) and hence the 'puzzling case', supposing that the mark-up is either interest inelastic or investment is hardly responsive to changes in demand caused by the distribution effects of interest rate variations.

If the rentiers' saving propensity is rather high and investment decisions are very inelastic with respect to demand but very elastic with respect to internal funds, the long-run equilibrium will tend to become unstable. The conditions for long-run instability are associated with short-run 'normal' negative effects of interest rate hikes on capacity utilization, capital accumulation and the profit rate.

The effects of interest rate variations on the equilibrium debt–capital ratio can be derived from equation (II.50):

$$\frac{\partial \lambda}{\partial i} = \frac{s_Z\left[\frac{h}{v}(1-\rho) - \beta\right] - \lambda\left[\beta(1-s_Z) - \rho\frac{h}{v}s_Z\right] + \frac{\partial h}{\partial i}\frac{1}{v}\{s_Z i[1-\rho(1+\lambda)-\alpha]\}}{i\left[\beta(1-s_Z) - \rho\frac{h}{v}s_Z\right]}. \tag{II.53}$$

First we consider the case of an interest-inelastic mark-up. With the conditions for a stable long-run equilibrium given, increasing interest rates will decrease the equilibrium debt–capital ratio if this ratio is very high in the initial equilibrium, more precisely if $\lambda > \frac{s_Z\left[\frac{h}{v}(1-\rho)-\beta\right]}{\beta(1-s_Z) - \rho\frac{h}{v}s_Z}$.[39] However, if interest rates increase when the equilibrium debt–capital ratio is still low, i.e. $\lambda < \frac{s_Z\left[\frac{h}{v}(1-\rho)-\beta\right]}{\beta(1-s_Z) - \rho\frac{h}{v}s_Z}$, this ratio will be rising. If $\lambda = \frac{s_Z\left[\frac{h}{v}(1-\rho)-\beta\right]}{\beta(1-s_Z) - \rho\frac{h}{v}s_Z}$ in the initial equilibrium, variations in the interest rate will not affect the equilibrium debt–capital ratio.[40] If the parameter constellation in our model implies an unstable long-run equilibrium, rising interest rates will always trigger falling equilibrium debt–capital ratios.[41]

In the case of an interest-elastic mark-up our results are slightly modified. The additional effect running through a variation of the mark-up and the profit share may be either negative or positive, depending on the values of the parameters α and ρ in the investment function, and on the initial debt–capital ratio. The extent to which this additional effect influences the direction and the magnitude of the total effect of interest rate variations on the debt–capital ratio depends on the initial interest rate. In the present model, the relation between the interest rate and the equilibrium debt–capital ratio, therefore, does not only depend on the parameters of the saving and the investment function, but also on initial conditions, i.e. on the debt–capital ratio in the initial equilibrium in the case of a stable long-run equilibrium and also on the level from which interest rates start to change in the case of an interest-elastic mark-up.[42]

From the analysis so far it has become clear that the short- and long-run effects of interest rate policies in our model may depend on the rentiers' propensity to save, the elasticities of investment with respect to capacity utilization and to internal funds, and on initial values of the interest rate and the equilibrium debt–capital ratio. This is summarized in equations (II.53)–(II.56) which display the long-run effects of interest rate variations on the endogenous variables of the model:

$$\frac{\partial\lambda}{\partial i} = \frac{s_Z\left[\frac{h}{v}(1-\rho)-\beta\right]-\lambda\left[\beta(1-s_Z)-\rho\frac{h}{v}s_Z\right]+\frac{\partial h}{\partial i}\frac{1}{v}\{s_Z i[1-\rho(1+\lambda)-\alpha]\}}{i\left[\beta(1-s_Z)-\rho\frac{h}{v}s_Z\right]}, \tag{II.53}$$

$$\frac{\partial u}{\partial i} = \frac{\left(\lambda+i\frac{\partial\lambda}{\partial i}\right)(1-s_Z-\rho)-\frac{\partial h}{\partial i}(1-\rho)\frac{u}{v}}{\frac{h}{v}(1-\rho)-\beta}, \tag{II.54}$$

$$\frac{\partial g}{\partial i} = \frac{\left(\lambda+i\frac{\partial\lambda}{\partial i}\right)\left[\beta(1-s_Z)-\rho\frac{h}{v}s_Z\right]-\frac{\partial h}{\partial i}\beta\frac{u}{v}}{\frac{h}{v}(1-\rho)-\beta}, \tag{II.55}$$

$$\frac{\partial r}{\partial i} = \frac{\left(\lambda+i\frac{\partial\lambda}{\partial i}\right)\frac{h}{v}(1-s_Z-\rho)-\frac{\partial h}{\partial i}\beta\frac{u}{v}}{\frac{h}{v}(1-\rho)-\beta}. \tag{II.56}$$

Model behaviour in the face of interest rate variations: a simple case

In what follows, we will trace the short- and long-run effects of changing interest rates through the model. Only stable goods market equilibria will be considered, but the potential long-run instability of the debt–capital ratio is taken into account. For the sake of simplicity, our analysis of the effects on real variables is confined to the accumulation rate, and only the case of an interest-inelastic mark-up is discussed explicitly. The chosen simplifications have the advantage that the model behaviour following interest rate variations only depends on the rentiers' propensity to save (s_z), the investment elasticities with respect to capacity utilization (β) and to internal funds (ρ), and on the initial equilibrium debt–capital ratio (λ) (Table II.2).

If $\beta(1 - s_Z) - \rho\frac{h}{v}s_Z > 0$, the long-run equilibrium debt–capital ratio will be stable. This requires that the rentiers' propensity to save is rather low and that investment is very responsive to capacity utilization, but very inelastic with respect to internal funds. These conditions imply, first, an equal distribution of financial wealth across the economy. Assuming that the propensity to consume declines with rising income, a more equal distribution of financial wealth – and hence yields from financial wealth – will amount to a lower average propensity to save. Secondly, a stable long-run equilibrium implies stable conditions of finance for firms, so that in the face of variations in internal funds, triggered by changes in

Table II.2 Effects of interest rate variations with an interest-inelastic mark-up in the extended Rowthorn–Dutt–Amadeo model

			$\beta(1 - s_Z) - \rho\frac{h}{v}s_Z$	
			+	–
1. Interest rate and equilibrium accumulation rate in the short run	$\frac{\partial g}{\partial i}$, λ exogenous, equation (II.45)		+	–
2. Interest rate and long-run equilibrium debt–capital ratio	$\frac{\partial \lambda}{\partial i}$, equation (II.53)	–, if $\lambda >$ 0, if $\lambda =$ +, if $\lambda <$	$\dfrac{s_Z\left[\frac{h}{v}(1-\rho)-\beta\right]}{\beta(1 - s_Z) - \rho\frac{h}{v}s_Z}$	–
3. Debt–capital ratio and accumulation rate	$\frac{\partial g}{\partial \lambda}$, i constant, equation (II.42)		+	–
4. Interest rate and equilibrium accumulation rate in the long run	$\frac{\partial g}{\partial i}$, λ endogenous, equation (II.55)		+	+
5. Stability of long-run equilibrium debt–capital ratio	$\frac{\partial \hat{\lambda}}{\partial \lambda}$, i constant, equation (II.51)		– (stable)	+ (unstable)

the interest rate or in the debt–capital ratio, creditors do not change their willingness to long-term finance and debtors do not change their willingness to invest very much. If this is the case, the 'principle of increasing risk' and hence internal funds will only have a small effect on investment. Decisions to invest are more determined by sales expectations of firms than by the risks associated with increasing debt finance. We may expect that these conditions rather prevail in a bank-based financial system than in a capital-market-based system. Bank-based systems are characterized by long-term relations between firms and creditors which are more stable than the short-term relations dominating in capital-market-based systems (Grabel 1997). Thirdly, conditions for a stable long-run equilibrium can also be assumed to prevail in periods of rapid and stable capital accumulation with stable sales expectations having a high weight for investment decisions rather than in periods of stagnation with uncertain sales and profit expectations.

When the interest rate rises in a constellation with a long-run stable debt–capital ratio, in the short run, with a given debt–capital ratio, the rate of capital accumulation will increase. In the long run, the debt–capital ratio will also vary with the direction of variation depending on the initial debt–capital ratio. The rate of accumulation in the long-run stable constellation moves in the same direction as the debt–capital ratio. Taking the direct and indirect effects of changing interest rates – via changing debt–capital ratios – into account, the equilibrium rate of capital accumulation will rise in the long run.

If $\beta(1 - s_Z) - \rho\frac{h}{v}s_Z < 0$, the long-run equilibrium will be unstable. This constellation requires a high rentiers' propensity to save, a low elasticity of investment with respect to capacity utilization and an elastic responsiveness to changes in internal funds. These conditions will be given, if financial wealth and the yields from financial assets are unequally distributed across the economy and if fragile relationships between the financial sector and non-financial business dominate. Variations in interest rates, and hence in internal funds, then have significant effects on the willingness to finance and the willingness to invest. The 'principle of increasing risk' has a dominant effect on investment whereas changes in capacity utilization are of minor importance. We may expect these conditions to prevail in capital-market-based financial systems (Grabel 1997). Prolonged periods of economic stagnation with uncertain sales and profit expectations should also be conducive to this constellation.

If interest rates increase in a parameter constellation yielding a long-run unstable debt–capital ratio, in the short run, with a given debt–capital ratio, capital accumulation will decrease. The long-run equilibrium debt–capital ratio will also fall. A falling equilibrium debt–capital ratio should then have a stimulating effect on the equilibrium accumulation rate, countervailing the short-run effect. In the long run, the equilibrium rate of capital accumulation will rise, also in the unstable case.

However, the interpretation of the effects of rising interest rates under the conditions of an unstable long-run equilibrium has to take into account that changing interest rates will trigger an unstable disequilibrium process with respect to the debt–capital ratio and to capital accumulation, so that the new equilibrium will not be reached. Starting from a long-run equilibrium debt–capital ratio, rising interest rates cause falling short-run equilibrium accumulation rates and a falling equilibrium debt–capital ratio in the long run. Since the actual debt–capital ratio then exceeds the new long-run equilibrium ratio, the instability of this equilibrium means cumulative deviation of the actual from the equilibrium debt-capital-ratio. Therefore, the actual debt-capital-ratio will increase and further diverge from its new equilibrium value.

This unstable disequilibrium process is hence characterized by falling accumulation rates and rising debt–capital ratios, both triggered by an increasing interest rate. Therefore, we get a macroeconomic 'paradox of debt', as already argued in Steindl (1952, pp. 113–22).[43] Because of an increasing interest rate, and hence decreasing internal funds, firms cut down investment in order to reduce debt–capital ratios and interest payments. The macroeconomic effect of this individual behaviour, however, is such that the actual debt–capital ratios and hence interest payments will increase, internal funds will decrease inducing firms to further cut down investment, and so on.[44] If interest rates fall, the cumulative disequilibrium process will be in the opposite direction: A falling interest rate induces a rising short-run equilibrium rate of capital accumulation, an increasing equilibrium debt–capital ratio and hence falling actual debt–capital ratios which will then further stimulate investment, and so on.

When the 'paradox of debt' prevails, Kalecki's 'principle of increasing risk', i.e. a co-movement of investment and indebtedness finally setting a limit to accumulation, is irrelevant at the macroeconomic level, as was already noted by Kalecki (1937) himself. The 'paradox of debt' also invalidates the macroeconomic relevance of Minsky's (1975, 1977) 'financial instability hypothesis' in so far as it is related to the financing of real investment. Minsky has to rely on a co-movement of investment and debt, finally leading to a breakdown in investment due to increasing financial fragility. Our results for the unstable case also question the Post-Keynesian structuralist views discussed in chapter 6, arguing that commercial banks endogenously increase interest rates because of increasing indebtedness of firms when investment *rises*. From our analysis it rather follows that commercial banks might increase lending rates in the face of rising debt–capital ratios and *falling* investment.

13.3 The Bhaduri/Marglin model extended[45]

The basic model

In this chapter we introduce the extensions related to the debt–capital ratio, the mark-up and to the saving function into the Bhaduri/Marglin approach. We obtain the following model:

$$r = hu\frac{1}{v}, \tag{II.1b}$$

$$\lambda = \frac{B}{pK}, \tag{II.35}$$

$$p = [1 + m(i)]wl, \quad m > 0, \frac{\partial m}{\partial i} \geq 0, \tag{II.36}$$

$$h = 1 - \frac{1}{1 + m(i)}, \quad \frac{\partial h}{\partial i} \geq 0, \tag{II.37}$$

$$\sigma = h\frac{u}{v} - i\lambda(1 - s_Z), \quad 0 < s_Z < 1, \tag{II.38}$$

$$g = \frac{\Delta K}{K} = \frac{I}{K} = \alpha + \beta u + \tau h - \theta\lambda i, \;\; \alpha, \beta, \tau, \theta > 0, \;\; g > 0 \text{ for } r - i > 0, \tag{II.57}$$

$$g = \sigma, \tag{II.10}$$

$$\frac{\partial\sigma}{\partial u} - \frac{\partial g}{\partial u} > 0 \quad \Rightarrow \quad \frac{h}{v} - \beta > 0. \tag{II.58}$$

This model differs from the extended Rowthorn–Dutt–Amadeo model discussed above only with respect to the investment function in equation (II.57), which then also implies a different goods market stability condition in equation (II.58). Based on Kalecki's 'principle of increasing risk', the rate of interest and the debt–capital ratio have a negative impact on investment because of their adverse effects on internal means of finance. This negative effect is added to the positive effects of the profit share and the rate of capacity utilization in a linear way. The parameter α stands for the motivation to accumulate, which derives from the competition of firms independently of the development of distribution, effective demand, monetary or financial variables. The intensity of the influence of effective demand is indicated by β, whereas τ shows the weight of distribution struggle and θ the impact of debt and the interest rate. To induce investors to demand real capital goods instead of financial assets, the expected rate of profit has to exceed the rate of interest in financial markets. This extended model hence preserves the independent positive effect of the profit share on investment which is characteristic for the Bhaduri/Marglin model.

Short-run equilibrium

Assuming the debt–capital ratio to be given and constant in the short run, the equilibrium values (*) for capacity utilization, capital accumulation and the rate of profit in the short run are as follows:

$$u^* = \frac{\lambda i(1 - s_Z - \theta) + \alpha + \tau h}{\dfrac{h}{v} - \beta}, \tag{II.59}$$

$$g^* = \frac{\lambda i\left[\beta(1 - s_Z) - \theta\dfrac{h}{v}\right] + \dfrac{h}{v}(\alpha + \tau h)}{\dfrac{h}{v} - \beta}, \tag{II.60}$$

$$r^* = \frac{\dfrac{h}{v}[\lambda i(1 - s_Z - \theta) + \alpha + \tau h]}{\dfrac{h}{v} - \beta}. \tag{II.61}$$

With a constant debt–capital ratio, we get the following reactions of the equilibrium values in the face of changing interest rates:

$$\frac{\partial u}{\partial i} = \frac{\lambda(1 - s_Z - \theta) + \dfrac{\partial h}{\partial i}\left(\tau - \dfrac{u}{v}\right)}{\dfrac{h}{v} - \beta}, \tag{II.62}$$

$$\frac{\partial g}{\partial i} = \frac{\lambda\left[\beta(1 - s_Z) - \theta\dfrac{h}{v}\right] + \dfrac{\partial h}{\partial i}\dfrac{1}{v}(\tau h - \beta u)}{\dfrac{h}{v} - \beta}, \tag{II.63}$$

$$\frac{\partial r}{\partial i} = \frac{\dfrac{h}{v}\lambda(1 - s_Z - \theta) + \dfrac{\partial h}{\partial i}\dfrac{1}{v}(\tau h - \beta u)}{\dfrac{h}{v} - \beta}. \tag{II.64}$$

If only stable short-run equilibria are considered, the short-run effects of interest rate variations depend again on the interest rate elasticity of the mark-up (and hence of the profit share), on the parameters in the saving and investment functions, i.e. the rentiers' saving propensity and the elasticities of investment with respect to debt and the interest rate, to the profit share and to capacity utilization, and may also be affected by the debt–capital ratio (Table II.3).

In the case of a rigid mark-up, the reaction of the equilibrium values to changes in the interest rate is mainly determined by the rentiers' propensity to save and by the debt and interest elasticity of investment. If the rentiers' saving propensity is rather high and the debt service elasticity of investment is high as well, rising interest rates will cause falling rates of capacity utilization, profit and capital accumulation. A low responsiveness of investment to demand reinforces the negative impact on equilibrium capital accumulation. This is again the 'normal case' usually expected in Post-Keynesian models.

If investment, however, is hardly affected by debt and interest payments, and the propensity to save out of interest income is low, there may arise regimes of accumulation with positive responses throughout the endogenously determined equilibrium values. A high responsiveness of investment to demand reinforces the positive impact on equilibrium capital accumulation. Again, this is the 'puzzling case'.

With a rigid mark-up, the debt–capital ratio does not affect the direction of change of the equilibrium values, but only affects the extent of

Table II.3 Responses of the profit share, the rate of capacity utilization, the rate of accumulation and the rate of profit to a variation in the interest rate in the extended Bhaduri/Marglin model: stable short-run equilibria

	$\frac{\partial u}{\partial i}$	$\frac{\partial g}{\partial i}$	$\frac{\partial r}{\partial i}$
$\frac{\partial h}{\partial i}=0$	$\frac{\partial u}{\partial i}>0$, if $\lambda(1-s_Z-\theta)>0$	$\frac{\partial g}{\partial i}>0$, if $\lambda\left[\beta(1-s_Z)-\theta\frac{h}{v}\right]>0$	$\frac{\partial r}{\partial i}>0$, if $\frac{h}{v}\lambda(1-s_Z-\theta)>0$
$\frac{\partial h}{\partial i}>0$	$\frac{\partial u}{\partial i}>0$, if $\lambda(1-s_Z-\theta)+\frac{\partial h}{\partial i}\left(\tau-\frac{u}{v}\right)>0$	$\frac{\partial g}{\partial i}>0$, if $\lambda\left[\beta(1-s_Z)-\theta\frac{h}{v}\right]+\frac{\partial h}{\partial i}\frac{1}{v}(\tau h-\beta u)>0$	$\frac{\partial r}{\partial i}>0$, if $\frac{h}{v}\lambda(1-s_Z-\theta)+\frac{\partial h}{\partial i}\frac{1}{v}(\tau h-\beta u)>0$

change: The lower the debt–capital ratio, the smaller will be the effects of interest rate variations. With a zero debt–capital ratio and a rigid mark-up, a change in the interest rate will not affect the short-run equilibrium position at all, as long as the interest rate remains below the profit rate and the restriction in equation (II.56) is fulfilled. These results are similar to those of the extended Rowthorn–Dutt–Amadeo model above.

In the case of an interest-elastic mark-up the debt–capital ratio may affect the direction of change of the equilibrium position caused by an interest rate variation. In general, the lower the debt–capital ratio is, the lower are the direct effects interest rate variations have on investment and on rentiers' consumption and the more important are the effects exerted by the redistribution of income between profits and wages on consumption and investment. These effects differ from the extended Rowthorn–Dutt–Amadeo model due to the specification of the investment function.

With an increasing mark-up following rising interest rates there will be an indirect positive impact on capacity utilization, capital accumulation and the profit rate running through distribution, if investment is very elastic with respect to the profit share and very inelastic with respect to capacity utilization. This may then dampen and perhaps even over-compensate a directly negative impact rising interest rates have on investment, or reinforce a directly positive impact. Therefore, in the case of an interest-elastic mark-up, the debt–capital ratio may be of utmost importance for the direction into which changes in monetary policy push the economy.

Long-run equilibrium

In the long run, the debt–capital ratio is endogenous again and has also feedback effects on the other variables of the system. We follow the same procedure as in the extended Rowthorn–Dutt–Amadeo model, start with equation (II.35) and assume away inflation, i.e. the mark-up may change but not the price level. For the growth rates of the variables it therefore follows that:

$$\hat{\lambda} = \hat{B} - \hat{K} = \hat{B} - g. \tag{II.47}$$

Since additional long-term credit granted in each period (ΔB) is equal to rentiers' saving in this period,

$$\Delta B = S_Z = s_Z iB, \tag{II.48}$$

it follows for the growth rate of debt:

$$\hat{B} = \frac{\Delta B}{B} = s_Z i. \tag{II.49}$$

For the long-run equilibrium debt–capital ratio ($\hat{\lambda} = 0$) we get from equations (II.47), (II.49) and (II.60):

$$\lambda^* = \frac{s_Z i\left(\frac{h}{v} - \beta\right) - \frac{h}{v}(\alpha + \tau h)}{i\left[\beta(1 - s_Z) - \theta\frac{h}{v}\right]}. \tag{II.65}$$

The stability condition can be derived applying equations (II.47), (II.49) and (II.60):

$$\frac{\partial\hat{\lambda}}{\partial\lambda} = \frac{-i\left[\beta(1 - s_Z) - \theta\frac{h}{v}\right]}{\frac{h}{v} - \beta}. \tag{II.66}$$

From this it follows for the stability of the debt–capital ratio:[46]

$$\frac{\partial\hat{\lambda}}{\partial\lambda} < 0, \text{ if } \beta(1 - s_Z) - \theta\frac{h}{v} > 0. \tag{II.67}$$

The long-run equilibrium tends to be stable, if the rentiers' saving propensity is low and investment decisions are very elastic with respect to changes in capacity utilization but very inelastic with respect to changes in debt services. This is the parameter constellation which also favours a 'puzzling' positive effect of interest rate increases on capacity utilization, capital accumulation and the profit rate in the short run, as in Lavoie's (1995a) 'Minsky-Steindl model' and in our extended Rowthorn–Dutt–Amadeo model. If the rentiers' saving propensity is rather high and investment decisions are very inelastic with respect to demand but very elastic with respect to debt and the interest rate, the long-run equilibrium tends to become unstable. Deviations from equilibrium will generate a long-run debt–capital ratio of either unity or zero. The conditions for long-run instability are associated with short-run 'normal' negative effects of interest rate hikes on capacity utilization, capital accumulation and the profit rate.

The effects of interest rate variations on the equilibrium debt–capital ratio can be derived from equation (II.65):

$$\frac{\partial\lambda}{\partial i} = \frac{s_Z\left(\frac{h}{v} - \beta\right) - \lambda\left[\beta(1 - s_Z) - \theta\frac{h}{v}\right] + \frac{\partial h}{\partial i}\frac{1}{v}[i(s_Z + \theta\lambda) - \alpha - 2\tau h]}{i\left[\beta(1 - s_Z) - \theta\frac{h}{v}\right]}. \tag{II.68}$$

First, we consider again the case of an interest-inelastic mark-up. With the conditions for a stable long-run equilibrium given, increasing interest rates will decrease the equilibrium debt–capital ratio, if this ratio is very high in the initial equilibrium, more precisely if $\lambda > \frac{s_Z\left(\frac{h}{v} - \beta\right)}{\beta(1 - s_Z) - \theta\frac{h}{v}}$.[47] However, if interest rates increase when the equilibrium debt–capital ratio is still low, i.e. $\lambda < \frac{s_Z\left(\frac{h}{v} - \beta\right)}{\beta(1 - s_Z) - \theta\frac{h}{v}}$, this ratio will be rising. If $\lambda = \frac{s_Z\left(\frac{h}{v} - \beta\right)}{\beta(1 - s_Z) - \theta\frac{h}{v}}$ in the initial equilibrium, variations in the interest rate will not affect the equilibrium debt–capital ratio. These results are different from Lavoie's (1995a) 'Minsky–Steindl model' which shows a uniquely positive relationship between the interest rate and the debt–capital ratio in the case of a stable long-run equilibrium, but they are similar to our extended Rowthorn–Dutt–Amadeo model discussed above. If the parameter constellation in the extended Bhaduri/Marglin model implies an unstable long-run equilibrium, rising interest rates will always trigger falling equilibrium debt–capital ratios, as in Lavoie's (1995a) 'Minsky–Steindl model' and in our extended Rowthorn–Dutt–Amadeo model.[48]

In the case of an interest-elastic mark-up, our results are slightly modified. When the conditions for a stable long-run equilibrium are given, a positive relation between the interest rate and the debt–capital ratio becomes more likely, if investment decisions are quite inelastic with respect to unit profits and if in the initial equilibrium the interest rate is already very high, so that $i(s_Z + \theta\lambda) - \alpha - 2\tau h > 0$. With a high elasticity of investment with respect to unit profits and a low interest rate in the initial equilibrium, i.e. $i(s_Z + \theta\lambda) - \alpha - 2\tau h < 0$, an interest-elastic mark-up will make a negative relation between the interest rate and the debt–capital ratio more likely. If the long-run equilibrium is unstable, a low unit labour cost elasticity of investment and a high interest rate in initial equilibrium will reinforce the negative relation between the interest rate and the debt–capital ratio. If the unit labour cost elasticity of investment is very high and increasing interest rates start from a low level, the negative relation between interest rate and debt–capital ratio may be dampened or even be reversed.

In the extended Bhaduri/Marglin model, the relation between the interest rate and the equilibrium debt–capital ratio, therefore, does not only depend on the parameters of the saving and the investment function, but also on initial conditions, i.e. on the debt–capital ratio in the initial equilibrium in the case of a stable long-run equilibrium and on the level from which interest rates start to change when the mark-up is interest-elastic. These path-dependence features are similar to the extended Rowthorn–Dutt–Amadeo model analysed above.

From the analysis so far it has become clear that also in the extended Bhaduri/Marglin model the short- and long-run effects of interest rate policies may depend on the coefficients in the saving and the investment function, the rentiers' propensity to save, the elasticity of investment with respect to debt and the interest rate, to capacity utilization and to unit profits, on the interest rate elasticity of the mark-up, and on initial values of the interest rate and the equilibrium debt–capital ratio. This is summarized in equations (II.68)–(II.71) which display the long-run effects of interest rate variations on the endogenous variables of the model:

$$\frac{\partial \lambda}{\partial i} = \frac{s_Z\left(\frac{h}{v} - \beta\right) - \lambda\left[\beta(1 - s_Z) - \theta\frac{h}{v}\right] + \frac{\partial h}{\partial i}\frac{1}{v}[i(s_Z + \theta\lambda) - \alpha - 2\tau h]}{i\left[\beta(1 - s_Z) - \theta\frac{h}{v}\right]}, \tag{II.68}$$

$$\frac{\partial u}{\partial i} = \frac{\left(\lambda + i\frac{\partial \lambda}{\partial i}\right)(1 - s_Z - \theta) + \frac{\partial h}{\partial i}\left(\tau - \frac{u}{v}\right)}{\frac{h}{v} - \beta}, \tag{II.69}$$

$$\frac{\partial g}{\partial i} = \frac{\left(\lambda + i\frac{\partial \lambda}{\partial i}\right)\left[\beta(1 - s_Z) - \theta\frac{h}{v}\right] + \frac{\partial h}{\partial i}\frac{1}{v}(\tau h - \beta u)}{\frac{h}{v} - \beta}, \tag{II.70}$$

$$\frac{\partial r}{\partial i} = \frac{\frac{h}{v}\left(\lambda + i\frac{\partial \lambda}{\partial i}\right)(1 - s_Z - \theta) + \frac{\partial h}{\partial i}\frac{1}{v}(\tau h - \beta u)}{\frac{h}{v} - \beta}. \tag{II.71}$$

Model behaviour in the face of interest rate variations: a simple case

Also for the extended Bhaduri/Marglin model we will trace the short- and long-run effects of changing interest rates through the model. Again: only stable goods market equilibria will be considered, but potential long-run instability of the debt–capital ratio is taken into account, the analysis of the effects on real variables is confined to the accumulation rate, and only the case of an interest-inelastic mark-up is discussed explicitly. The chosen simplifications make our results directly comparable to those derived in the extended Rowthorn–Dutt–Amadeo model above and in Lavoie's (1995a) 'Minsky–Steindl model'. The simplifying assumptions have the advantage that in this model the model behaviour following interest rate variations also depends only on three parameters: the rentiers' propensity to save (s_Z), the investment elasticities with respect to capacity utilization (β) and with respect to debt and interest costs (θ), and on the initial equilibrium debt–capital ratio (λ) (Table II.4).

Table II.4 Effects of interest rate variations with an interest-inelastic mark-up in the extended Bhaduri/Marglin model

		$\beta(1-s_Z)-\theta\frac{h}{v}$	
		+	−
1. Interest rate and equilibrium accumulation rate in the short run	$\frac{\partial g}{\partial i}$, λ constant, equation (II.63)	+	−
2. Interest rate and long-run equilibrium debt–capital ratio	$\frac{\partial \lambda}{\partial i}$, equation (II.68)	$\begin{cases} -, \text{ if } \lambda > \\ 0, \text{ if } \lambda = \\ +, \text{ if } \lambda < \end{cases} \frac{s_Z\left(\frac{h}{v}-\beta\right)}{\beta(1-s_Z)-\theta\frac{h}{v}}$	−
3. Debt–capital ratio and accumulation rate	$\frac{\partial g}{\partial \lambda}$, i constant, equation (II.60)	+	−
4. Interest rate and equilibrium accumulation rate in the long run	$\frac{\partial g}{\partial i}$, λ variable, equation (II.70)	+	+
5. Stability of long-run equilibrium debt–capital ratio	$\frac{\partial \hat{\lambda}}{\partial \lambda}$, i constant, equation (II.66)	− (stable)	+ (unstable)

If $\beta(1-s_Z)-\theta\frac{h}{v}>0$, the long-run equilibrium debt–capital ratio will be stable. This requires that the rentiers' propensity to save is rather low and that investment is very responsive to capacity utilization, but very inelastic with respect to interest payments and debt. These conditions are similar to those derived in the extended Rowthorn–Dutt–Amadeo model. They imply an equal distribution of financial wealth across the economy and stable conditions of finance. If this is the case, the 'principle of increasing risk' will only have little effect on investment. Decisions to invest are rather determined by sales expectations of firms than by the risks associated with increasing debt finance.

When the interest rate rises in a constellation with a long-run stable debt–capital ratio, the rate of capital accumulation will increase in the short run. The long-run variation of the debt–capital ratio will depend on the initial debt–capital ratio. The rate of accumulation in the long-run stable constellation moves in the same direction as the debt–capital ratio. Taking the direct and indirect effects of changing interest rates – via changing debt–capital ratios – into account, the equilibrium rate of capital accumulation will also rise in the long run.

If $\beta(1-s_Z)-\theta\frac{h}{v}<0$, the long-run equilibrium will be unstable. Similar to the extended Rowthorn–Dutt–Amadeo model, this constellation requires a high rentiers' propensity to save, a low elasticity of investment with respect to capacity utilization and an elastic responsiveness to changes in the interest rate or in the debt–capital ratio. These conditions will be given, if financial wealth is unequally distributed across the economy and if fragile relations between the financial sector and non-financial business dominate. The 'principle of increasing risk' has a dominant effect on investment whereas changes in capacity utilization are of minor importance. Prolonged periods of economic stagnation with uncertain sales and profit expectations should also be conducive to this constellation.

If interest rates increase in a parameter constellation yielding a long-run unstable debt–capital ratio, in the short run, with a given debt–capital ratio, capital accumulation will decrease. The long-run variable equilibrium debt–capital ratio will also go down. A falling debt–capital ratio should then have a stimulating effect on the equilibrium accumulation rate, countervailing the short-run effect. In the long run, the equilibrium rate of capital accumulation will rise, also in the unstable case.

However, also in the extended Bhaduri/Marglin model the interpretation of the effects of rising interest rates under the conditions of an unstable long-run equilibrium has to take into account that changing interest rates will trigger an unstable disequilibrium process, so that the new equilibrium will not be reached, similar to the extended Rowthorn–Dutt–Amadeo model discussed above: Starting from a long-run equilibrium position, rising interest rates cause falling accumulation rates in the short run and a falling equilibrium debt–capital ratio in the long run. Since the actual debt–capital ratio then exceeds the new long-run equilibrium ratio, the instability of this equilibrium means cumulative deviation of the actual from the equilibrium debt–capital ratio. Therefore, the actual debt–capital ratio will increase and finally approach unity. This unstable disequilibrium process is hence characterized by falling accumulation rates and rising debt–capital ratios, both triggered by an increasing interest rate. Again, we get a macroeconomic 'paradox of debt'. When interest rates fall, the cumulative disequilibrium process is in the opposite direction: Falling interest rates induce rising rates of capital accumulation and falling debt–capital ratios. If the 'paradox of debt' prevails, Kalecki's 'principle of increasing risk' is irrelevant at the macroeconomic level, also in the extended Bhaduri/Marglin model.

14
Interest Rate, Distribution and Accumulation in Post-Keynesian Models: Summary and Conclusions of Part II

In the second part of the book we have introduced the monetary interest rate, mainly determined by central bank policies, into Post-Keynesian models of distribution and growth in the tradition of Nicholas Kaldor, Joan Robinson and Michal Kalecki. We have argued that the monetary theories of Kaldor, Robinson and Kalecki have provided the basis for – or are at least compatible with – the Post-Keynesian monetary theory which has been outlined in chapter 6 and applied in this part. Kaldor and Robinson as well as Kalecki suppose that the rate of interest is an exogenous variable for the income-generating and growth process. The volume of credit and the stock of money adjust endogenously to the requirements of finance and circulation. The rate of interest is a monetary phenomenon which has both short- and long-run effects on the real economy. These monetary theories, however, were not incorporated into their own models by the founding mother and fathers of Post-Keynesian distribution and growth theories.

In order to integrate Post-Keynesian monetary theory into the models of distribution and growth we have outlined a simple model economy, including a full description of a monetary circuit. Then, this model has been used to analyse the effects of changes in the interest rate in the different variants of Post-Keynesian distribution and growth theory.

In the Kaldor–Robinson model, assuming full utilization of the capital stock in the long run, changes in the interest rate have uniquely inverse effects on the rates of capital accumulation and profit. However, the Kaldor–Robinson model suffers from serious limitations: the assumptions of continuous full utilization of the capital stock and income shares being a passive or residual variable of capitalists' investment and consumption spending. But also in the Kaleckian distribution and growth models, assuming a long-run variable rate of capacity utilization and income shares being determined by active distribution conflict, variations in the rate of interest have uniquely adverse effects on the rates of capacity utilization, capital accumulation and profit. This is true for different variants of the Kaleckian model, the 'stagnationist' Rowthorn–Dutt–Amadeo model and the Bhaduri/Marglin model with different potential accumulation regimes.

These unique results in all the models of Post-Keynesian distribution and growth theory have been possible, because the effects of the interest rate have only been introduced into the investment functions of the models. The negative impact of changes in the interest rate on investment in these models is mainly exerted through firms' internal funds for investment finance and the related access to external funds in incomplete financial markets, and less through opportunity costs of real investment. Rising creditor's and debtor's risk *à la* Keynes, or the 'principle of increasing risk' *à la* Kalecki, associated with increasing investment under the conditions of given own capital or given retained profits, constitute a constraint for capital accumulation working through the finance channel.

However, these unique results cannot be sustained if further effects of changing interest rates are considered. This has been shown in the extensions of the Rowthorn–Dutt–Amadeo and the Bhaduri/Marglin models. First, firms' stock of debt has been explicitly integrated and the long-run dynamics of the debt–capital ratio have been studied. Secondly, potential effects of changing interest rates on distribution between gross profits and wages have been taken into account, allowing for an interest-elastic mark-up in firms' pricing. Thirdly, the effects of changing interest rates and interest payments as well as changes in the mark-up on aggregate saving and consumption have been considered.

Basically, our results in the extended Rowthorn–Dutt–Amadeo as well as in the extended Bhaduri/Marglin model are quite similar to each other, but also to other Kaleckian 'monetary' models, based on different accumulation functions, which may, but need not, be necessarily 'wage-led'. But there are also some differences.

Taken the debt–capital ratio as given, short-run equilibrium effects of interest rate variations on capacity utilization, capital accumulation and the rate of profit are not unique, but depend on parameter values of the model, as in Dutt (1992, 1995) and in Lavoie (1992a, pp. 363–71; 1993, 1995a, pp. 164–73). In our models these are the parameters in the saving and investment function, and the initial debt–capital ratio in the case of an interest-elastic mark-up. Depending on the values of these parameters, the effects of interest rate variations on the real equilibrium may be either negative throughout ('normal case'), mixed or even positive throughout ('puzzling case').

A low rentiers' saving propensity, a low elasticity of investment with respect to debt services or internal funds and a high elasticity with respect to capacity utilization are generally conducive to a positive effect of rising interest rates on capacity utilization, capital accumulation and the profit rate, and hence to the 'puzzling case'. The 'normal case' becomes more likely, the higher the rentiers' saving propensity, the higher the elasticity of investment with respect to debt services or internal funds and the lower the investment responsiveness to capacity utilization.

In the case of an interest-inelastic mark-up, the degree of indebtedness does not affect the direction of the influence interest rate variations have on the real short-run equilibrium. In the case of an interest-elastic mark-up, however, the degree of indebtedness may have an impact on the direction into which interest rate policies push the economy. Therefore, the degree of indebtedness already has to be taken into account when analysing the short-run effects of monetary policies. Different from the extended Bhaduri/Marglin model, in the extended Rowthorn–Dutt–Amadeo model the 'normal case' for the effects of interest rate variations on the real equilibrium will become generally more likely, if the mark-up is interest-elastic. This is due to the more 'wage-led' feature of the investment function in this model.

We also find that – similar to Lavoie's (1995a, pp. 164–73) 'Minsky–Steindl model' – that long-run stability of the debt–capital ratio is associated with the short-run 'puzzling case', in both the extended Rowthorn–Dutt–Amadeo model and the extended Bhaduri/Marglin model. But unlike Lavoie's 'Minsky–Steindl model', we have some path dependence of interest rate effects on the equilibrium debt–capital ratio in our models. The parameter constellation yielding the short-run 'puzzling case' and a long-run stable debt–capital ratio has been associated with equal distribution of financial wealth, long-term stable relations between the financial sector and non-financial business, as prevalent in bank-based financial systems, and with periods of rapid capital accumulation with stable sales and profit expectations of firms.

The short-run 'normal case' is associated with the long-run instability of the debt–capital ratio and with the macroeconomic 'paradox of debt' in both of our extended Kaleckian models. This 'paradox of debt' has also been found in other monetary extensions of Kaleckian distribution and growth models of different types (Dutt 1992, 1995; Lavoie 1995a, pp. 164–73). The parameter constellation yielding the short-run 'normal case' and a long-run unstable debt–capital ratio giving rise to the 'paradox of debt' is more likely with unequal distribution of financial wealth, unstable relations between the financial sector and non-financial business, as prevalent in capital-market-based systems, and in periods of stagnation with uncertain sales and profit expectations of firms.

Taken together, we can conclude that the general results of Kaleckian 'monetary' models of distribution and growth, related to the dependence of the short-run real effects of interest rate variations on the historically and institutionally given parameter values in the model, on the one hand, and to the long-run instability of the debt–capital ratio and to the 'paradox of debt', on the other hand, seem to be quite robust with respect to the concrete specification of the investment function in these models. Monetary extensions of 'wage-led' models share these general characteristics with models which allow for different regimes of accumulation. Since the parameter values in the models are of the utmost importance for the concrete short- and long-run model behaviour, the Kaleckian 'monetary' models of distribution require an empirical and historical analysis in order to determine these values. This is therefore a precondition for the analysis of the real effects of monetary policies via changes in the interest rate.

In the models discussed so far, the inflationary impact of distribution conflict has been excluded from the analysis. Distribution conflict and monetary policies setting the interest rate have been assumed to affect the mark-up in firms' pricing, and hence distribution between firms, rentiers' and workers' households, but not the inflation rate. This simplification has allowed us to gain important insights into the effects of changes in the interest rate on distribution, economic activity, capital accumulation and debt. However, the analysis has to be extended in order to cover the inflationary consequences of distribution conflict, on the one hand, and the effects of monetary policy interventions reacting upon deviation of actual inflation from some inflation target, on the other hand. This will be done in the following part of the book.

Part III
Distribution Conflict, Inflation and Monetary Policy in a Credit Economy

15
Distribution Conflict, Inflation and Monetary Policy in a Credit Economy: Introduction to Part III

In the third part of the book we will introduce the inflationary consequences of distribution conflict and monetary policy reactions fighting inflation acceleration, omitted in the previous part, into the monetary Kaleckian distribution and growth models developed in chapter 13, the extended Rowthorn–Dutt–Amadeo model and the extended Bhaduri/Marglin model. In undertaking this analysis, we shall address and clarify two important problems in Kaleckian models: First, which is the role of an 'inflation barrier' or a 'Non-Accelerating Inflation Rate of Unemployment' (NAIRU) in these kind of models and how are these models related to modern mainstream macroeconomic New Consensus models which are built on the notion of a NAIRU determining long-run equilibrium unemployment? Secondly, how can we cope with the possibility of a deviation of the long-run equilibrium rate of capacity utilization from the 'normal rate' of utilization conceived by firms when planning new investment in capital stock? Can the main results of the Kaleckian models, the 'paradox of thrift' and at least the possibility of a 'paradox of costs', be sustained if this problem is addressed? And how are the results of the Kaleckian distribution and growth models related to orthodox Classical and Marxian results?

In Chapter 16 the extended monetary Rowthorn–Dutt–Amadeo model will be supplemented with conflict inflation and the role of a NAIRU will be discussed. The short-run stability of a NAIRU will be examined, taking into account real debt effects of accelerating and decelerating inflation usually neglected in Post-Keynesian models of conflict inflation and in New Consensus models, and the short-run effectiveness of monetary policy interventions applying the interest rate tool will be analysed. The problem of long-run endogeneity of the NAIRU will be addressed integrating the long-run distribution effects of central banks' real interest rate variations into the model. Finally some implications for wage bargaining and monetary policies will be outlined.

In chapter 17, the problem of a persistent deviation of the equilibrium rate of capacity utilization from the 'normal rate' of utilization in Kaleckian models of distribution and growth will be addressed, applying the extended monetary Bhaduri/Marglin model supplemented with conflict inflation. We assess this problem following the approach of Dumenil/Levy (1999) who consider the 'normal rate' of utilization in a monetary production economy as the rate which is associated with price stability. Since inflation in the monetary Kaleckian models is driven by distribution conflict, the 'normal rate' of utilization is associated with the consistent distribution claims of firms and labourers. Taking into account real debt effects of changes in inflation and distribution effects of monetary policy interventions, we will discuss the short-run stability of the 'normal rate' and address the issue of long-run endogeneity. In general, we will show that in a Kaleckian monetary distribution and growth model, which takes the major features of a capitalist credit economy seriously, the 'normal rate' of capacity utilization is endogenous to distribution conflict and monetary policy intervention in the long run. And we will also show that major Kaleckian results, in particular the paradox of costs, can be retained for both the short and the long run.

16
A Kaleckian Alternative to the New Consensus on Monetary Policy and Wage Bargaining: Trying to Make Sense of the NAIRU[1]

16.1 Introduction

The idea of a NAIRU is at the core of modern New Keynesian and New Consensus models of monetary policy analysis.[2] In these models the NAIRU is determined by structural factors of the labour market, the wage bargaining process, and the social benefit system. Due to 'micro-founded' rigidities, short-run unemployment determined by the goods market may deviate from long-run equilibrium unemployment given by the NAIRU. However, New Keynesian and New Consensus models suppose a perhaps slow, but stable adjustment mechanism of the actual unemployment rate to the NAIRU, either through a real balance effect or through a monetary policy reaction function. A downward-sloping Phillips curve is valid in the short run, but in the long run effective demand and hence monetary policies have no effect on the NAIRU, and the long-run Phillips curve becomes vertical again. All that monetary policy can do is stabilize output and employment in the short run and stabilize inflation in the long run (Fontana/Palacio-Vera 2005).

In the standard New Consensus model, short-run unemployment has no effect on the NAIRU. However, within the New Keynesian approach, some models have been advanced in which short-run unemployment determined by the goods market affects the NAIRU through the phenomenon of 'hysteresis' (Ball 1999; Blanchard/Summers 1987, 1988). Applying union wage bargaining or insider–outsider models, persistent unemployment and an increasing share of long-term unemployment in total unemployment, with the associated loss of skills and access to firms by the long-term unemployed, will decrease the pressure of a given rate of unemployment on labour unions' or insiders' target real wage and hence on nominal wage demands. This requires an increasing total rate of unemployment in order to stabilize inflation. The economic policy implications of this amended New Keynesian approach, however, are quite straightforward: prevent unemployment in the short run by means of applying appropriate monetary policies, and reduce the existing NAIRU by means of structural reforms in the labour market and the social benefit system, which reduce workers' nominal wage demands and hence inflation pressure, and therefore allow for more expansive monetary policies.

Post-Keynesians have reacted differently to the New Keynesian NAIRU approach. On the one hand, some have rejected the idea of a NAIRU altogether and have insisted that unemployment in the short and in the long run is determined by the 'principle of effective demand' (Galbraith 1997; Davidson 1998). On the other hand, in Post-Keynesian models the cause of accelerating inflation is usually attributed to unresolved conflict over the distribution of income, in particular between capital and labour.[3] This implies that, although employment is determined by effective demand in the short and in the long run, in every moment in time there may be some sort of 'inflation barrier' (Robinson 1962, p. 59) for the increase in economic activity. In what follows, we attempt to contribute to an integration of a conflicting claims theory of inflation with a long-run determination of unemployment by effective demand. This will give rise to a Post-Keynesian interpretation of the NAIRU which will allow us to examine its short-run stability and long-run endogeneity properties.

Within Post-Keynesian theory, Sawyer (2001c, 2002, 2006) has argued that the NAIRU may only be a weak attractor for actual unemployment determined by effective demand, without analysing the stability of the adjustment process in detail. Stockhammer (2004a) has investigated the stability of the NAIRU, focussing on distribution effects of employment variations – and not on inflation effects – applying the distribution and growth model in the tradition of Bhaduri/Marglin (1990). He has shown that only in a profit-led growth regime the NAIRU is generally stable. Sawyer (2001c, 2002) and Arestis/Sawyer (2004, pp. 73–99, 2005) have demonstrated that the NAIRU will become endogenous to actual unemployment if the long-run effects of current investment on capital stock and on productivity growth are taken into account. Lavoie's (2004) Post-Keynesian amendment of the New Consensus model also relies on a positive relation between capital stock growth and productivity growth, and between output growth and labour supply, which makes the natural rate of growth and the NAIRU endogenous to actual growth and actual unemployment.[4]

Although Post-Keynesian models of distribution and growth with conflict inflation, and also some modern New Keynesian and New Consensus NAIRU models, explicitly or implicitly rely on a credit economy in which credit and the stock of money are endogenous, they do not explicitly analyse the implications of debt and costs of debt (interest) on the stability and the endogeneity of the NAIRU. This is a serious limitation, because the effects of accelerating inflation or disinflation/deflation on firms' debt–capital ratio might considerably affect their investment decisions. This was already pointed out by Fisher (1933) and Keynes (1936, p. 264). Real debt effects might hence affect the stability of the NAIRU in the short run, and might contribute to endogeneity in the long run. And central banks' variations in the real interest rate, although perhaps effective in the short run when it comes to putting a halt to accelerating inflation, may have long-run effects on firms' costs of production and hence on the NAIRU, which then might contradict the stabilization of inflation (Lavoie 1992a, pp. 402–4).

We will address these problems applying the monetary extension of the Rowthorn–Dutt–Amadeo model as developed in chapter 13 and integrating conflict inflation and monetary policy interventions into this model. First we shall recapitulate the basic model. Then conflict inflation will be added to the model and the 'Stable Inflation Rate of Employment' (SIRE) will be distinguished from the 'Goods market Equilibrium Rate of Employment' (GERE). The short-run stability of the SIRE will be investigated, without and with monetary policy interventions affecting the real interest rate, and it will be shown that the SIRE is not generally stable. Next, the long-run effects of variations in the real interest rate on the SIRE and the GERE will be discussed and the endogeneity problem will be addressed. Finally the results will be summarised and some conclusions for monetary policies and wage bargaining will be drawn.

16.2 The basic model

The basic model applied in this chapter is the extended monetary Rowthorn–Dutt–Amadeo model developed in Section 13.2. For convenience, the closed economy, one-good model with constant production coefficients and without economic activity by the state is summarized again by the following equations:

$$r = hu\frac{1}{v}, \qquad \text{(III.1)}$$

$$p = [1 + m(i)]\frac{w}{y}, \qquad m > 0, \ \frac{\partial m}{\partial i} \geq 0, \qquad \text{(III.2)}$$

$$h = \frac{\Pi}{pY} = 1 - \frac{1}{1 + m(i)}, \qquad \frac{\partial h}{\partial i} \geq 0, \qquad \text{(III.3)}$$

$$\lambda = \frac{B}{pK}, \qquad \text{(III.4)}$$

$$\sigma = \frac{\Pi - Z + S_Z}{pK} = h\frac{u}{v} - i\lambda(1 - s_Z), \quad 0 < s_Z < 1, \qquad \text{(III.5)}$$

$$g = \alpha + \beta u + \rho\left(h\frac{u}{v} - i\lambda\right), \qquad \alpha, \beta, \rho, > 0, \quad \rho < 1, \qquad \text{(III.6)}$$

$$g = \sigma, \qquad \text{(III.7)}$$

$$\frac{\partial \sigma}{\partial u} - \frac{\partial g}{\partial u} > 0 \Rightarrow (1 - \rho)\frac{h}{v} - \beta > 0. \qquad \text{(III.8)}$$

With given production coefficients the capital potential output ratio (v) is a constant, so that the rate of profit (r) in equation (III.1) is determined by the profit share (h) and the rate of capacity utilization (u). Firms set prices (p) according to a mark-up (m) on unit labour costs, which can be calculated from the nominal wage rate (w) and labour productivity (y), which is also constant up to full capacity output (equation (III.2)). The profit (Π) share in nominal output (pY) is determined by the mark-up (equation (III.3)).

The interest rate (i) is an exogenous variable controlled by the central bank. Considering the distribution effects of interest rate variations, we shall now assume that the mark-up in equation (III.2) – and hence the profit share in equation (III.3) – is interest-inelastic in the short run, but that it is interest-elastic in the long run. As the mark-up on variable costs has to cover the firms' actual and imputed interest payments, the minimum mark-up is affected by the interest rate. For the same reason, the rate of interest determines the minimum rate of profit on real investment in the long run.

In the short run, however, there need not be an immediate positive impact of interest rate variations on the mark-up, the profit share and the profit rate, but we rather suppose a direct effect on internal funds of the firm and hence on investment demand and employment. If changes in the interest rate are lasting, the mark-up and the profit share will have to change in the same direction, because in the long run firms can only sustain those production processes which yield the minimum rate of profit determined by the interest rate. Note that for a long-run effect on the mark-up and the profit share, it is again a change in the interest rate and not in the actual interest payments which is relevant, because we assume that firms are well aware of imputed interest costs on own capital – that is, on accumulated retained earnings.

Recall that in the extended Rowthorn–Dutt–Amadeo model long-term finance of the capital stock (pK) is provided by retained earnings of firms or by long-term credit (B) granted by rentiers' households, directly or through banks. Equation (III.4) defines the debt–capital ratio (λ).

In equation (III.5) for the saving rate (σ), which relates total saving to the nominal capital stock, a classical saving hypothesis is assumed, i.e. workers do not save. The part of profits retained is completely saved by definition. The part of profits distributed to rentiers' households, i.e. the interest payment on the stock of debt, is used by those households according to their propensity to save (s_Z). Therefore, total saving comprises retained profits (Π-Z) and saving out of interest income (S_Z).

In equation (III.6) we have the Kaleckian accumulation function with a positive relationship between capital accumulation (g) and capacity utilization, on the one hand, and internal funds, on the other hand. Internal funds are given by the difference between the rate of profit and the rate of interest times the debt–capital ratio. Therefore, the rate of interest and the debt–capital ratio both have a negative impact on investment because they adversely affect internal funds.

The goods market equilibrium is determined in equation (III.7), and equation (III.8) defines the stability condition. The goods market equilibrium values (*) for capacity utilization, capital accumulation, and the rate of profit are as follows:

$$u^* = \frac{i\lambda(1 - s_Z - \rho) + \alpha}{\frac{h}{v}(1 - \rho) - \beta}, \tag{III.9}$$

$$g^* = \frac{i\lambda\left[\beta(1 - s_Z) - \rho\frac{h}{v}s_Z\right] + \alpha\frac{h}{v}}{\frac{h}{v}(1 - \rho) - \beta}, \tag{III.10}$$

$$r^* = \frac{\frac{h}{v}[i\lambda(1 - s_Z - \rho) + \alpha]}{\frac{h}{v}(1 - \rho) - \beta}. \tag{III.11}$$

16.3 Employment, wage bargaining and inflation: the GERE and the SIRE

With constant productivity of labour, capacity utilization determined by the goods market equilibrium also determines employment (E), and with a given labour force (LF) also the employment rate (e = E/LF), which, in what follows, we term the 'Goods market Equilibrium Rate of Employment' (GERE). An increase in capacity utilization is associated with a proportional increase in the GERE. Generally, in Kaleckian and Post-Keynesian distribution and growth models, full utilization of productive capacity determined by the capital stock will not mean full employment of labour. In order to keep things as simple as possible, however, we will assume in this chapter that the rate of capacity utilization and the employment rate are equal (u = e) and that hence full utilization of capacity is associated with full employment.[5] Under these conditions the rate of unemployment [$\psi = (LF - E)/LF)$] is determined by the rate of capacity utilization:

$$u = e = 1 - \psi. \tag{III.12}$$

Inflation in Kaleckian and Post-Keynesian models is determined by conflict over income distribution between capital and labour, as mentioned above. Figure III.1 displays a simple 'conflicting claims' model of employment and inflation assuming constant production coefficients and a constant mark-up.

Although wage bargaining is concerned with money wage rates, it is assumed that labour unions intend to achieve a certain real wage rate – and with labour productivity given or productivity growth correctly anticipated a certain wage share. The labour unions' 'target real wage rate' (w_b^r) depends positively on the employment rate, and with our assumptions mentioned above therefore on the rate of capacity utilization, because unemployment has a negative impact on union bargaining power:

$$w_b^r = \phi + \varepsilon u. \tag{III.13}$$

At this stage we assume that unions do not consider the macroeconomic effects of their nominal wage demands. There is co-ordination neither between unions in different firms or industries, nor between wage bargaining parties and central banks. Full employment is therefore associated with a union target real wage rate equal to labour productivity (y). Therefore, unemployment has the function to curtail distribution claims of workers (Kalecki 1971, pp. 156–64).

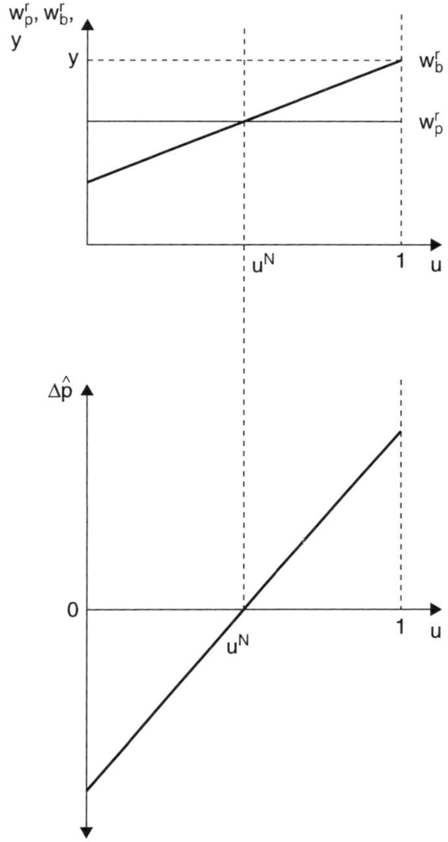

Figure III.1 Employment rate and distribution conflict: no wage bargaining coordination

The feasible real wage rate (w^r_p) is given by mark-up pricing of firms. From equation (III.2) we get for the 'target real wage rate' of firms:

$$w^r_p = \frac{w}{p} = \frac{y}{1+m}. \tag{III.14}$$

With the simplifying assumptions of a constant coefficient technology and a constant mark-up up to full capacity output, the feasible real wage rate curve in Figure III.1 is just a horizontal line. The unions' target real wage and the feasible real wage only coincide by accident. From equations (III.13) and (III.14), and making use of equation (III.3), we get for the employment rate (e^N), and hence the rate of capacity utilization (u^N), which allow for the consistency of the target real wage rates of labour unions and firms:

$$u^N = e^N = \frac{\frac{y}{1+m} - \phi}{\varepsilon} = \frac{y(1-h) - \phi}{\varepsilon}. \qquad \text{(III.15)}$$

Only if the goods market equilibrium generates an employment rate of $e^* = u^* = u^N$, will the distribution claims of labourers and firms be compatible. Whenever the GERE deviates from u^N we get rising or falling inflation rates (and finally deflation). This can easily be shown as follows. Assume that wage bargaining parties determine the growth rate of nominal wages ($\hat{w}$) according to:

$$\hat{w}_t = \hat{p}_{t-1} + \hat{y}_t + \varepsilon(u_t^* - u^N). \qquad \text{(III.16)}$$

Wage inflation is therefore determined by past inflation, (correctly anticipated) productivity growth, the attempt to improve distribution whenever the employment rate exceeds some threshold, and nominal wage moderation whenever the employment rate is below this threshold. Price setting of firms follows wage setting by wage bargainers. It is therefore firms' pricing decisions which determine distribution at any rate. From equation (III.2) we get for the inflation rate ($\hat{p}$):

$$\hat{p}_t = (1 \hat{+} m)_t + \hat{w}_t - \hat{y}_t. \qquad \text{(III.17)}$$

If firms do not vary the mark-up, and productivity growth is either correctly anticipated by firms and labour unions or zero, we get:

$$\hat{p}_t = \hat{p}_{t-1}, \text{ only if: } u_t^* = u^N. \qquad \text{(III.18)}$$

The unemployment rate $[\psi^N = (LF - E^N)/LF = 1 - e^N = 1 - u^N]$ associated with this 'Stable Inflation Rate of Employment' (SIRE) may therefore be termed a 'Non-Accelerating Inflation Rate of Unemployment' (NAIRU). It defines a distribution equilibrium between the claims of workers and those of firms.

16.4 The short-run stability of the NAIRU/the SIRE

Discussing the stability of the NAIRU or the SIRE, we shall proceed in two steps. First, the issue of stability without monetary policy interventions will be considered. Then, the effects of monetary policy applying the interest rate tool whenever the GERE deviates from the SIRE will be analysed.

No monetary policy intervention

In older New Keynesian models with an exogenous stock of money, the stability of the NAIRU is achieved by a real balance effect.[6] Falling (rising) nominal wages and hence price inflation whenever unemployment is above (below) the NAIRU is assumed not to affect nominal demand, but only real demand. This will then bring back real demand to a level consistent with the NAIRU. However, since in our model the stock of money is endogenous, Keynes or Pigou effects cannot work as stabilisers.

Stockhammer (2004a) has discussed another potential stabilization mechanism of the NAIRU in a Post-Keynesian distribution and growth model making use of the Bhaduri/Marglin (1990) distinction between wage-led and profit-led growth regimes. Following a suggestion by the late Kalecki (1971, pp. 156–64), distribution is assumed to be affected by unemployment: Rising (falling) unemployment causes a falling (rising) wage share. A change in distribution then feeds back on demand, output and unemployment. Therefore, in a profit-led regime the NAIRU will always be stable, because falling (rising) unemployment reduces (increases) the profit share and hence investment, output and employment. In a wage-led regime stability depends on the relative adjustments of accumulation and distribution whenever unemployment deviates from the NAIRU.

However, the distribution effects of a changing employment rate, or rate of capacity utilization, as supposed by Stockhammer (2004a), cannot be taken for granted: A rising employment rate will surely cause increasing nominal wage demands by workers, but it may also trigger rising profit claims by firms and hence rising mark-ups.[7] And as firms set prices in the goods markets after nominal wages have been set in the labour market, we could also suppose a rising profit share accompanying rising rates of capacity utilization and employment due to firms' improved sales conditions, at least in a closed economy. If this is assumed, the NAIRU in Stockhammer's (2004a) model will be stable in the wage-led regime, whereas in the profit-led regime stability will depend on relative adjustments of accumulation and distribution.

We will not try to resolve this issue here and continue to assume that distribution between wages and gross profits is not affected by changes in the rates of capacity utilization and employment. In what follows we will rather discuss a presumably more important effect in a credit economy: the real debt effect associated with rising/falling inflation rates which was already highlighted by Fisher (1933) and by Keynes (1936, p. 264).

Let us assume that the stock of firms' debt is not indexed to changes in the inflation rate. Accelerating inflation will therefore decrease the debt–capital ratio defined in equation (III.4), decelerating inflation will increase this ratio. If monetary policy does not respond to changes in the inflation rate, and does not vary the nominal interest rate accordingly, also real interest rates will fall in the face of accelerating inflation and will rise when inflation decelerates. Taken together, this implies that the interest–capital ratio $[i\lambda = (iB)/(pK) = Z/(pK)]$ will fall when inflation rises, and will rise when inflation falls. Given that changes in the real interest rate do not affect the mark-up and hence the profit share in the short run, the effects of changes in the interest–capital ratio on the GERE can be determined from equation (III.9):

$$\frac{\partial u}{\partial (i\lambda)} = \frac{1 - s_Z - \rho}{\frac{h}{v}(1 - \rho) - \beta}. \qquad \text{(III.9a)}$$

If only stable goods market equilibria are considered, equation (III.9a) shows that the effects of changes in the interest–capital ratio on the GERE depend on the parameters in the saving and investment function of the model. If the rentiers' propensity to consume $(1\text{-}s_Z)$ is smaller than firms' investment elasticity related to internal funds (ρ), rising indebtedness and rising real interest payments will have a negative effect on the GERE. This can again be called the 'normal case' (Lavoie 1995a), usually expected in Post-Keynesian theory. An increasing interest–capital ratio of firms will have a negative impact on the goods market equilibrium.

If the conditions of the 'normal case' prevail, the SIRE will be unstable. Whenever the GERE exceeds the SIRE, accelerating inflation will cause falling debt–capital ratios and falling real interest rates, and hence a rising GERE, moving the economy farther away from stable inflation. If the GERE falls short of the SIRE, decelerating inflation and finally deflation will cause a rising debt–capital ratio and rising real interest rates, and hence a falling GERE. The economy will be trapped in a downward spiral of disinflation/deflation, rising real indebtedness of the firm sector and a falling GERE. Therefore we get the macroeconomic 'paradox of debt' again, here associated with cumulative inflation or disinflation/deflation.[8] With decelerating inflation and rising interest–capital ratios, firms individually reduce investment in order to confine the burden of debt, with the macroeconomic effect that disinflation or deflation is reinforced and the interest–capital ratio keeps on rising.

With accelerating inflation, firms individually will increase debt and investment, with the macroeconomic effect of further acceleration of inflation and a further decrease in the interest–capital ratio.

If the rentiers' propensity to consume exceeds firms' investment elasticity with respect to internal funds, a rising interest–capital ratio of firms will be associated with an increasing GERE. This is the 'puzzling case' (Lavoie 1995a) again, usually not expected in Post-Keynesian theory. If the conditions of the 'puzzling case' prevail, the SIRE will be stable. Rising (falling) inflation rates will trigger falling (rising) debt–capital ratios and falling (rising) real interest rates, which will now cause a falling (rising) GERE.[9] The GERE will therefore adjust to the SIRE.

Monetary policy intervention

In our 'normal case', stabilizing the SIRE requires monetary policy intervention applying the monetary interest rate tool. Also modern New Keynesian and, in particular, the New Consensus models rely on monetary policy to adjust actual unemployment to the NAIRU and to stabilize the inflation rate.[10] In these models the (real) rate of interest is the monetary policy instrument, which implies that it is no longer assumed that monetary policy controls the stock of (high-powered) money and that the latter is endogenous to the whole economic process (Arestis/Sawyer 2004, pp. 10–72). Whenever unemployment falls short of the NAIRU, and inflation accelerates, the central bank is supposed to increase nominal interest rates such that real interest rates rise, which should then adversely affect aggregate demand and hence employment. If unemployment is above the NAIRU, the central bank should lower nominal interest rates such that real interest rates decrease, which should increase aggregate demand and hence employment. In order to have a stable NAIRU, monetary policy interventions have to be symmetric and their effects have to be assumed to be symmetric as well. If these conditions are fulfilled, what central banks can achieve is output stabilization in the short run and stable inflation rates in the long run (Fontana/Palacio-Vera 2005).[11]

In the 'normal case' in our model, however, in order to stabilize the SIRE, central banks do not only have to change real rates of interest by means of varying the nominal rate, but the change in the real interest rate has to be sufficient to overcompensate the counter-effects of the change in the firms' debt–capital ratio on the GERE. In general, this is not a problem in a situation of rising inflation, because there is no upper limit for the nominal interest rate set by the central bank. But in a situation of falling inflation or even deflation, central banks may not be able

Table III.1 The short-run stability of the 'Stable Inflation Rate of Employment' (SIRE)

	$1 - s_Z - \rho$	
	– ('normal case')	+ ('puzzling case')
No monetary policy intervention	*unstable*	*stable*
Monetary policy intervention	*stable*, if change in real interest rate over-compensates change in the debt–capital ratio, otherwise *unstable*	*unstable*, if change in real interest rate over-compensates change in the debt–capital ratio, otherwise *stable*

to reduce the nominal rate of interest by a sufficient amount to decrease real rates and to over-compensate the restrictive demand effects of rising debt–capital ratios, because there is a zero lower bound for the nominal interest rate. Therefore, in this situation central banks may be unable to adjust the GERE to the SIRE, and the economy may be trapped in a deflationary recession. In the 'normal case', therefore, the NAIRU can generally only be considered an 'inflation barrier' which has to be enforced by the central banks, but central banks may be incapable to adjust actual unemployment to the NAIRU whenever the former exceeds the latter.

In the 'puzzling case', monetary policy interventions, which follow the New Keynesian/New Consensus advice and increase the real rate of interest in the face of rising inflation and decrease it in the face of falling inflation or deflation, will have a destabilizing effect. This may over-compensate the stabilizing effect exerted by the change in the debt–capital ratio and may cause a further deviation of the GERE from the SIRE. Table III.1 summarizes our results with respect to short-run stability of the SIRE.

16.5 The long-run endogeneity of the NAIRU/the SIRE

The endogeneity of the NAIRU, that is the adjustment of the NAIRU to the actual rate of unemployment determined by the goods market in the case of a persistent deviation of the two rates, has been discussed within New Keynesian models under the heading of 'hysteresis' (Blanchard/Summers 1987; Ball 1999). Applying union wage bargaining or insider–outsider models, persistent unemployment and an increasing share of long-term unemployment in total unemployment, with the associated loss of skills and access to firms by the long-term unemployed, will decrease the pressure of a given rate of unemployment on labour unions' or insiders' target real wage, and hence on nominal wage demands. The labour unions' target real wage curve in Figure III.1 will rotate upwards (ε in equations (III.13), (III.15) and (III.16) will increase), the SIRE will decline, and the NAIRU will increase.

Arestis/Sawyer (2004, pp. 73–99, 2005) and Sawyer (2001c, 2002) have discussed another source of endogeneity of the NAIRU: the effect of current investment on capital stock and productivity growth.[12] Whereas investment in the short run determines effective demand and hence the GERE, net investment will also increase the capital stock and will therefore affect maximum employment if it is restrained by the capital stock. And it will also affect the NAIRU or the SIRE, if it is assumed that firms increase the mark-up when actual output approaches full capacity output. In order to simplify our model, we have excluded this by means of assuming a constant mark-up and full utilization of capital stock being associated with full employment. However, in the real world this is not necessarily the case, and Arestis/Sawyer have therefore made an important point: Low investment not only causes a low GERE, but also decreases the SIRE by restraining the capital stock and output capacity.

But investment is not limited to only affect the size of the capital stock, it will also affect productivity growth, if we assume that technical progress is embodied in physical investment and/or that there are increasing returns to scale.[13] In our model, increasing productivity (growth) will shift the firms' target real wage curve in Figure III.1 downwards and the SIRE in equation (III.15) will increase. This, however, supposes that labour unions do not adjust their target real wage rate when productivity growth increases. But this cannot be taken for granted, if labour unions target a certain wage share and can correctly anticipate productivity growth as we have assumed in equation (III.16). If this is the case, productivity growth will have no effect on the SIRE or the NAIRU. Therefore, the effect of productivity growth on the NAIRU depends on labour unions' or workers' aspirations to participate in increasing productivity.

In what follows, we will trace another source of endogeneity which is associated with the distributional effects of monetary policy responses to accelerating or decelerating inflation rates. Assume for the reasons given above that persistent changes in the real interest rate are in the long run accompanied by changes in the mark-up in the same direction. In our model this has two effects.

First, changes in the mark-up affect the firms' target real wage rate: An increasing (decreasing) mark-up shifts the firms' target real wage curve in Figure III.1 downwards (upwards) and the SIRE decreases (increases). From equation (III.15) we get for the effect of a change in the mark-up and hence in the profit share on the SIRE:

$$\frac{\partial u^N}{\partial h} = -\frac{y}{\varepsilon} < 0. \tag{III.15a}$$

Secondly, changes in the mark-up and thus in distribution between wages and gross profits have an additional effect on the goods market equilibrium and hence on the GERE. From equation (III.9) we get:

$$\frac{\partial u}{\partial h} = -\frac{\frac{1-\rho}{v}u}{\frac{h}{v}(1-\rho)-\beta} < 0. \tag{III.9b}$$

The effect of a change in the mark-up and in the profit share on the GERE is negative. Raising the mark-up when interest rates increase will have a positive impact on firms' internal funds but will simultaneously reduce consumption demand, sales and hence capacity utilization (and the GERE), which will then negatively feed back on internal funds. Furthermore, lower capacity utilization will also have a negative impact on investment decisions.

Let us now discuss the implications for the effects of monetary policy interventions. We start with the 'normal case' from Table III.1. Assume that the GERE exceeds the initial SIRE at u_1^N in Figure III.2. Since accelerating inflation and a falling interest–capital ratio of firms is a stimulus for effective demand, the GERE will further increase and inflation acceleration will speed up. In order to stabilize the rate of inflation, central banks have to increase nominal interest rates in order to raise real interest rates by a sufficient amount to over-compensate the demand-stimulating effects of falling debt–capital ratios. Therefore, in the short run the central bank can bring back the GERE to the SIRE at u_1^N. In the long run, however, a higher real interest rate will induce firms to increase the mark-up. This will shift the firms' target real wage curve down from w_{p1}^r to w_{p2}^r and reduce the SIRE to u_2^N. The redistribution at the expense of labour will also reduce the GERE. Three scenarios are possible depending on the relative effects of changes in distribution on the GERE and on the SIRE in equations (III.9b) and (III.15a).

1. If, by accident, $\partial u/\partial h = \partial u^N/\partial h$, the reduction of the GERE caused by an increasing mark-up will make this new rate coincide with the SIRE at u_2^N, so that the economy gets to rest at a stable SIRE.

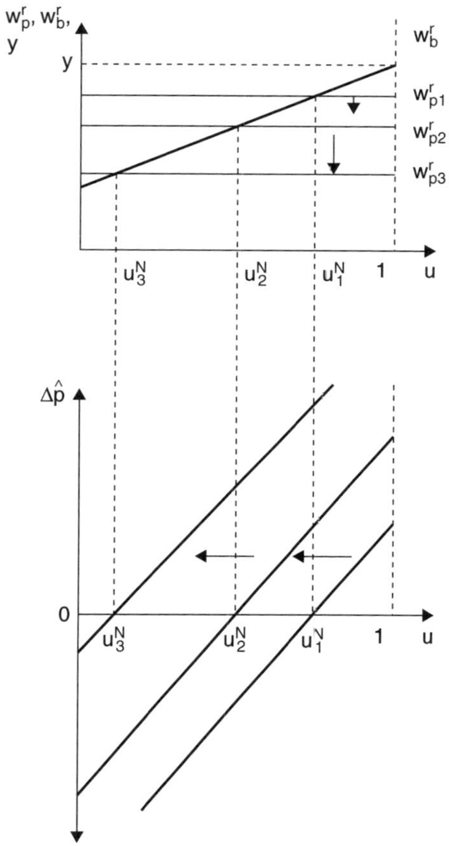

Figure III.2 Long-run endogeneity of the Stable Inflation Rate of Employment (SIRE) caused by monetary policy intervention: the horizontal 'long-run Phillips curve'

2. If $|\partial u/\partial h| > |\partial u^N/\partial h|$, the effective demand effect of redistribution at the expense of labour will make the GERE fall below u_2^N and we get falling inflation rates. This should then make central banks reduce real interest rates, making the GERE increase to u_2^N in the short run. In the long run, firms then reduce mark-ups, the firms' target real wage curve shifts upwards, and effective demand is stimulated by redistribution in favour of labour. The SIRE as well as the GERE will increase, with the latter now overshooting the former and monetary policy will have

to intervene again. This oscillation may converge to a stable SIRE between u_2^N and u_1^N, but may also generate stable oscillation around that SIRE, or the oscillation may even explode, depending on the degree of over- and undershooting of the GERE with respect to the SIRE and the concomitant change in the real interest rate required for the short-run adjustment of the GERE to the SIRE.

3. If $|\partial u/\partial h| < |\partial u^N/\partial h|$, the effective demand effect of redistribution at the expense of labour is weak, so that the GERE remains above u_2^N. We will get accelerating inflation again, inducing the central bank to increase real interest rates, forcing the GERE down to u_2^N in the short run. In the long run, firms will again increase mark-ups, which will shift their target real wage curve down to w_{p3}^T and the SIRE will decline to u_3^N. The GERE will also decline, because of the redistribution of income at the expense of labour, but will remain above u_3^N, inflation will accelerate anew and central banks will have to intervene again.

Equation (III.9b) shows that the effective demand effect of redistribution between wages and gross profits becomes weaker when the GERE decreases. This implies that a development according to scenario 3 becomes more likely the lower the GERE declines.

Scenario 3 is shown in Figure III.2: Stable inflation is associated with a declining SIRE. The long-run 'Phillips curve' becomes horizontal because of the nature of monetary policy interventions.[14] In this scenario, monetary policy is only able to stabilize the inflation rate in the long run at the expense of a continuously decreasing GERE. Monetary policy interventions trigger a process in which stabilizing inflation in the short run by means of increasing real interest rates and slowing down the economy re-establishes the inflation problem in the long run, when the full distribution effects of real interest rate variations are felt. In the long run, this scenario describes a latent tendency towards stagflation.

Note that scenario 3 also works in reverse: If the central bank intends to improve the GERE, in the short run lowering real interest rates will be associated with accelerating inflation. In the long run, however, a falling mark-up increases the SIRE. And since the demand effect of redistribution in favour of labour is not too strong, so that the GERE does not exceed the SIRE, there is again room for manoeuvre for the central bank to cut real interest rates.

Let us now briefly discuss the short-run 'puzzling case' from Table III.1. In this case a deviation of the GERE from the SIRE is self-correcting in the short run without monetary policy intervention. If the GERE exceeds

u_1^N in Figure III.2, the reduction in consumption demand caused by the devaluation of rentiers' assets will over-compensate the stimulation of firms' investment demand caused by a falling interest–capital ratio. If central banks simply hold the nominal interest rate constant, they will support this adjustment process and the economy will return to u_1^N.

If, however, central banks try to fight accelerating inflation rates by means of increasing the real interest rate, as recommended by the New Keynesian and the New Consensus models, they will delay the convergence process towards u_1^N in the short run.[15] The long-run effect of an increasing real interest rate will reduce the SIRE to u_2^N. This will again accelerate inflation. The redistribution at the expense of labour caused by an increasing mark-up, however, will have a dampening effect on the GERE shifting it towards u_2^N. Again, we have three scenarios depending on the relative effects of changes in distribution on the GERE and on the SIRE (equations (III.9b) and (III.15a)):

1. If, by accident, $\partial u/\partial h = \partial u^N/\partial h$, the GERE will coincide with u_2^N and the economy will get to rest at this lower stable SIRE.
2. If $|\partial u/\partial h| > |\partial u^N/\partial h|$, the GERE falls below u_2^N and we will get disinflation, short-run real interest rate cuts delaying the convergence process towards u_2^N, which will in the long run decrease the mark-up moving the SIRE upwards. Redistribution in favour of labour will stimulate demand and employment and will make the GERE exceed the SIRE, and so on. The outcome of this process will again depend on the degree of over- and undershooting of the GERE with respect to the SIRE and on the degree of (now disturbing) monetary policy interventions.
3. If $|\partial u/\partial h| < |\partial u^N/\partial h|$, the redistribution effect at the expense of labour income on demand is weak, the GERE will remain higher than u_2^N. Inflation will accelerate, central banks will increase real interest rates, disturbing the short-run convergence process towards u_2^N and decreasing the SIRE to u_3^N.

Since the effective demand effect of redistribution between wages and gross profits becomes weaker when the employment rate goes down (equation (III.9b)), we obtain again that scenario 3 becomes the more likely the lower the GERE drops: The long-run 'Phillips curve' again becomes horizontal, as in Figure III.2.

Let us finally add that, whatever case we consider and whatever scenario comes into existence, in the long run the SIRE and hence the NAIRU are endogenous to monetary policy's real interest rate manipulation in our model. Therefore, in our approach the NAIRU is a direct result of monetary policy interventions.

16.6 Results and implications for monetary policy and wage bargaining

In a Kaleckian distribution and growth model with endogenous money and inflation generated by distribution conflict, we have shown that monetary policy is either an unnecessary or a costly tool to control inflation in the short run. Taking into account the real debt effects of inflation acceleration or deceleration, the NAIRU will be stable in the 'puzzling case' with a propensity to consume out of rentiers' income exceeding the sensitivity of investment with respect to internal funds. In this case, inflation-targeting monetary policies raising real interest rates in the face of accelerating inflation will disturb the adjustment to stable inflation rates. In the 'normal case' of a rentiers' propensity to consume falling short of firms' elasticity of investment with respect to internal funds, the NAIRU will be unstable. Inflation-targeting monetary policies applying the interest rate tool will be able to contain accelerating inflation. There are, however, some doubts whether monetary policies will be able to fight decelerating inflation and finally deflation because there is a zero lower bound for the nominal interest rate. In this case, therefore, the NAIRU is merely an 'inflation barrier' enforced by monetary policies, but there is no guarantee that monetary policies will always be able to adjust unemployment determined by the goods market to the NAIRU, as is assumed in New Keynesian or New Consensus models.

In the long run, variations in the real interest rate will affect the firms' target real wage rate and the NAIRU becomes endogenous to monetary policy. This direct channel of endogeneity supplements those channels already discussed in the literature: labour market hysteresis and capital stock effects on the NAIRU. In the 'normal' as well as in the 'puzzling case', inflation-targeting monetary policies raising the real interest rate in the face of accelerating inflation will raise the NAIRU. This bears the risk of a continuously increasing NAIRU in order to keep inflation under control, which may yield a horizontal long-run Phillips curve and latent stagflation. Taking these effects into account, monetary policy raising real interest rates can be considered an inappropriate tool to control inflation in the long run.

According to our analysis, monetary policy should rather aim at low real interest rates in the short and in the long run. This allows for a long-run increase in the SIRE and hence a reduction in the NAIRU, in any case.

In the 'puzzling case', lower real interest rates will decrease the GERE in the short run, but the real debt effects associated with disinflation will finally adjust the GERE to the higher SIRE in the long run. In the 'normal case', lowering real interest rates will increase the GERE in the short run which might trigger acceleration of inflation. This, however, will be dampened or even be wiped out as soon as the long-run increase in the SIRE becomes effective.

If short-run accelerating inflation in the face of an increasing GERE is to be avoided, the causes of inflation should be addressed directly. Therefore, policy makers should resort to incomes policy and apply wage bargaining co-ordination as an appropriate tool. As recent research on the interaction of independent central banks and wage bargaining institutions has shown, effectively co-ordinated wage bargaining is able to internalize negative macroeconomic wage externalities (Franzese 2001a, 2001b; Hein 2002, 2004c): In economies with a high degree of 'effective' wage bargaining co-ordination, the reduction of inflation rates has been accompanied by less employment losses than in economies with a low degree of co-ordination.

Effective wage bargaining co-ordination is characterized by a high degree of horizontal bargaining co-ordination between industries (pattern bargaining, state imposed or sponsored co-ordination, intra-associational co-ordination). In order to solve the implementation problem of collective agreements and to prevent negative or positive wage drift, 'effective' bargaining co-ordination also has to include a high degree of vertical co-ordination within industries (high level of union and bargaining agreement coverage, legal enforceability of collective agreements, peace obligations) (Kittel/Traxler 2001). The influence of effective co-ordination of wage bargaining on the SIRE in our model is shown in Figure III.3.

With effective wage bargaining co-ordination, the labour unions' target real wage curve has a horizontal part. Between u_1^N and u_2^N the bargaining parties are able to accept the feasible real wage rate and to exhaust the scope for distribution, taking into account the inflation objective of the central bank. By means of effectively co-ordinated wage bargaining a constant inflation rate becomes compatible with a range of GEREs. The SIRE or the NAIRU as the short-run limit to employment are no longer unique. Contrary to prevailing propositions, in our Kaleckian approach a reduction of the NAIRU and an increase in the SIRE can be attained by means of organizing the labour market and co-ordinating the bargaining parties, and does not require decentralization of wage bargaining and deregulation of labour markets, as advocated

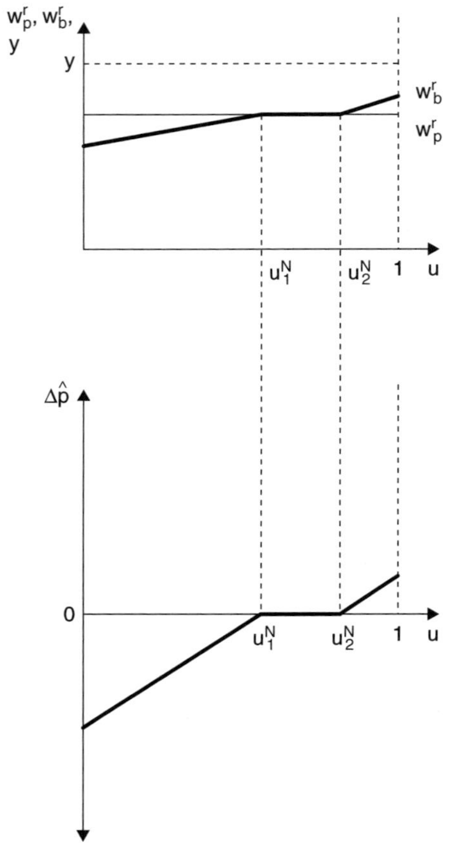

Figure III.3 Employment rate and distribution conflict: effective wage bargaining co-ordination

by New Keynesian or New Consensus models. A high degree of effective wage bargaining co-ordination should also have the additional virtue that increasing unemployment will not cause immediate disinflation or deflation, with its potentially negative impacts on effective demand and the GERE, in the 'normal case' of our model.

17

On the (In-)stability and the Endogeneity of the Normal Rate of Capacity Utilization in a Post-Keynesian/Kaleckian 'Monetary' Distribution and Growth Model[16]

17.1 Introduction

The Kaleckian models of distribution and growth discussed so far have been criticized by some Neo-Marxian and Neo-Ricardian authors (Auerbach/Skott 1988; Committeri 1986), because the equilibrium rate of capacity utilization in these models may deviate permanently from firms' target rate of utilization, the long-run 'normal rate', without any tendency to adjustment.[17] This deviation seems to be inconsistent with the requirement that firms' investment decisions should be based on expectations of some 'normal rate' of utilization with regard to new productive equipment. Therefore, firms are supposed to adjust productive capacity to demand in the long run, and capacity utilization should be equal to firms' target rate of utilization in a 'fully adjusted long-run position'.

Dumenil/Levy (1999) have even argued that taking into account the adjustment of the goods market equilibrium rate of capacity utilization to the long-run 'normal rate' yields a synthetic model which displays Keynesian/Kaleckian properties in the short run, but regains Classical properties in the long-run fully adjusted position. Therefore, in the long run both the paradox of thrift and the paradox of costs, although valid in the short run, disappear. The adjustment mechanisms Dumenil/Levy (1999) apply and the results they derive are similar to those proposed in the New Consensus macroeconomic model:[18] Deviations of the goods market equilibrium rate of capacity utilization from the 'normal rate' trigger rising (or falling) prices which make monetary policies intervene bringing the economy back to the 'normal rate' of utilization in the long run, which is then associated with stable prices.

Post-Keynesians/Kaleckians have reacted differently to the Neo-Marxian/Neo-Ricardian critique. Whereas Chick/Caserta (1997) have argued that a 'provisional' goods market equilibrium may be more important than a fully adjusted long-run position when it comes to analysing a monetary production economy characterized by continuous change in historical time, others have proposed different adjustment mechanisms between the 'normal' and the goods market equilibrium rate of capacity utilization. Commendatore (2005), Dutt (1997), Lavoie (1996b) and Park (1997) have argued that the firms' notion of the 'normal rate' of utilization is slowly increased (decreased) when the actual rate is persistently higher (lower) than the 'normal rate'. In a model with full-cost pricing Lavoie (2002) has made the target rate of return calculated on the basis of 'normal' utilization adjust to the actual rate of return which depends on the goods market equilibrium rate of utilization. And adding conflict inflation to this model, Lavoie (2002, 2003b) has shown that firms' target rate of return becomes endogenous and equilibrium capacity utilization is not necessarily the standard or 'normal rate' underlying target rate of return pricing – that is, capacity utilization remains endogenous. Cassetti (2006) has further extended the analysis and has included the rate of capital scrapping as an additional adjustment variable whenever the equilibrium rate of capacity utilization deviates from the 'normal rate'. All these papers show that under certain conditions the main propositions of the Kaleckian model, the paradox of thrift and the paradox of costs, may still hold.

Although these Kaleckian models discuss important adjustment processes, they are far from complete. In particular, although they contain distribution struggle and inflation arising from unresolved conflict, they omit to discuss major effects of rising or falling inflation on demand and hence on capacity utilization. In a credit economy these effects are associated with the influence of changing inflation on firms' real debt position (Fisher 1933; Keynes 1936, p. 264). And these models also lack a discussion of monetary policy effects on distribution and demand in a credit economy. The present chapter attempts to bridge some of these gaps applying a similar analysis as in the previous chapter.

We start from the Dumenil/Levy (1999) notion that the long-run 'normal rate' of capacity utilization in a monetary production economy should be associated with stable inflation. But, unlike Dumenil/Levy (1999), we take a closer look at the causes of changing inflation in a monetary production economy, which remain unclear in their model and which we see originating from unresolved distribution conflict. In addition, unlike Dumenil/Levy (1999) and the Kaleckian models referred to above, we integrate the feedbacks of changing inflation on demand into our model. And we fully take account of the short-run and long-run demand and distribution effects of monetary policies applying the interest rate tool in order to fight rising or falling inflation rates. Our discussion is based on the monetary extension of the Bhaduri/Marglin (1990) model, as developed in chapter 13. Besides wage-led growth, this model also allows for profit-led growth, as Dumenil/Levy (1999) suppose for the long run.

The chapter is organized as follows. First, we shall present the basic model, add conflict inflation to the model, and shall distinguish the 'Stable Inflation Rate of Capacity Utilization' (SIRCU), as the long-run 'normal rate' of utilization, from the 'Goods market Equilibrium Rate of Capacity Utilization' (GERCU). Then we shall discuss the short-run stability properties of the SIRCU, with and without monetary policy interventions, before the endogeneity issue of the 'normal rate' will be addressed focusing on the long-run adjustments of GERCU and SIRCU. Finally, the validity of the paradox of thrift and the paradox of costs within our model will be discussed.

17.2 The basic model

The basic model applied in this chapter is the extended monetary Bhaduri/Marglin model developed in section 13.3. It is based on the same premises as the extended Rowthorn–Dutt–Amadeo model applied in the previous chapter, the only difference being the investment function in equation (III.19) and therefore also the stability condition in equation (III.20). For convenience, the model is summarized by the following equations again:

$$r = hu\frac{1}{v}, \qquad \text{(III.1)}$$

$$p = [1 + m(i)]\frac{w}{y}, \qquad m > 0, \frac{\partial m}{\partial i} \geq 0, \qquad \text{(III.2)}$$

$$h = \frac{\Pi}{pY} = 1 - \frac{1}{1 + m(i)}, \qquad \frac{\partial h}{\partial i} \geq 0, \qquad \text{(III.3)}$$

$$\lambda = \frac{B}{pK}, \qquad \text{(III.4)}$$

$$\sigma = \frac{\Pi - Z + S_Z}{pK} = h\frac{u}{v} - i\lambda(1 - s_Z), \quad 0 < s_Z < 1, \qquad \text{(III.5)}$$

$$g = \alpha + \beta u + \tau h - \theta\lambda i, \quad \alpha, \beta, \tau, \theta > 0, \quad g > 0 \text{ for } r - i > 0, \qquad \text{(III.19)}$$

$$g = \sigma, \qquad \text{(III.7)}$$

$$\frac{\partial\sigma}{\partial u} - \frac{\partial g}{\partial u} > 0 \Rightarrow \frac{h}{v} - \beta > 0. \qquad \text{(III.20)}$$

The rate of profit (r) in equation (III.1) is determined by the profit share (h) and the rate of capacity utilization (u), assuming the capital–potential output ratio (v) to be constant. Firms set prices (p) according to a mark-up (m) on unit labour costs (equation (III.2)). Unit labour costs are given by the nominal wage rate (w) and constant labour productivity (y). The share of profits (Π) in nominal output (pY) is determined by the mark-up (equation (III.3)). The mark-up in equation (III.2) – and hence the profit share in equation (III.3) – is interest-inelastic in the short run but interest-elastic in the long run. Long-term finance of the capital stock (pK) is provided by retained earnings of firms or by long-term credit (B) granted by rentiers' households, directly or through banks, and equation (III.4) defines the debt–capital ratio (λ). In equation (III.5) for the saving rate (σ), a classical saving hypothesis is assumed. Total saving comprises retained profits (Π-Z) and saving out of interest income (S_Z). Capital accumulation in equation (III.19) is positively affected by the rate of capacity utilization and by the profit share, and negatively by firms' interest payments, and hence by the interest rate and the debt–capital ratio. The goods market equilibrium is determined in equation (III.7), and equation (III.20) defines the stability condition. The goods market equilibrium values (*) for capacity utilization, capital accumulation, and the rate of profit are as follows:

$$u^* = \frac{\lambda i(1 - s_Z - \theta) + \alpha + \tau h}{\frac{h}{v} - \beta}, \qquad \text{(III.21)}$$

$$g^* = \frac{\lambda i\left[\beta(1 - s_Z) - \theta\frac{h}{v}\right] + \frac{h}{v}(\alpha + \tau h)}{\frac{h}{v} - \beta}, \qquad \text{(III.22)}$$

$$r^* = \frac{\frac{h}{v}[\lambda i(1 - s_Z - \theta) + \alpha + \tau h]}{\frac{h}{v} - \beta}. \qquad \text{(III.23)}$$

17.3 Capacity utilization, wage bargaining, inflation and monetary policy intervention: the GERCU and the SIRCU

With constant productivity of labour and a given labour supply, the 'Goods Market Equilibrium Rate of Capacity Utilization' (GERCU) in equation (III.21) determines a certain rate of employment, and hence unemployment. An increase in the GERCU is associated with a proportional increase in employment and the employment rate. Generally, in Kaleckian and Post-Keynesian distribution and growth models full utilization of productive capacity determined by the capital stock will not mean full employment of labour.

In chapter 16 we have developed a Kaleckian 'conflicting claims' model of employment and inflation assuming constant production coefficients and a constant mark-up, which can now be applied again (Figure III.1, p. 139). Recall that, although wage bargaining is concerned with money wage rates, we have assumed that labour unions intend to achieve a certain real wage rate – and with labour productivity given or productivity growth correctly anticipated a certain wage share. The labour unions' target real wage rate (w_b^r) depends positively on the employment rate. With our assumptions from above, the labourers' target real wage rate is positively related to the rate of capacity utilization:

$$w_b^r = \phi + \varepsilon u. \tag{III.13}$$

In this chapter we assume that labour unions do not consider the macroeconomic effects of their nominal wage demands. There is neither co-ordination between unions in different firms or industries nor between wage bargaining parties and monetary policy.

Also recall that the feasible real wage rate (w_p^r) is given by mark-up pricing of firms. From equation (III.2) we get for the target real wage rate of firms:

$$w_p^r = \frac{w}{p} = \frac{y}{1+m}. \tag{III.14}$$

For the rate of capacity utilization (u^N), which allows for consistent target real wage rates of labour unions and firms we get the already familiar result:

$$u^N = \frac{\frac{y}{1+m} - \phi}{\varepsilon} = \frac{y(1-h) - \phi}{\varepsilon}. \tag{III.15}$$

Only if the GERCU is equal to u^N, will the distribution claims of labourers and firms be compatible. Whenever the GERCU deviates from u^N

we get rising or falling inflation rates (and finally deflation). Therefore equation (III.15) also defines a 'Stable Inflation Rate of Capacity Utilization' (SIRCU). In a monetary production economy this rate of capacity utilization can be considered to be the 'normal rate'.

17.4 Short-run stability of the SIRCU and monetary policy interventions

Discussing the short-run stability of the SIRCU, we have to take a look at the effects of rising or falling inflation on the GERCU, and therefore we can follow the procedure already applied in chapter 16. Let us assume again that firms set prices in the goods market after nominal wages in the labour market have been set, so that under the condition of a constant mark-up distribution between capital and labour does not change when the GERCU diverges from the SIRCU. And let us also assume again that the stock of firms' debt is not indexed to changes in the inflation rate. Rising inflation rates will therefore decrease the debt–capital ratio defined in equation (III.4), falling inflation rates will increase this ratio.

If monetary policy does not respond to changes in the inflation rate and does not vary the nominal interest rate accordingly, real interest rates will fall in the face of accelerating inflation and will rise when inflation decelerates. Taken together, this implies that the interest–capital ratio $[i\lambda = (iB)/(pK) = Z/(pK)]$ will fall when inflation rises and will rise when inflation falls. Given that changes in the real interest rate do not affect the mark-up and hence the profit share in the short run, the effects of changes in the interest–capital ratio on the GERCU can be determined from equation (III.21) as follows:

$$\frac{\partial u}{\partial(i\lambda)} = \frac{1 - s_Z - \theta}{\frac{h}{v} - \beta}. \tag{III.21a}$$

If only stable goods market equilibria are considered, equation (III.21a) shows that the effects of changes in the interest–capital ratio on the GERCU depend on the parameters in the saving and investment function of the model.

If the rentiers' propensity to consume $(1 - s_Z)$ exceeds the firms' investment elasticity with respect to the interest–capital ratio (θ), rising real debt–capital ratios of firms and rising real interest rates will be associated with an increasing GERCU. This is again the 'puzzling case'. If the conditions of the 'puzzling case' prevail, the SIRCU will be stable: Rising (falling) inflation rates will trigger falling (rising) debt–capital ratios of firms and falling (rising) real interest rates which will then cause a falling (rising) GERCU. The GERCU will therefore adjust to the SIRCU.

If the rentiers' propensity to consume is smaller than firms' investment elasticity related to the interest–capital ratio, rising indebtedness and rising real interest payments will have a negative effect on the GERCU. We get the 'normal case'. If the conditions of the 'normal case' prevail, the SIRCU will be unstable: Rising (falling) inflation will cause falling (rising) real debt–capital ratios of firms and falling (rising) real interest rates, which will now cause a rising (falling) GERCU, moving the economy farther away from the SIRCU.

In the 'normal case', stabilizing the SIRCU requires monetary policy intervention, as suggested by Dumenil/Levy (1999) and also by modern New Consensus models. Note again that, different from New Consensus models, in our model central banks do not only have to change real interest rates by means of varying the nominal rate, but the change in the real interest rate has to be sufficient to over-compensate the counter-effects of the change in the firms' debt–capital ratio on the GERCU. In general, this is not a problem in a situation of rising inflation, because there is no upper limit for the nominal interest rate set by the central bank. But as we have already argued above, in a situation of falling inflation or even deflation, central banks may not be able to reduce the nominal rate of interest by a sufficient amount to decrease real rates and to over-compensate the restrictive demand effects of rising debt–capital ratios, because of the zero lower bound for the nominal interest rate. Therefore,

Table III.2 The short-run stability of the 'Stable Inflation Rate of Capacity Utilization' (SIRCU)

	$1 - s_Z - \theta$	
	– ('normal case')	+ ('puzzling case')
No monetary policy intervention	*unstable*	*stable*
Monetary policy intervention	*stable*, if change in real interest rate over-compensates change in the debt–capital ratio, otherwise *unstable*	*unstable*, if change in real interest rate over-compensates change in the debt–capital ratio, otherwise *stable*

in this situation central banks may not be able to adjust the GERCU to the SIRCU and the economy may be trapped in a deflationary recession.

In the 'puzzling case', monetary policy interventions, which follow the Dumenil/Levy (1999)/New Consensus advice and increase the real rate of interest in the face of rising inflation and decrease it in the face of falling inflation or deflation, will have a destabilizing effect. This may over-compensate the stabilizing effect exerted by the change in the debt–capital ratio and may cause a further deviation of the GERCU from the SIRCU. Table III.2 summarizes our results with respect to short-run stability of the SIRCU or to the 'normal rate' of capacity utilization.

17.5 The long-run endogeneity of the SIRCU

In the 'normal case' we have monetary policies which can enforce short-run adjustment when the GERCU deviates from the SIRCU, provided that there is sufficient room of manoeuvre to vary real interest rates. In the long run, however, the distribution effect of persistent changes in the interest rate will make the SIRCU endogenous to short-run deviations of the GERCU. Assume for the reasons given in chapter 16 that persistent changes in the real interest rate are accompanied by changes in the mark-up in the same direction in the long run. In the present model this has again two effects:

First, changes in the mark-up affect the firms' target real wage rate: An increasing (a decreasing) mark-up shifts the firms' target real wage curve in Figure III.1 downwards (upwards) and the SIRCU decreases (increases). From equation (III.15) we get:

$$\frac{\partial u^N}{\partial h} = -\frac{y}{\varepsilon} < 0. \qquad \text{(III.15a)}$$

Secondly, changes in the mark-up and hence in distribution between wages and profits have an additional long-run effect on the goods market equilibrium and hence on the GERCU, which adds to the short-run effect of monetary policy intervention. From equation (III.21) we get:

$$\frac{\partial u}{\partial h} = \frac{\tau - \frac{u}{v}}{\frac{h}{v} - \beta}. \qquad \text{(III.21b)}$$

Unlike the results in chapter 16 based on the Rowthorn–Dutt–Amadeo approach, the long-run effect of a change in the profit share on the GERCU is not unique in the present model based on the Bhaduri/Marglin approach. It rather depends on the elasticity of investment with respect to the profit share and on the initial GERCU, which has been established by the short-run effects of monetary policy interventions. A high profit share elasticity of investment and a low initial GERCU will be conducive to a positive relation between the profit share and the GERCU, and we will see *profit-led expansion*:

$$\frac{\partial u}{\partial h} > 0, \text{ if: } \tau - \frac{u}{v} > 0. \tag{III.21c}$$

A low profit share elasticity of investment and a high initial GERCU, however, will give rise to a negative relation between the profit share and the GERCU, and we will see *wage-led expansion*:

$$\frac{\partial u}{\partial h} < 0, \text{ if: } \tau - \frac{u}{v} < 0. \tag{III.21d}$$

Let us now discuss the short- and long-run effects of monetary policy interventions in the 'normal case' (Table III.2) of our model. Assume that by accident the GERCU exceeds the initial SIRCU at u_1^N in Figure III.4, which is essentially the same as Figure III.2. Since rising inflation, a declining debt–capital ratio and falling real interest rates stimulate effective demand, the GERCU will further increase and inflation will speed up. In order to stabilize the inflation rate, central banks have to increase nominal interest rates in order to raise real interest rates by a sufficient amount to over-compensate the demand-stimulating effects of falling debt–capital ratios. Therefore, in the short run the central bank can bring back the GERCU to the SIRCU at u_1^N. In the long run, however, a higher real interest rate will induce firms to increase the mark-up. This will shift the firms' target real wage curve down from w_{p1}^r to w_{p2}^r and reduce the SIRCU to u_2^N. The redistribution at the expense of labour will also affect the GERCU. Here, we now have to distinguish between (A) wage-led and (B) profit-led regimes in order to discuss the further process:

(A) In the wage-led regime three scenarios (A.1–A.3) are possible, depending on the relative (both negative) effects of changes in the mark-up on the GERCU and on the SIRCU in equations (III.15a) and (III.21b):

(A.1) If by accident $\partial u/\partial h = \partial u^N/\partial h$, the reduction of the GERCU caused by an increasing mark-up will make this new rate coincide with u_2^N, so that the economy gets to rest in a stable SIRCU at u_2^N.

(A.2) If $|\partial u/\partial h| > |\partial u^N/\partial h|$, the effective demand effect of redistribution at the expense of labour will make the GERCU fall below u_2^N and we get falling inflation rates. This should make monetary policies reduce real interest rates, making the GERCU increase to u_2^N in the short run. In the

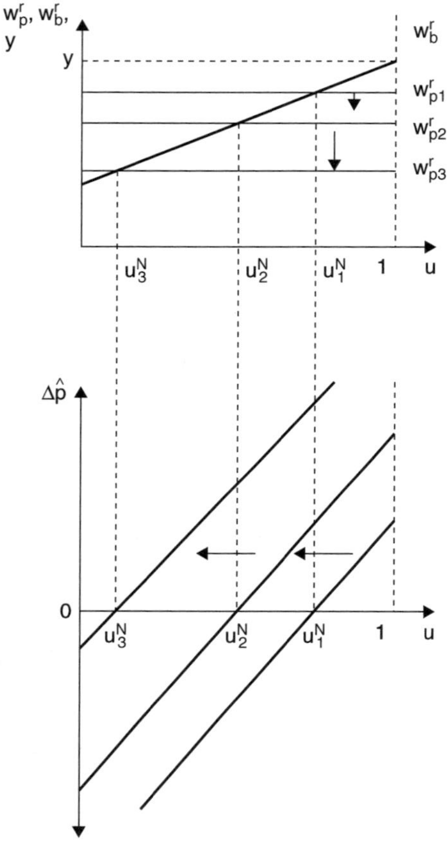

Figure III.4 Long-run endogeneity of the Stable Inflation Rate of Capacity Utilization (SIRCU) caused by monetary policy intervention

long run, firms then reduce mark-ups, which will increase the SIRCU as well as the GERCU, with the latter now overshooting the former, and monetary policy has to intervene again. This oscillation may converge to a stable SIRCU between u_2^N and u_1^N, but it may also generate stable or exploding oscillation around that SIRCU, depending on the degree of over- and undershooting of the GERCU with respect to the SIRCU and the concomitant change in the real interest rate required for the short-run adjustment of the GERCU to the SIRCU.

(A.3) If $|\partial u/\partial h| < |\partial u^N/\partial h|$, the negative effective demand effect of redistribution at the expense of labour is weak, so that the GERCU remains above u_2^N. Again we get accelerating inflation inducing the central bank to increase real interest rates, forcing the GERCU down to u_2^N in the short run. In the long run, firms again increase the mark-up which shifts their target real wage curve down to w_{p3}^r and makes the SIRCU decline to u_3^N. The effective demand effect of redistribution also makes the GERCU fall, but it remains above u_3^N, inflation accelerates anew and central banks have to intervene again.

(B) If the economy is in a profit-led regime, the long-run distribution effect of rising interest rates, which have brought down the GERCU to the SIRCU in the short run, will again increase the GERCU to a level above the old SIRCU at u_1^N. The gap between the GERCU and the new SIRCU at u_2^N might therefore be even wider than in the situation we have started from. Inflation will speed up again, inducing monetary policies to increase real interest rates once more, which will be able to bring down the GERCU to the lower SIRCU at u_2^N in the short run. The long-run distribution effect will reduce the SIRCU to u_3^N but will increase the GERCU, and inflation will accelerate again.

From equation (III.21b), we get that the lower the GERCU, the more likely the wage-led scenario (A.3) and finally the profit-led scenario (B) will become. This is what is shown in Figure III.4: The rate of capacity utilization which stabilizes the inflation rate (at whatever level) becomes horizontal because of the nature of monetary policy interventions. In these scenarios, monetary policy is only able to stabilize the inflation rate in the long run at the expense of a continuously decreasing SIRCU, because monetary policy interventions trigger a process in which stabilizing inflation in the short run by means of increasing real interest rates and slowing down the economy re-establishes the inflation problem in the long run when the full distribution effects of real interest rate variations are felt. Therefore, if monetary policies combat inflation by means of raising real interest rates, they will become a cause of the problem of stagflation.

Note that scenarios (A.3) and (B) also work in reverse: If the central bank intends to improve the GERCU, in the short run lowering real interest rates will be associated with rising inflation rates. In the long run, however, a falling mark-up increases the SIRCU. And since the long-run demand effect of redistribution in favour of labour is either not too strong (scenario A.3) or even negative (scenario B), so that the GERCU remains below the new SIRCU, there is again room for manoeuvre for the central bank to cut real interest rates. Since this process is associated with a gradually increasing rate of capacity utilization, monetary policies lowering real interest rates and increasing the GERCU in the short run and the SIRCU in the long run can contribute to a transformation of a profit-led regime into a wage-led regime.

Summing up so far, the 'normal rate' of capacity utilization, the SIRCU, is endogenous to monetary policies determining the real interest rate in our model. In the 'puzzling case', the GERCU adjusts to the SIRCU because of the 'puzzling' real debt effects on demand and capacity utilization. In the 'normal case' no such adjustment can be supposed and monetary policy interventions are indicated. In the short run, these will always be able to adjust the GERCU to SIRCU from above, but for an adjustment from below a sufficient room of manoeuvre for reducing real interest rates is required, and cannot be taken for granted. In the long run, distribution effects of changing interest rates will make the SIRCU endogenous to monetary policy, and demand effects triggered by redistribution will have a further influence on the GERCU. This will give rise to adjustment processes of the two rates which will not necessarily lead to a stable equilibrium. It may rather generate complex disequilibrium processes of interacting GERCUs and SIRCUs, which are driven by monetary policy interventions in the face of deviation of these two rates and concomitant changes in inflation rates. These disequilibrium processes may either lead to converging, constant or exploding oscillations of the GERCU around a SIRCU moving there and back, or to a disequilibrium process of continuously falling (or rising) GERCUs and SIRCUs.

17.6 The paradox of thrift and the paradox of costs

Paradox of thrift

Discussing the central features of Kaleckian models of distribution and growth we begin with the paradox of thrift. If we start from the coincidence of a goods market equilibrium with a distribution equilibrium ($u^* = u^N$), a change in the rentiers' propensity to save will only affect the GERCU inversely, but will have no effect on the SIRCU. From equation (III.21) we get for the change in the GERCU the well-known paradox of thrift outcome:

$$\frac{\partial u}{\partial s_Z} = -\frac{\lambda i}{\frac{h}{v} - \beta} < 0. \tag{III.21e}$$

A falling (rising) rentiers' propensity to save will increase (decrease) the GERCU which will then exceed (fall short of) the SIRCU and will therefore trigger rising (falling) inflation rates. In the 'puzzling case', the change in inflation rates will re-adjust the GERCU to the SIRCU and the economy will return to the former equilibrium. Therefore, in this case a change in the propensity to save will not have any effect on this joint equilibrium.

In the 'normal case', the deviation of the GERCU from the SIRCU will not be self-correcting, but will trigger cumulative divergence and will hence trigger monetary policy intervention. Here the scenarios discussed above apply. Therefore, inflation-targeting monetary policy intervention will question the 'paradox of thrift' in the long run without being necessarily able to re-establish a new joint equilibrium of GERCU and SIRCU: Rising (falling) inflation caused by a decreasing (increasing) rentiers' saving propensity will trigger a rising (falling) real interest rate, and hence a rising (falling) mark-up and a falling (rising) SIRCU in the long run, to which monetary policy will then again try to adjust the GERCU. Also note, that a higher (lower) rentiers' propensity to save will make the 'normal case' more (less) likely (equation (III.21b)).

Paradox of costs

To assess the relevance of the paradox of costs let us start again from a joint equilibrium of GERCU and SIRCU and assume that the mark-up and hence the profit share vary. This affects both the GERCU and the SIRCU as shown in equations (III.15a) and (III.21b). A falling (rising) mark-up will cause a rising (falling) SIRCU and in the wage-led regime a rising (falling) GERCU, whereas in the profit-led regime we get a falling (rising) GERCU. In the 'puzzling case', however, the GERCU will adjust to the new SIRCU in both the wage-led and the profit-led regime due to the 'puzzling' real debt effects on demand and capacity utilization. Therefore, in the 'puzzling case' the paradox of costs is generally valid, although in our model we have started from the Bhaduri/Marglin (1990) distinction between wage-led and profit-led expansion.

In the 'normal case', the discussion in section 17.5 applies. In the wage-led scenario (A.1) the paradox of costs is fully valid and a new joint equilibrium of GERCU and SIRCU is established. In the wage-led scenario (A.2) with a strong effect of redistribution on the GERCU, a falling (rising) mark-up will trigger increasing (decreasing) inflation and hence monetary policy intervention which in the long run will make the mark-up increase (decrease) again. Depending on the extent of the required interest rate variations, this effect may invalidate the paradox of costs without necessarily leading to a new joint goods market and distribution equilibrium. In the wage-led scenario (A.3) and in the profit-led scenario (B) with either a weak or even a negative (positive) demand effect of a falling (rising) mark-up, falling (rising) inflation rates will induce monetary policies to cut (raise) interest rates, which in the long run will reinforce the initial redistribution. Here the paradox of costs is fully valid and is even accelerated by real interest rate variations without leading to a new joint equilibrium of GERCU and SIRCU.

17.7 Conclusions

Starting from the problem of a persistent divergence of the equilibrium rate of capacity utilization from the 'normal rate' of utilization without endogenous adjustments in Kaleckian models of distribution and growth, we have followed the approach proposed by Dumenil/Levy (1999) to consider the 'normal rate' of utilization in a monetary production economy as the rate which is associated with stable inflation. But, unlike Dumenil/Levy (1999), we have taken a closer look at the causes of changing inflation, which remain unclear in their model and which we have originating from unresolved distribution conflict between capital and labour. And also unlike Dumenil/Levy (1999) and their Kaleckian critics, we have integrated the feedbacks of changing inflation on demand via real debt effects, and we have fully taken account of the short-run and long-run demand and distribution effects of monetary policies applying the interest rate tool in order to fight rising or falling inflation rates. Our discussion has been based on a monetary extension of the Bhaduri/Marglin (1990) model in order to allow for potential profit-led growth, as Dumenil/Levy (1999) have it for the long run.

We have shown that in such a model the adjustment of capacity utilization to the 'normal rate' may, but need not necessarily, require monetary policy interventions. And if monetary policy interventions applying the interest rate tool are necessary, this will affect the 'normal rate' of utilization which will therefore become endogenous to the economic process. However, with monetary policy interventions, the establishment of a joint goods market and distribution equilibrium with stable inflation cannot be taken for granted. Generally, we will get complex disequilibrium processes of interacting 'normal' and goods market equilibrium rates of utilization, which are driven by monetary policy interventions in the face of deviations of these two rates and concomitant changes in inflation rates.

With respect to the main results of Kaleckian models, we have found that changes in the propensity to save either have no long-run effects on the joint distribution and goods market equilibrium, and hence on the 'normal rate' of utilization, or that the paradox of thrift is invalidated by monetary policy interventions which are triggered by changes in the inflation rate following a change in demand. The paradox of costs, however, with only a minor exception, is valid also in the long run, when the adjustment of the 'normal rate' takes place, although we have allowed for the possibility of profit-led expansion in the short and in the long run.

Generally, we have shown that in a model which takes the major features of a credit economy seriously, the 'normal rate' of capacity utilization is endogenous to distribution conflict and monetary policy intervention in the long run. And we have also shown that some major Kaleckian results can be retained for the short and the long run. Therefore, we do not necessarily have to be 'Keynesian in the short term and classical in the long term', as suggested by Dumenil/Levy (1999).

18
Summary and Conclusions: Money, Distribution Conflict and Capital Accumulation

The present book attempts to contribute to 'monetary analysis' and to the research programme of a 'monetary theory of production'. In particular, we have tried to contribute to a synthesis of Post-Keynesian monetary theory and Post-Keynesian models of distribution and growth. The focus has been on the distribution and growth effects of monetary policies applying the interest rate tool in a modern credit money economy, which is characterized by the autonomy of investment from saving also in the long run, by latent under-utilization of productive capacities, and by conflict over distribution of the social product.

In order to situate our analysis in the history of economic thought and into the development of economic paradigms we have started in the first part with a survey of the different paradigms in economics applying Schumpeter's distinction between 'real analysis' and 'monetary analysis'. In chapter 3 we argued that Classical orthodoxy, Neoclassical economics, Neoclassical Synthesis, Monetarist, New Classical, but also today's mainstream New Keynesian and New Consensus theories follow 'real analysis'. In the long run – in New Classical theory also in the short run – the economic equilibrium is determined by real forces only. Relative prices, income distribution, output, employment and growth are determined by 'real analysis'. Monetary variables, the quantity of base money or the base rate of interest controlled by the central bank, have real effects in the short run when nominal rigidities prevail, at the most. These real effects, however, are confined to short-run disequilibria, and in the long run monetary variables are neutral with respect to real outcomes. In long-run equilibrium, monetary policies can only affect the price level or inflation. Therefore, in long-run equilibrium the Classical dichotomy between the monetary and the real sphere, as well as Say's law are assumed to hold. The real rate of profit, or the 'natural rate of interest', determines the monetary rate of interest. Money is neutral with respect to output, employment, distribution and growth.

Classical heterodoxy (Banking School, Neo-Ricardian monetary theory of distribution), Marx's, Keynes's and Post-Keynesian theories, however, pursue 'monetary analysis', as has been argued in chapters 4–6. Monetary variables are integral and indispensable elements of the total model and hence also of the determination of long-run equilibrium. In this sense, money is fundamentally non-neutral. Although there are significant differences between Classical heterodoxy, Marx's, Keynes's and Post-Keynesian approaches, these theories share the view that modern capitalist economies should be considered as credit money economies. In such an economy, the rate of interest is an exogenous variable for the processes of income generation and capital accumulation and is not automatically and uniquely affected by these processes. The volume of credit and the quantity of money are endogenous variables determined by the creditworthy demand for credit and payment conventions. The demand for credit is mainly affected by firms' production and investment decisions and the associated requirements of external finance.

In modern credit money economies, firms' investment is the driving force of the economic process and is mainly determined by the expected profit rate and the interest rate. Investment might also be affected by the financial position of the firm (own capital, retained earnings) influencing firms' access to external long-term finance in incompletely competitive financial markets. From a macroeconomic point of view, investment is not limited by saving, but generates the adequate amount of saving via changes in prices and distribution and/or via effects on output and capacity utilization. Say's law is therefore rejected by all the proponents of 'monetary analysis' and is replaced by a kind of 'principle of effective demand'. The level of employment is determined by monetary policies, the asset market and the goods market. From the perspective of the labour market, employment is a 'given' variable which is not determined in this market. The labour market rather sets the nominal wage rate which is a crucial variable for the price level and hence for inflation.

The schools of 'monetary analysis' differ, however, when it comes to the explicit analysis of the effects of monetary policy on distribution, economic activity and growth, as we have summarized in chapter 7. In Keynes's and in Post-Keynesian monetary theories, the exogenous monetary interest rate determines functional income and economic activity in a unique way in long-run equilibrium, taking the state of expectations as given. The rate of profit on real investment is equal to the real long-term monetary interest rate, and the real wage rate becomes a residual variable. Simultaneously, the rate of interest determines the volume of reproducible capital goods, and hence output and capital accumulation, adversely. Although it has been admitted that this equilibrium may never be reached by an economy moving through historical time, in Keynes's and in Post-Keynesian theories it has not been made clear convincingly how distribution effects of interest rate variations interact with the direct effects on investment and capital accumulation in long-period equilibrium.

In Classical heterodoxy, in particular in the Neo-Ricardian monetary theory of distribution, the monetary rate of interest also determines a unique distribution equilibrium in the long run. The rate of interest is not equal to the real rate of profit, but the latter is derived by summing up the rate of interest and the rate of profit of enterprise which is assumed to be given in the face of variations in the interest rate. Therefore, changes in the rate of interest have a unique effect on the rate of profit. The output and accumulation effects of variations in the rate of interest, however, are not uniquely determined in long-period equilibrium, because the rate of interest is not associated with a unique volume of investment. The distribution effects of changes in the interest rate rather exert contradicting cost and demand effects on investment and capital accumulation. The total effect on investment and growth then depends on the relative strength of these effects.

In the monetary interpretation of Marx's economics we have obtained an indeterminate effect of interest rate variations on economic activity for similar reasons as in Neo-Ricardian monetary theory. But we have a different influence on functional income distribution in this approach. Since the rate of profit of enterprise is considered to be a variable which is affected by distribution conflict, Marx deals with a three-party conflict between rentiers or financial capital, firms or industrial capital, and wage labour. He supposes that changes in the rate of interest affect industrial profits and hence leave real wages untouched, the latter being determined in the distribution conflict between industrial capitalists and labourers.

In the second part of the book we have investigated deeper into the effects of changes in the monetary rate of interest on income distribution and capital accumulation, taking into account the main elements of 'monetary analysis' as developed in the Neo-Ricardian monetary theory of distribution, in Marx's monetary analysis and in Post-Keynesian monetary theory. For this reason we have introduced the monetary interest rate, mainly determined by central bank policies, into Post-Keynesian demand-driven models of distribution and growth in the tradition of

Nicholas Kaldor, Joan Robinson and Michal Kalecki. After a brief review of the contributions of Robinson, Kaldor and Kalecki to monetary theory and of their distribution and growth models in chapter 9, we have outlined a simple model economy, including a full description of a monetary circuit, in chapter 10. This model was then used to analyse and to compare the effects of changes in the interest rate in the different variants of Post-Keynesian distribution and growth theory in chapters 11 and 12. Finally, the model has been extended to cover the approaches to the distributive effects of monetary policies outlined above, and also some long-run debt dynamics in chapter 13.

As summarized in chapter 14, we have demonstrated that in the Kaldor–Robinson model, assuming full utilization of the capital stock in the long run, changes in the interest rate have uniquely inverse effects on the rates of capital accumulation and profit. However, in our view, this model suffers from serious limitations associated with the assumptions of full utilization of the capital stock in long-period growth equilibrium and the real wage rate being a passive and residual variable. But also in the Kaleckian distribution and growth models, assuming a long-run variable rate of capacity utilization and income shares being determined by distribution conflict, variations in the rate of interest have uniquely inverse effects on the rates of capacity utilization, capital accumulation and profit. This is true for different variants of the Kaleckian model, the 'stagnationist' Rowthorn–Dutt–Amadeo model and the Bhaduri/Marglin model which allows for wage-led or profit-led accumulation regimes. These unique results in the Post-Keynesian distribution and growth models have been possible, because the effects of the interest rate have only been introduced into the investment functions of the models first.

Extending the different variants of the Kaleckian model and considering further effects of changing interest rates, these unique results cannot be sustained. First, firms' stock of debt has been explicitly integrated and the long-run dynamics of the debt–capital ratio have been discussed. Secondly, potential effects of changing interest rates on distribution between gross profits and wages have been taken into account, allowing for an interest-elastic mark-up in firms' pricing, as proposed by the Neo-Ricardian monetary theory of distribution. Thirdly, the effects of changing interest rates and interest payments, as well as changes in the mark-up on aggregate saving and consumption have been considered, too.

Generally, our results for the extended Rowthorn–Dutt–Amadeo model and for the extended Bhaduri/Marglin model are quite similar, but they also differ in some details. Taking the debt–capital ratio as given, short-run equilibrium effects of interest rate variations on capacity utilization, capital accumulation and the rate of profit are not unique, but depend on parameter values of the model. In our models these are the parameters in the saving and investment function, and the initial debt–capital ratio in the case of an interest-elastic mark-up. Depending on the values of these parameters, the effects of interest rate variations on the real equilibrium may be either negative throughout ('normal case'), mixed or even positive throughout ('puzzling case').

We have shown that a low rentiers' saving propensity, a low elasticity of investment with respect to debt services or internal funds and a high elasticity with respect to capacity utilization are generally conducive to a positive effect of rising interest rates on capacity utilization, capital accumulation and the profit rate, and hence to the 'puzzling case'. The 'normal case' becomes more likely, the higher the rentiers' saving propensity, the higher the elasticity of investment with respect to debt services or internal funds, and the lower the investment responsiveness to capacity utilization.

In the case of an interest-inelastic mark-up, the degree of indebtedness does not affect the direction of influence interest rate variations have on the real equilibrium. In the case of an interest-elastic mark-up, however, the degree of indebtedness may have an impact on the direction into which interest rate policies push the economy. Therefore, we have argued that the degree of indebtedness has already to be taken into account when analysing the short-run effects of monetary policies.

We have also discovered that long-run stability of the debt–capital ratio is associated with the short-run 'puzzling case', in both the extended Rowthorn–Dutt–Amadeo model and the extended Bhaduri/Marglin model. Unlike other monetary Kaleckian distribution and growth models, there is also some path dependence of interest rate effects on the equilibrium debt–capital ratio in our extended models.

In both our extended Kaleckian models, the short-run 'normal case' is associated with long-run instability of the debt–capital ratio and with the macroeconomic 'paradox of debt'. It can be assumed that the parameter constellation yielding the short-run 'normal case' and a long-run unstable debt–capital ratio giving rise to the 'paradox of debt' is more likely with unequal distribution of financial wealth, unstable relations between the financial sector and non-financial business, as prevalent in capital market-based systems, and in periods of stagnation with uncertain sales and profit expectations.

Taken together, our general results of the Kaleckian 'monetary' distribution and growth models, related to the dependence of the short-run real effects of interest rate variations on the historically and institutionally given parameter values of the model, on the one hand, and related to the long-run instability of the debt–capital ratio and to the 'paradox of debt', on the other hand, seem to be quite robust with respect to the concrete specification of the investment function in these models. Monetary extensions of 'wage-led' or 'stagnationist' models share these general characteristics with models which allow for different regimes of accumulation.

In the Post-Keynesian models discussed in the second part of the book, the inflationary impact of distribution conflict has been excluded from the analysis. Distribution conflict and monetary policies setting the interest rate have been assumed to affect the mark-up in firms' pricing, and hence distribution between firms, rentiers' and workers' households, but not the inflation rate. In the third part of the book we have then taken into account the inflationary consequences of distribution conflict and monetary policy reactions fighting inflation acceleration or deceleration.

In chapter 16, the role of an 'inflation barrier' or a 'Non-Accelerating-Inflation-Rate-of-Unemployment' (NAIRU) in monetary Kaleckian distribution and growth models has been discussed and the relationship to modern mainstream macroeconomic New Consensus models, building on the idea of a NAIRU as long-run equilibrium unemployment, has been clarified. For this purpose the extended monetary Rowthorn–Dutt–Amadeo model has been supplemented with conflict inflation and the role of a NAIRU as a short-run 'inflation barrier' has been analysed. In particular, we have taken into account real debt effects of accelerating and decelerating inflation, which have usually been neglected in other Post-Keynesian and in New Keynesian models. The short-run stability of a NAIRU has been examined, and the effectiveness of monetary policy interventions applying the interest rate tool has been questioned. It has been demonstrated that in the short run monetary policy interventions in order to put a brake on accelerating inflation when unemployment falls short of the NAIRU are either unnecessary or costly in terms of employment. We have also argued that central banks may be incapable to stimulate the economy when unemployment exceeds the NAIRU and the economy experiences cumulative disinflation and finally deflation. Taking into account that changes in the interest rate affect firms' cost of production and hence distribution conflict, it has also been shown that in the long run restrictive monetary policies bear the risk of continuously increasing the NAIRU in order to keep inflation under control. The long-run Phillips curve may therefore become horizontal and the short-run NAIRU becomes endogenous to actual unemployment and to monetary policy interventions fighting accelerating or decelerating inflation rates.

We have argued that instead of relying on monetary policies, the cause of inflation should be directly addressed by incomes policies. Wage bargaining co-ordination could be applied as an appropriate policy tool.

In chapter 17, the problem of a persistent deviation of the long-run equilibrium rate of capacity utilization from the 'normal rate' of utilization conceived by firms when planning new investment in capital stock has been assessed, and the sustainability of the main results of the Kaleckian models, the 'paradox of thrift' and at least the possibility of a 'paradox of costs', have been evaluated. We have approached these issues applying the extended monetary Bhaduri/Marglin model supplemented with conflict inflation. We have followed an approach proposed by Dumenil/Levy (1999) who consider the 'normal rate' of utilization in a monetary production economy as the rate which is associated with price stability. Since inflation in the monetary Kaleckian models is driven by distribution conflict, the 'normal rate' of utilization has been associated with consistent income claims of firms and labourers. Taking into account real debt effects of changes in inflation and distribution effects of monetary policy interventions again, we have discussed the short-run stability of the 'normal rate' and we have addressed the issue of long-run endogeneity. Generally, we have shown that in a Kaleckian monetary distribution and growth model, which takes the major features of a capitalist credit money economy seriously, the 'normal rate' of capacity utilization is endogenous to distribution conflict and monetary policy intervention in response to changes in conflict inflation, in the long run. And we have also demonstrated that major Kaleckian results, in particular the paradox of costs, can be retained for the short and the long run in this model.

Taken together, we hope to have demonstrated that 'monetary analysis', as contained in Post-Keynesian monetary theories, but also in the Neo-Ricardian monetary theory of distribution and in Marx's monetary analysis, can be integrated into Post-Keynesian models of distribution of growth in a consistent and convincing way. In particular, the Kaleckian distribution and growth models have turned out to be an adequate basis to start from, because these models have already taken on board major features of modern credit money economies – the long-run independence of investment from saving, the latent under-utilization of productive capacities also in the long run, and the conflict over the distribution of income.[1] Addressing the question of investment finance, and integrating endogenous money and credit, as well as an exogenous interest rate into these models should have made them more convincing. Since the parameter values in the models are of utmost importance for the concrete short- and long-run model behaviour, Kaleckian monetary distribution and growth models require empirical and historical analysis in order to determine these parameter values, as a precondition for the analysis of the real effects of monetary policies. Therefore, more empirical research in this area should be undertaken.[2]

However, also our theoretical models require further development. The monetary distribution and growth models presented in this book have been closed economy models without economic activity of the state and without technical change. The models should therefore be expanded in order to address open economy issues, economic activity of the state and technical change, too. As the survey by Blecker (2002) has shown, Kaleckian models have recently covered these areas, but without explicit integration of money, credit, finance and interest rates.[3]

Furthermore, the treatment of the financial sector in our models so far has been quite basic and elementary, because we have only dealt with credit and retained profits, but we have not explicitly discussed the role of the stock market for investment finance, for instance. Therefore, the monetary distribution and growth models have to be further developed in order to be able to contribute to our understanding of the distribution and growth effects associated with the recent trends towards 'financialization' of non-financial business, increasing shareholder-value orientation in those economies which formerly have been dominated by bank-based financial systems, and increasing importance of consumer debt based on notional wealth effects generated by stock market and housing market booms.[4]

Simultaneously to the integration of money, credit and interest into Post-Keynesian distribution and growth models, a contribution to a Post-Keynesian alternative to New Consensus macroeconomics has been provided in this book. In further research this should be synthesized with the other Post-Keynesian critique of the New Consensus model and of the NAIRU being the long-run equilibrium unemployment rate determined by structural characteristics of the labour market and the social benefit system, already alluded to in chapter 16.[5] This should give rise to a 'Post-Keynesian consensus' in which monetary policy is non-neutral, both in the short and the long run, in which the NAIRU is merely a short-run 'inflation barrier', but not the equilibrium to which the actual unemployment rate is attracted in the short run, neither by market forces nor by monetary policy interventions in any case, and in which the 'inflation barrier' becomes itself endogenous to the development of actual unemployment through different channels. Also in this area further research is required in order to assess the role of monetary and fiscal policies as well as wage bargaining in modern credit money economies and to derive convincing economic policy recommendations.[6]

Notes

Notes from Part I

1 See also Rogers (1989) on this distinction.
2 In Adam Smith (1776, pp. 37–46, 286–330) money was considered as commodity money which is introduced in order to facilitate commodity exchange minimizing transaction costs and allowing for the deepening of the division of labour and, hence, for faster productivity growth. The general level of prices is given by relative production costs of the money commodity and the commodities to be circulated. If paper money without intrinsic value is introduced, commodity money is pushed out of circulation, and there is no increase in the general price level. On monetary theory in Classical economics see further, for instance, Lapavitsas (1998) and Roncaglia (2005, pp. 196–203).
3 See Clower (1999), Hahn (1982), Hellwig (1993), Lucas (1996), Niehans (1978), and Rogers (1989, pp. 45–72).
4 See Coddington (1976), Snowdon/Vane (2005, pp. 101–47), and Tobin (1993).
5 See Friedman (1968, 1970, 1972), as well as Rogers (1989, pp. 136–57), Smithin (2003a, pp. 40–62) and Snowdon/Vane (2005, pp. 163–97).
6 See Lucas (1972, 1976), as well as Laidler (1986, 1988), Smithin (2003a, pp. 69–78), and Snowdon/Vane (2005, pp. 219–71).
7 See Kydland/Prescott (1982), Plosser (1989), and Snowdon/Vane (2005, pp. 294–343).
8 See Gordon (1990), Greenwald/Stiglitz (1987, 1993, 2003), Mankiw (1992), Romer (1993), and Snowdon/Vane (2005, pp. 357–432) on New Keynesian theory. On the New Consensus model see Carlin/Soskice (2006, pp. 27–172), Clarida/Gali/Gertler (1999), McCallum (2001), Meyer (2001), Romer (2000), Snowdon/Vane (2005, pp. 419–427), Taylor (2000), and Walsh (2002).
9 See also Fontana (2006), Pivetti (1991, pp. 87–90), Rogers (1989, pp. 21–44), and Trautwein (2000).
10 On the Banking School see Lapavitsas (1998) and Pivetti (1991, pp. 74–9).
11 On the notions and meanings of 'endogenous money' in different theories see Palley (2002). We use the notion of 'endogenous money' as credit and money being endogenously created on demand by the banking sector in a credit economy.
12 See Ciccarone (1998), Panico (1985), and in particular Pivetti (1985, 1987a, 1987b, 1991, 2001). For a survey of the Neo-Ricardian or Sraffian research programme see Aspromourgos (2004).
13 This chapter draws on Hein (2004b, 2006a).
14 See Shaikh (1978a, 1983a) for surveys of Marxian crisis theories. The early attempts by Fritsch (1968) and De Brunhoff (1976) to reconstruct Marx's theory of money and credit remained without major consequences for Marxian theories of accumulation and crisis.

15 See Alexander (1940), Dillard (1984), Fan-Hung (1939), Foley (1986a), Kenway (1980), Rogers (1989), Rotheim (1991), and Sardoni (1986, 1987).
16 See Argitis (2001), Evans (1997), Graziani (1997), Lapavitsas (1994, 1997, 2000a, 2000b), Lapavitsas/Saad-Filho (2000), Matthews (1996), Mollo (1999), Sardoni (1997a, 1997b), and Williams (1992, 2000).
17 There is, however, no agreement on this point of view in Marxian economics. De Brunhoff (1976), Crotty (1987), Evans (1997), Foley (1983, 1986b), and Weeks (1981) hold that Marx's commodity theory of money is a correct, albeit historically restricted starting point for the analysis of money and therefore not applicable to modern economies. Lapavitsas (2000a) and Lapavitsas/Saad-Filho (2000) do not only consider commodity money to be an appropriate starting point for Marx's theory of money and credit, but also argue that anchoring the monetary system on a money commodity would stabilize capitalist reproduction, also in modern times.
18 Therefore, there is also no reason to assume, as does Marx (1867, pp. 141–4), that 'universal money', money for international transactions, has to be a commodity.
19 In Marx's commodity money system, however, there seems to be an effect of the quantity of money on the level of prices as soon as the money commodity in circulation is replaced by paper money (Marx 1867, pp. 125–30). An increase in the supply of paper money should increase the level of prices measured in units of paper money, because a unit of paper money now represents less units of the money commodity in circulation. This quantity theory relation, however, can only be sustained, if the representative of the money commodity is only used for circulation purposes. But this need not be the case. According to Marx (1867, p. 130), the role of 'money as money', which includes the function of money as a store of value (hoard), may also be assumed by the money representative. Hence, there need not be a strict relationship between the quantity of paper money and the price level, because the amount of paper money in hoards may be variable, and the quantity theory collapses.
20 Ricardo's version of Say's law differs from the Neoclassical version, because it is neither associated with full employment of labour nor is there an economic mechanism equating saving and investment. Ricardo's version of Say's law simply implies that saving and investment are identical (Garegnani 1978, 1979).
21 On Marx's rejection of Say's law in the formulation of Ricardo and the 'possibility theory of crisis' as opposed to a theory of the actual crisis see more explicitly Kenway (1980) and Sardoni (1987, pp. 26–36, 1997b).
22 See Sowell (1972) for an overview of the 'general glut' controversy.
23 The role of credit in economic crisis is explored in more detail by Marx in *Capital*, Vol. III (Marx 1894, pp. 476–519), where he shows that the credit system may exacerbate economic crisis.
24 For a more extensive treatment of the schemes of reproduction see Hein (1997, pp. 136–55), Kenway (1987) and recently Trigg (2006).
25 See Hein (1997, pp. 136–55), Sweezy (1942) and Trigg (2006) for an extensive discussion.
26 See also De Brunhoff (1976, pp. 60–72) and Foley (1986b, pp. 86–9). Lapavitsas (2000a) and Mollo (1999), however, do not seem to be aware that

hoarding and dishoarding of a money commodity can only play a limited role for money endogeneity in a growing economy.

27 We therefore disagree with Lapavitsas (1997, 2000b) and Lapavitsas/Saad-Filho (2000) who consider the credit system in Marx's theory to be mainly a mechanism for the internal reallocation of idle funds among industrial and commercial capitalists.

28 In this respect Marx agrees with the Banking point of view in the 'banking–currency controversy' (Lapavitsas 1994; Mollo 1999).

29 See also Argitis (2001) and Pivetti (1987a) on the relation between profits of enterprise and interest in Marx's theory.

30 This objection can also be applied to Panico's (1980) attempt to reformulate Marx's approach in a production price model.

31 See Argitis (2001), Panico (1980, 1988) and Pivetti (1987a) for similar results with respect to Marx's theory of the rate of interest and Sardoni (1997a) for some ambiguities in Marx's reasoning.

32 Of course, there may be feedbacks from accumulation to distribution in those models. See Amadeo (1986a) and Marglin (1984a) for more specific formulations.

33 For the short-run version of the profit-squeeze approach explaining trade cycles see the seminal paper by Goodwin (1967), for the long-run version explaining economic stagnation see Glyn/Sutcliffe (1972) and the more recent work in the 'Social Structure of Accumulation' approach, i.e. Gordon/Weisskopf/Bowles (1987). For the 'falling-rate-of-profit-due-to-rising-organic-composition-of-capital' theories see Catephores (1989, pp. 166–187) and Shaikh (1978a, 1978b, 1983b, 1987). For a critique of the necessity of a falling rate of profit due to technical change in a model with prices of production instead of labour values see Van Parijs (1980).

34 See Amadeo (1986a) and Marglin (1984a) for comparisons of the orthodox Marxian model with Post-Keynesian models. For a more detailed discussion of Post-Keynesian models of growth and distribution see Lavoie (1992a, pp. 282–347). In Hein (2004a, pp. 59–87, 133–219) an extensive discussion of the orthodox Marxian model, the models by Kaldor and Robinson as well as different variants of the Kaleckian model is provided.

35 Whereas Robinson (1962) only assumes full utilization of the capital stock on the equilibrium growth path, Kaldor (1957, 1961) also assumes full employment of labour.

36 To achieve this, the propensity to save out profits of course has to exceed the propensity to save out of wages.

37 See also Bertocco (2005), Fontana/Gerrard (2002), and Rotheim (1981, 1991).

38 Of course, in a Neoclassical model this endogenous mechanism is the rate of interest in the capital market equilibrating leakages from the circuit (saving) and injections into it (investment).

39 See Eatwell (1983a, 1983b) and the contributions in Eatwell/Micate (1983) for an assessment of the Neoclassical elements in Keynes's theory.

40 In the *General Theory* (Keynes 1936, pp. 230–1) argues '...that money has, both in the long and the short period, a zero, or at any rate a very small, elasticity of production...' and '...that it has an elasticity of substitution equal, or nearly equal, to zero...'.

41 See Keynes (1973, pp. 201–23, 229–33), Hawtrey (1937), Ohlin (1937a, 1937b), and Robertson (1937, 1938a, 1938b, 1940).

42 On the debate in the 1980s see Asimakopulos (1983, 1985, 1986a, 1986b, 1986/87), Davidson (1986/87), Graziani (1984, 1988), Kregel (1986/87), Richardson (1986), Snippe (1985), Terzi (1986, 1986/87), and Wray (1988b). For the more recent debate see the references in chapter 10 below.

43 On the Post-Keynesian research programme see the surveys by Arestis (1996a), Arestis/Dunn/Sawyer (1999), Eichner (1978a), Eichner/Kregel (1975), Fontana/Gerrard (2006), Hamouda/Harcourt (1988), Harcourt (1987, 2001) and the books by Arestis (1992), Carvalho (1992), Davidson (1994, 2002), Eichner (1978b), Harcourt (2006), Holt/Pressman (2001), Lavoie (1992a, 2006a) and Palley (1996a). On the history of Post-Keynesianism see especially King (2002). On a recent debate on 'what Post-Keynesianism really is', spawned by Davidson's (2003–4) critique of King's (2002) book, see Davidson (2005), Dow (2005), Fontana (2005), King (2005), and Lavoie (2005, 2006b).

44 On the work of Kalecki see Sawyer (1985) and on the relevance of Kaleckian economics for the Post-Keynesian research programme see the contributions in King (1996).

45 Starting point of this controversy had been Robinson (1953). For surveys see Harcourt (1969, 1994), Kurz (1987a), Kurz/Salvadori (1997, pp. 427–67), Pasinetti (2000), and Pasinetti/Scazzieri (1987). On the still existing relevance see recently Cohen/Harcourt (2003).

46 See for instance Harrod (1939, 1948), Kaldor (1955/56, 1957, 1961), Kaldor/Mirrless (1962), and Robinson (1956, 1962). Surveys on Post-Keynesian growth and distribution theories can be found in Hein (2004a, pp. 133–76) and Lavoie (1992a, pp. 282–96).

47 See the basic models by Bhaduri/Marglin (1990), Dutt (1984, 1987) and Rowthorn (1981). For surveys see Hein (2004a, pp. 177–219) and Lavoie (1992a, pp. 297–347).

48 On monetary elements in the early work of Kaldor and Robinson see Lavoie (1999), Rochon (1999, pp. 143–50, 2000, 2001a) and Vernengo/Rochon (2001). On the monetary theory in Kalecki's writing see Arestis (1996b), Dymski (1996) and Sawyer (1985, pp. 88–107, 2001a, 2001b).

49 See Kaldor (1970, 1982, 1985), Moore (1988, 1989) and Lavoie (1984, 1992a, pp. 149–216).

50 In the Pasinetti theorem (Pasinetti 1974, pp. 103–20) the rate of interest on accumulated workers' saving equals the rate of profit in long-run natural growth equilibrium. For a discussion and extension of the Pasinetti theorem including a government sector see Panico (1997). He derives positive effects of both the rate of interest and the real rate of growth on the normal rate of profit.

51 See, among others, in particular Dutt (1989, 1992, 1995), Dutt/Amadeo (1993), Epstein (1992, 1994), Hein (1999, 2006b, 2006d, 2007), Lavoie (1992a, pp. 347–71, 1993, 1995a), Lavoie/Godley (2001/2), Lavoie/Rodriguez/Seccareccia (2004), Lima/Meirelles (2006), and Taylor (1985, 2004, pp. 272–8).

52 In an edited book by Setterfield (2002) on Post-Keynesian growth theory there is no contribution dealing explicitly with the role of the interest rate, credit

and finance in growth. The same is true for a 'Symposium on Demand Led Growth' in the *Review of Political Economy*, Vol. 15 (1), 2003. In a recent Festschrift for Edward Nell, edited by Argyros/Forstater/Mongiovi (2004), only two out of twenty contributions deal with monetary issues.

53 Money being a social relation which is based on creditor–debtor contracts guaranteed by a social institution (the state) does not imply that money is the creature of the state coming into existence through taxing capabilities of the state defining the unit of tax payments, as modern chartalism supposes (Goodhart 1998; Wray 1998). For a discussion of the deficiencies of chartalism, see Rochon/Vernengo (2003).

54 See the Berlin school of Monetary Keynesianism, for instance Riese (1986), but also Chick (1996) and Lavoie (1996a).

55 See more detailed Smithin (2003a, pp. 25–35, 152–73). According to his view, the notion of a hierarchy of promises to pay and an inverse hierarchy of interest rates is not only valid within a currency area but it can also be applied to the relationship between different currencies and central banks issuing these currencies. See also Herr (1992).

56 Post-Keynesian and Monetary Circuit literature distinguishes between 'finance' and 'funding' (Carvalho 1992, p. 151) or between 'initial finance' und 'final finance' (Graziani 1989, p. 7; Lavoie 1992a, p. 159). Whereas 'finance' or 'initial finance' means the creation of short-run credit in order to initiate a production process, 'final finance' or 'funding' means the use of income generated by the production process in order to long-term finance newly produced investment goods, either through stocks and shares or through long-term credit. For a more detailed analysis see chapter 10.

57 For a survey on the relationship between the rate of interest and investment in Post-Keynesian and Neo-Ricardain models see, for instance, McKenna/Zannoni (1990). On the investment theories in Keynes and in Kalecki and the respective differences see Arena (1996), Fazzari/Mott (1986/87) and Lopez/Mott (1999).

58 See in particular the work by Minsky (1975, 1977) as well as the surveys by Crotty (1992) and Fazzari/Mott (1986/87).

59 See also Steindl (1952, pp. 113–24), who assumes an effect of the 'gearing ratio', the relationship between capital stock and own capital, on investment.

60 Dealing with the role of own capital in his *Theory of Economic Dynamics*, Kalecki (1954, pp. 91–5) neglects rising interest rates due to 'increasing risk' associated with increasing investment already for the single firm and rather supposes credit rationing.

61 A more detailed discussion of the required amount of finance for production and investment purposes and the sources of 'initial' and 'final' finance is provided in chapter 10 where we will analyse a monetary circuit.

62 On endogenous money in Post-Keynesian theory see Cottrell (1994), Fontana (2003, 2004a), Hewitson (1995), Howells (1995b), Lavoie (1984, 1992a, pp. 149–216, 1994), Moore (1989), Rochon (1999, 2001a), and Smithin (2003a, pp. 98–104, 121–7).

63 What exactly this base rate is depends on institutional circumstances under which central banks operate.

64 On the discussion between 'horizontalists' and 'structuralists' see the surveys by Fontana (2003, 2004a), Palley (1994, 1996b), and Pollin (1991).

65 Major elements of the horizontalist view have already been developed by Le Bourva in the French debate of the 1950s (Lavoie 1992b). On an English translation of this contribution see Le Bourva (1992).
66 See Wolfson (1996) for an elaboration of a Post-Keynesian theory of credit rationing based on asymmetric expectations of borrowers and lenders in a world with fundamental uncertainty. Credit rationing may occur due to differences in expectations between borrowers and lenders. Wolfson shows that credit standards and interest rates are both increased, if commercial banks' state of confidence decreases. Credit rationing and increasing spreads are then moving together.
67 See also Palley (1996b).
68 See, for instance, Herr (1988b, 1993), Howells (1995a, 1995b), Minsky (1975), Palley (1994, 1996b), and Wray (1990, 1992a, 1992b, 1995).
69 For a description of the variables, see the explanation of Figure I.1.
70 For a description of the variables, see again the explanation of Figure I.1. See also Palley (1996b).

Notes from Part II

1 Surveys of Post-Keynesian growth and distribution theories can be found in Hein (2004a, pp. 133–219) and Lavoie (1992a, pp. 282–347). For recent developments see the contributions in Setterfield (2002) and in Argyros/Forstater/Mongiovi (2004).
2 Mark-up pricing in the banking sector, i.e. commercial banks marking up the central bank's base rate in order to determine market rates of interest, is therefore irrelevant in Kalecki's approach (Sawyer 2001a).
3 For empirical analysis based on the Bhaduri/Marglin model see Bowles/Boyer (1995), Ederer/Stockhammer (2007), Hein/Krämer (1997), Hein/Vogel (2007), Marglin/Bhaduri (1990, 1991), Naastepad (2006), Naastepad/Storm (2007), Onaran/Stockhammer (2004, 2005, 2006), and Sawyer (1997).
4 See, among others, in particular Dutt (1989, 1992, 1995), Dutt/Amadeo (1993), Epstein (1992, 1994), Hein (1999, 2004a, pp. 221–38, 2006b, 2007), Hein/Ochsen (2003), Lavoie (1992a, pp. 347–71, 1993, 1995a), Lavoie/Godley (2001/2), Lavoie/Rodriguez/Seccareccia (2004), Lima/Meirelles (2006), Smithin (1997, 2003a, pp. 131–51, 2003b), and Taylor (1985, 2004, pp. 272–8).
5 Note that this assumption is different from the one in the Kaldor–Robinson model where labour supply is taken as given or assumed to be growing at a constant rate (Marglin 1984a, 1984b, pp. 103–9).
6 On the Monetary Circuit School see Bossone (2001, 2003), Fontana/Realfonzo (2006), Gnos (2007), Graziani (1989, 1994, 1996, 2003), Lavoie (1992a, pp. 149–69, 1994), Parguez (1996), Parguez/Seccareccia (2000), Realfonzo (2003), Seccareccia (1996, 2003), and the contributions in Fontana/Realfonzo (2005). On the relationship between Monetary Circuit School and Post-Keynesianism see Deleplace/Nell (1996), Fontana (2000), and Rochon (1999, 2003).
7 This view on the tasks of commercial bank sector is similar to New Keynesian work (Greenwald/Stiglitz 2003, pp. 43–103). On the role of commercial banks in the Monetary Circuit School see, in particular, Bossone (2001, 2003).

8 We shall not consider the role of the state in a monetary circuit. For the sake of simplicity there are no taxes, no credit demand by the state, no public investment, public transfers or public interest payments. See Lavoie (1992a, pp. 165–9) for some basic considerations with respect to the integration of the state into a monetary circuit model.
9 For a more detailed treatment see the discussion of Post-Keynesian monetary theories in chapter 6.
10 See Graziani (1989), Lavoie (1992a, pp. 151–7), and Seccareccia (1996, 2003) for similar analyses.
11 See Lavoie (1992a, pp. 161–165, 2003a), Rochon (2003), Rochon/Rossi (2004), and Rossi (2005) for models which contain the interaction between a central bank and commercial banks.
12 Depreciations and replacement investment are not considered, because we have assumed above, for the sake of simplicity, that the capital stock does not depreciate.
13 See also Nell (1996). A detailed treatment of monetary flows in Marx's (1885) schemes of reproduction in *Capital,* Vol. II, derives similar results (Hein 1997, pp. 136–55; Trigg 2006, pp. 33–49).
14 See Keynes (1973, pp. 201–23, 229–33), Hawtrey (1937), Ohlin (1937a, 1937b), and Robertson (1937, 1938a, 1938b, 1940).
15 Graphically, in Figure I.1 in chapter 6, the credit demand curve which describes the creditworthy loan demand as an inverse function of the loan rate of interest, shifts to the left. With a horizontal loan supply curve we get a lower amount of credit granted to firms at a given rate of interest.
16 Simplified 'Kaldor–Robinson', 'Cambridge', 'Neo-Keynesian' or 'Post-Keynesian' distribution and growth models can be found in Amadeo (1986a), Dutt (1987), Hein (2004a, pp. 149–76), Lavoie (1992a, pp. 284–96), and Marglin (1984a, 1984b, pp. 69–95), among others.
17 In his growth models, Kaldor also assumed full employment of labour, whereas Robinson, by and large, considered unemployment to persist also in long-run growth equilibrium.
18 The same is true for the relationship between the rate of capital accumulation and the wage rate. Faster accumulation is associated with a lower real wage rate, taking the technical conditions of production as given.
19 See Smithin (2003b) for a similar model. Lavoie (1995a) makes clear that the result for the Kaldor–Robinson model with competitive goods markets also applies to Eichner's (1980) model with oligopolistic markets and target-rate-of-return pricing. Eichner assumes that the target rate of return is given by the internal means of finance required for an intended rate of accumulation. There is hence no direct influence of the interest rate on the mark-up, the real wage and the rate of profit. But there are indirect effects. If we assume an accumulation function that makes the decisions to invest depend on the difference between the rate of profit and the interest rate, we will get for Eichner's model, which – like the Kaldor–Robinson model – assumes a normal rate of capacity utilization in the long period, a reduction in the rates of accumulation and profit and a rising real wage following an increase in the interest rate.
20 More extensive treatments of the basic Kaleckian distribution and growth models can be found in Blecker (2002), Hein (2004a, pp. 177–219), Lavoie (1992a, pp. 297–347), and Mott/Slattery (1994).

21 On the Rowthorn–Dutt–Amadeo model see Rowthorn (1981), Dutt (1984, 1987, 1990) and Amadeo (1986a, 1986b, 1987), but also Taylor (1985). On the Bhaduri/Marglin model see Bhaduri/Marglin (1990). For a similar model see Kurz (1994) and for further developments see Bhaduri (2006a).
22 See Lavoie (1992a, pp. 327–32, 1995b, 1996b, 2003b) for a review and discussion of the related literature.
23 On pricing and distribution see also Kalecki (1971, pp. 43–77) and Asimakopulos (1988).
24 In a more detailed analysis in which productivity differentials between firms, differences in the mark-up between industries, and open economy aspects are taken into account, nominal wage increases may affect income shares in a Kaleckian approach also when the mark-up remains constant. See Kalecki (1954, pp. 28–41; 1971, pp. 156–64), Sylos-Labini (1979), and Hein (2004a, pp. 178–88, 2005) for elements of such an analysis.
25 On Kaleckian and Post-Keynesian price theory see the overviews by Lavoie (1992a, pp. 129–48, 2001) and Lee (2003).
26 In the introduction to Kalecki's *Selected Essays on the Dynamics of the Capitalist Economy 1933–1970*, only published after he had passed away, we can read: 'It is interesting to notice that the theory of effective demand, already clearly formulated in the first papers, remains unchanged in all the relevant writings, as do my views on the distribution of national income. However, there is a continuous search for new solutions in the theory of investment decisions, where even the last paper represents – for better or for worse – a novel approach' (Kalecki 1971, p. viii). In the foreword to the English translation of his early works published in Poland in the 1930s, *Studies in the Theory of Business Cycles, 1933–1939*, there is a similar view: 'The studies also reflect the most essential features of my theory of the business cycle. I modified in my later work only the factors determining investment decisions (...)' (Kalecki 1969, p. 1). For a survey of investment functions in Kalecki's models see Steindl (1981).
27 On Kalecki's 'principle of increasing risk' see also chapter 6 as well as Arestis (1996b) and Sawyer (1985, pp. 101–6, 2001a).
28 In his latest work, Kalecki (1971, pp. 169–75) also attempted to introduce technical progress into the investment function. There, expected profitability of the latest capital stock vintages which incorporate a higher level of technical knowledge are of importance for investment decisions (Steindl 1981). Since we are assuming constant technical conditions of production in our model, we do not need to deal with this development.
29 In these New Keynesian models credit rationing, external finance premia and financial accelerators in economic downturns are derived. See Greenwald/Stiglitz (2003) for an overview and Stiglitz/Weiss (1981) on credit rationing, Bernanke/Blinder (1992) on external finance premia, Bernanke/Gertler (1995) on the bank-lending and the credit-channel of monetary transmission, and Bernanke/Gertler/Gilchrist (1996) and Gertler/Gilchrist (1993) on the financial accelerator.
30 See already Meyer/Kuh (1957) for empirical work on the effect of firms' internal funds on investment questioning the Modigliani/Miller (1958) theorem. More recent studies with similar results are Fazzari/Mott (1986/87), in particular Fazzari/Hubbard/Peterson (1988), and also Ndikumana (1999).

For surveys on the empirical work confirming the effect of internal funds on firms' investment see Hubbard (1998) and Schiantarelli (1996).

31 Our assumption is equivalent to assuming that dividend incomes, if they existed, would be completely reinvested into the firm.

32 This saving function is similar to the one used by Lavoie (1992a, p. 365, 1995a, p. 160), the only difference is that we explicitly consider the debt–capital ratio.

33 This section draws on Hein (2006b).

34 For similar results based on different Kaleckian models see Dutt (1992, 1995), Hein (1999), and Lavoie (1992a, pp. 363–71, 1993, 1995a).

35 If rising interest rates have a positive effect on the real equilibrium, however, it might be difficult for firms to raise mark-ups because rising mark-ups will require weak unions and hence rising unemployment – and not falling.

36 See chapter 16 for an introduction of conflict inflation and related real debt effects into the present model.

37 This does not imply that rentiers' saving is a precondition for credit and investment. On the contrary, rentiers' saving as well as firms' retained earnings are a result of production of investment and consumption goods initially financed by short-term credit, as we have shown in chapter 10 in our discussion of the monetary circuit.

38 Note that the stability of the goods market equilibrium implies $\frac{h}{v}(1-\rho)-\beta>0$.

39 From equation (II.53), assuming an interest-inelastic mark-up and the stability conditions for the short-run goods market equilibrium $\left[\frac{h}{v}(1-\rho)-\beta>0\right]$ and the long-run debt–capital ratio $\left[\beta(1-s_Z)-\rho\frac{h}{v}s_Z>0\right]$ to hold, we get: $\frac{\partial\lambda}{\partial i}=\frac{1}{i}\left\{\frac{s_Z\left[\frac{h}{v}(1-\rho)-\beta\right]}{\beta(1-s_Z)-\rho\frac{h}{v}s_Z}-\lambda\right\}$.

40 These results are different from Lavoie's (1995a, pp. 164–73) 'Minsky–Steindl model' who gets a uniquely positive relation between the interest rate and the debt–capital ratio in the case of a stable long-run equilibrium.

41 Assuming an interest-inelastic mark-up and the stability conditions for the short-run goods market equilibrium $\left[\frac{h}{v}(1-\rho)-\beta>0\right]$ to hold, we get from equation (II.53) if the long-run debt–capital ratio is unstable $\left[\beta(1-s_Z)-\rho\frac{h}{v}s_Z<0\right]$: $\frac{\partial\lambda}{\partial i}=\frac{1}{i}\left\{\frac{s_Z\left[\frac{h}{v}(1-\rho)-\beta\right]}{\beta(1-s_Z)-\rho\frac{h}{v}s_Z}-\lambda\right\}<0$.

42 These path-dependence features are absent from Lavoie's (1995a, pp. 164–73) 'Minsky–Steindl model'.

43 On the macroeconomic paradox of debt see also Dutt (1995) and Lavoie's (1995a, pp. 164–173) 'Minsky–Steindl model'.

44 This process may be reinforced if commercial banks – in the face of rising indebtedness of firms – start to increase market rates beyond the initial increase in the central bank's base rate.

45 This section draws on Hein (2007).

46 Note that the stability of the goods market equilibrium implies $\frac{h}{v}-\beta>0$.

47 From equation (II.68), assuming an interest-inelastic mark-up and the stability conditions for the short-run goods market equilibrium $\left[\frac{h}{v}-\beta>0\right]$

and the long-run debt–capital ratio $\left[\beta(1-s_Z)-\theta\frac{h}{v}>0\right]$ to hold, we get: $\frac{\partial\lambda}{\partial i}=\frac{1}{i}\left[\frac{s_Z\left(\frac{h}{v}-\beta\right)}{\beta(1-s_Z)-\theta\frac{h}{v}}-\lambda\right]$.

48 From equation (II.68), assuming an interest-inelastic mark-up, a stable short-run goods market equilibrium $\left[\frac{h}{v}-\beta>0\right]$ and an unstable long-run debt–capital ratio $\left[\beta(1-s_Z)-\theta\frac{h}{v}>0\right]$, we get: $\frac{\partial\lambda}{\partial i}=\frac{1}{i}\left[\frac{s_Z\left(\frac{h}{v}-\beta\right)}{\beta(1-s_Z)-\theta\frac{h}{v}}-\lambda\right]<0$.

Notes from Part III

1 This chapter draws on Hein (2006c).

2 See Ball/Mankiw (2002), Blanchard/Katz (1997), Carlin/Soskice (1990, pp. 133–66), Layard/Nickell/Jackman (1991, pp. 361–396), Mankiw (2001), and Stiglitz (1997) for New Keynesian discussions of the NAIRU, and Carlin/Soskice (2006, pp. 27–172), Clarida/Gali/Gertler (1999), McCallum (2001), Meyer (2001), Romer (2000), Snowdon/Vane (2005, pp. 419–427), Taylor (2000), and Walsh (2002) for New Consensus models. As already mentioned in chapter 3, these models are basically characterised by three equations: 1. an aggregate demand function derived from households' and firms' optimization behaviour which relates the output gap inversely to the real interest rate, 2. an expectations-augmented Phillips curve which makes the rate of inflation positively dependent on the output gap in the short run, and 3. a central bank reaction function in which the nominal interest rate set by the central bank is determined by the equilibrium real interest rate, by the output gap, and by the deviation of actual inflation from the inflation target (Taylor rule).

3 See Arestis/Sawyer (2004, pp. 73–87, 2005), Cassetti (2002), Lavoie (1992a, pp. 391–421, 2002), Rowthorn (1977), and Sawyer (2001c, 2002, 2006).

4 Setterfield's (2004) Post-Keynesian extension of the New Consensus model, however, assumes away an inflation barrier and hence a NAIRU. He asserts that there is a long-run stable relation between the rate of growth and the inflation rate, and hence no acceleration of inflation at a certain point.

5 This simplification precludes that the size of the capital stock may have an effect on the NAIRU, as in Arestis/Sawyer (2004, pp. 71–99, 2005) and Sawyer (2001c, 2002, 2006).

6 See Carlin/Soskice (1990, pp. 159–60) and Layard/Nickell/Jackman (1991, pp. 362–4) who rely on a Keynes effect within an IS–LM framework. Blanchard/Summers (1987) take nominal demand as given and implicitly rely on a Pigou effect.

7 See Arestis/Sawyer (2004, pp. 73–87, 2005) and Sawyer (2002, 2006) for conflicting claims models with an increasing mark-up when high levels of capacity utilization are achieved. See also Lavoie (1992a, pp. 391–7) for a discussion of different cases with respect to relative bargaining powers of firms and labour unions.

8 For the macroeconomic 'paradox of debt' in Kaleckian and Post-Kaleckian distribution and growth models with constant prices see chapter 13.

9 Even if we concede that in the face of accelerating inflation the behaviour of rentiers and firms may change, this will only temporarily inhibit the convergence process of the GERE towards the SIRE. Rentiers' consumption behaviour may change and the saving propensity out of rentiers' income may decline when inflation accelerates. For the 'puzzling case' to exist, however, the saving propensity of rentiers already has to be very low, so that there is only small room for manoeuvre. The same argument applies to the responsiveness of investment with respect to interest payments.

10 For the modern New Keynesian and New Consensus view see Carlin/Soskice (2006, pp. 27–172), Clarida/Gali/Gertler (1999), McCallum (2001), Meyer (2001), Romer (2000), Snowdon/Vane (2005, pp. 419–27), Taylor (2000), and Walsh (2002).

11 For a more extensive discussion of the New Consensus model from a Post-Keynesian perspective see Arestis (2006), Arestis/Sawyer (2004, 2006), Fontana (2006), Fontana/Palacio-Vera (2005), Lavoie (2004), Setterfield (2004), Palacio-Vera (2005), and Sawyer (2006).

12 See also Arestis/Biefang-Frisancho Mariscal (2000), Arestis/Baddeley/Sawyer (2006), and Rowthorn (1995, 1999).

13 The productivity-enhancing effects of investment in capital stock is pointed out in demand-led growth models. See Dutt (2003, 2006a), Kaldor (1957), Leon-Ledesma/Thirlwall (2002), and the papers in Setterfield (2002). Growth is primarily demand-driven because labour force and productivity growth respond to demand. This view has been applied by Lavoie (2004) in his Post-Keynesian alternative to the New Consensus models in which the natural rate of growth is endogenous to the actual rate of growth.

14 Our argument is different from Freedman/Harcourt/Kriesler's (2004) who also derive a horizontal long-run Phillips curve. They use the labour market hysteresis argument: In order to keep inflation down, a certain amount of short-term unemployment is required irrespective of long-term unemployment. But as short-term unemployed under the condition of persistent unemployment inevitably become long-term unemployed, the total rate of unemployment required to stabilise inflation has to increase.

15 Of course, central banks raising the real interest rates may also prevent the adjustment process, as we have argued above.

16 This chapter draws on Hein (2006d).

17 See Lavoie (1995b, 1996b, 2003b) for a review and discussion of the relevant literature.

18 See Lavoie/Kriesler (2005) on the similarity of the Dumenil/Levy (1999) model to the New Consensus model.

Notes from Summary and Conclusions

1 See Lavoie (2006b) for a similar view on the role of the Kaleckian distribution and growth models for the further development of heterodox theory.

2 For a preliminary but incomplete attempt see Hein/Ochsen (2003).

3 On technical progress and productivity issues see also the recent work by Bhaduri (2006b, 2006c), Cassetti (2003), Dutt (2003, 2006a), Lima (2000), and Naastepad (2006). On open economy issues see Bhaduri/Marglin (1990),

Blecker (1989, 1998), Cassetti (2002), Hein/Vogel (2007), McCombie/Roberts (2002), and, of course, Thirlwall (1979). For further contributions in these areas see also the papers in Argyros/Forstater/Mongiovi (2004) and Setterfield (2002).

4 See Boyer (2000), Bhaduri/Laski/Riese (2006), Dutt (2006b), Stockhammer (2004b, 2004c, 2005/6) and van Treeck (2007) for recent contributions in these areas. See also the stock-flow consistent modelling approach pioneered by Lavoie/Godley (2001/2) and Godley/Lavoie (2006).

5 See, for instance, Arestis (2006), Arestis/Sawyer (2004, 2005), Fontana (2006), Fontana/Palacio-Vera (2005), Lavoie (2004), Palacio-Vera (2005), Sawyer (2001c, 2002, 2006), Setterfield (2004), and Stockhammer (2004a, 2006).

6 For recent research and discussion in this area see Arestis/Sawyer (2006), Atesoglu/Smithin (2006), Davidson (2006), Fontana/Palacio/Vera (2002, 2004, 2006), Lavoie (1996c), Lima/Setterfield (2006), Monvoisin/Rochon (2006), Palley (2006), Rochon/Rossi (2006), Sawyer (2006), Seccareccia (1998), Setterfield (2006a, 2006b), and Smithin (2004).

References

Alexander, S. (1940) 'Mr. Keynes and Mr. Marx', *Review of Economic Studies*, 7: 123–35.

Amadeo, E.J. (1986a) 'Notes on capacity utilisation, distribution and accumulation', *Contributions to Political Economy*, 5: 83–94.

Amadeo, E.J. (1986b) 'The role of capacity utilisation in long period analysis', *Political Economy*, 2: 147–60.

Amadeo, E.J. (1987) 'Expectations in a steady-state model of capacity utilisation', *Political Economy*, 3: 75–89.

Arena, R. (1996) 'Investment decisions in circuit and post Keynesian approaches: a comparison', in G. Deleplace and E. Nell (eds), *Money in Motion* (Basingstoke: Macmillan).

Arestis, P. (1992) *The Post-Keynesian Approach to Economics* (Aldershot, Brookfield: Edward Elgar).

Arestis, P. (1996a) 'Post-Keynesian economics: towards coherence', *Cambridge Journal of Economics*, 20: 111–35.

Arestis, P. (1996b) 'Kalecki's role in post Keynesian economics: an overview', in J.E. King, (ed.), *An Alternative Macroeconomic Theory: The Kaleckian Model and Post-Keynesian Economics* (Boston: Kluiwer).

Arestis, P. (2006) 'New monetary policy and Keynes', *Intervention: Journal of Economics*, 3: 245–62.

Arestis, P., Baddeley, M., Sawyer, M. (2006) 'Is capital stock a determinant of unemployment?', in E. Hein, A. Heise and A. Truger (eds), *Wages, Employment, Distribution and Growth: International Perspectives* (Basingstoke: Palgrave Macmillan).

Arestis, P., Biefang-Frisancho Mariscal, I. (2000) 'Capital stock, unemployment and wages in the UK and Germany', *Scottish Journal of Political Economy*, 47: 487–503.

Arestis, P., Dunn, S.P., Sawyer, M. (1999) 'Post Keynesian economics and its critics', *Journal of Post Keynesian Economics*, 21: 527–49.

Arestis, P., Howells, P. (1996) 'Theoretical reflections on endogenous money: the problem with convenience lending', *Cambridge Journal of Economics*, 20: 539–51.

Arestis, P., Howells, P. (1999) 'The supply of credit money and the demand for deposits: a reply', *Cambridge Journal of Economics*, 23: 115–19.

Arestis, P., Sawyer, M. (2004) *Re-examining Monetary and Fiscal Policy for the 21st Century* (Cheltenham: Edward Elgar).

Arestis, P., Sawyer, M. (2005) 'Aggregate demand, conflict and capacity in the inflationary process', *Cambridge Journal of Economics*, 29: 959–74.

Arestis, P., Sawyer, M. (2006) 'The nature and role of monetary policy when money is endogenous', *Cambridge Journal of Economics*, 30: 847–60.

Argitis, G. (2001) 'Intra-capitalist conflicts, monetary policy and income distribution', *Review of Political Economy*, 13: 453–70.

Argyros, G., Forstater, M., Mongiovi, G. (eds) (2004) *Growth, Distribution, and Effective Demand* (Armonk, New York: M.E. Sharpe).

Asimakopulos, A. (1983) 'Kalecki and Keynes on finance, investment, and savings', *Cambridge Journal of Economics*, 7: 221–33.
Asimakopulos, A. (1985) 'Finance, savings and investment in Keynes's economics', *Cambridge Journal of Economics*, 9: 405–7.
Asimakopulos, A. (1986/87) 'Finance, liquidity, saving and investment', *Journal of Post Keynesian Economics*, 9: 79–90.
Asimakopulos, A. (1986a) 'Finance, investment, and saving: a reply to Terzi', *Cambridge Journal of Economics*, 10: 81–2.
Asimakopulos, A. (1986b) 'Richardson on Asimakopulos on finance: a reply', *Cambridge Journal of Economics*, 10: 199–201.
Asimakopulos, A. (1988) 'Post-Keynesian theories of distribution', in Asimakopulos, A. (ed.), *Theories of Income Distribution* (Boston: Kluiwer).
Aspromourgos, T. (2004) 'Sraffian research programmes and unorthodox economics', *Review of Political Economy*, 16: 179–206.
Atesoglu, H.S., Smithin, J. (2006) 'Inflation targeting in a simple macroeconomic model', *Journal of Post Keynesian Economics*, 28: 673–88.
Auerbach, P., Skott, P. (1988) 'Concentration, competition and distribution – a critique of theories of monopoly capital', *International Review of Applied Economics*, 2: 42–61.
Ball, L. (1999) 'Aggregate demand and long-run unemployment', *Brooking Papers on Economic Activity*, 2: 189–251.
Ball, L., Mankiw, N.G. (2002) 'The NAIRU in theory and practice', *Journal of Economic Perspectives*, 16(4): 115–36.
Bernanke, B.S., Blinder, A.S. (1992) 'The federal funds rate and the channels of monetary transmission', *American Economic Review*, 82: 901–21.
Bernanke, B.S., Gertler, M. (1995) 'Inside the black box: the credit channel of monetary policy transmission', *Journal of Economic Perspectives*, 9: 27–48.
Bernanke, B.S., Gertler, M., Gilchrist, S. (1996) 'The financial accelerator and the flight to quality', *The Review of Economics and Statistics*, 78: 1–15.
Bertocco, G. (2001) 'Is Kaldor's theory of money supply endogeneity still relevant?', *Metroeconomica*, 52: 95–120.
Bertocco, G. (2005) 'The role of credit in a Keynesian monetary economy', *Review of Political Economy*, 17: 489–511.
Bhaduri, A. (2006a) 'The dynamics of profit- and wage-led expansion: a note', in E. Hein, A. Heise and A. Truger (eds), *Wages, Employment, Distribution, and Growth: International Perspectives* (Basingstoke: Palgrave Macmillan).
Bhaduri, A. (2006b) 'Labour market flexibility and economic expansion', in E. Hein, A. Heise and A. Truger (eds), *Wages, Employment, Distribution and Growth: International Perspectives* (Basingstoke: Palgrave Macmillan).
Bhaduri, A. (2006c) 'Endogenous economic growth: a new approach', *Cambridge Journal of Economics*, 30: 69–83.
Bhaduri, A., Laski, K., Riese, M. (2006) 'A model of interaction between the virtual and the real economy', *Metroeconomica*, 57: 412–27.
Bhaduri, A., Marglin, S. (1990) 'Unemployment and the real wage: the economic basis for contesting political ideologies', *Cambridge Journal of Economics*, 14: 375–93.
Blanchard, O., Katz, L.F. (1997) 'What we know and do not know about the natural rate of unemployment', *Journal of Economic Perspectives*, 11(1): 51–72.

Blanchard, O., Summers, L.H. (1987) 'Hysteresis in unemployment', *European Economic Review*, 31: 288–95.

Blanchard, O., Summers, L.H. (1988) 'Beyond the natural rate hypothesis', *American Economic Review*, 78: 182–7.

Blecker, R.A. (1989) 'International competition, income distribution and economic growth', *Cambridge Journal of Economics*, 13: 395–412.

Blecker, R.A. (1998) 'International competitiveness, relative wages, and the balance-of-payment-constraint', *Journal of Post Keynesian Economics*, 20: 495–526.

Blecker, R.A. (2002) 'Distribution, demand and growth in neo-Kaleckian macro-models', in M. Setterfield (ed.), *The Economics of Demand-led Growth* (Cheltenham: Edward Elgar).

Bossone, B. (2001) 'Circuit theory of banking and finance', *Journal of Banking and Finance*, 25: 857–90.

Bossone, B. (2003) 'Thinking of the economy as a circuit', in L.-P. Rochon and S. Rossi (eds), *Modern Theories of Money* (Cheltenham: Edward Elgar).

Bowles, S., Boyer, R. (1995) 'Wages, aggregate demand, and employment in an open economy: an empirical investigation', in G.A. Epstein and H.M. Gintis (eds), *Macroeconomic Policy after the Conservative Era* (Cambridge: Cambridge University Press).

Boyer, R. (2000) 'Is a finance-led growth regime a viable alternative to Fordism? A preliminary analysis', *Economy and Society*, 29(1): 111–45.

Carlin, W., Soskice, D. (1990) *Macroeconomics and the Wage Bargain: A Modern Approach to Employment, Inflation and the Exchange Rate* (Oxford: Oxford University Press).

Carlin, W., Soskice, D. (2006) *Macroeconomics: Imperfections, Institutions and Policies* (Oxford: Oxford University Press).

Carvalho, F.J.C. de (1992) *Mr. Keynes and the Post Keynesians: Principles of Economics for a Monetary Production Economy* (Aldershot, Brookfield: Edward Elgar).

Cassetti, M. (2002) 'Conflict, inflation, distribution and terms of trade in the Kaleckian model', in M. Setterfield (ed.), *The Economics of Demand-led Growth* (Cheltenham: Edward Elgar).

Cassetti, M. (2003) 'Bargaining power, effective demand and technical progress: A Kaleckian model of growth', *Cambridge Journal of Economics*, 27: 449–64.

Cassetti, M. (2006) 'A note on the long-run behaviour of Kaleckian models', *Review of Political Economy*, 18: 497–508.

Catephores, G. (1989) *An Introduction to Marxist Economics* (Basingstoke: Macmillan).

Chick, V. (1996) *The Monetary Theory of Keynes and the Post Keynesians*, Discussion Paper in Economics, 96–109 (London: University College, London).

Chick, V., Caserta, M. (1997) 'Provisional equilibrium and macroeconomic theory', in P. Arestis, G. Palma and M. Sawyer (eds), *Markets, Unemployment and Economic Policy: Essays in Honour of Geoff Harcourt*, vol. 2 (London, New York: Routledge).

Ciccarone, G. (1998) 'Prices and distribution in a Sraffian credit economy', *Review of Political Economy*, 10: 399–413.

Clarida, R., Gali, J., Gertler, M. (1999) 'The science of monetary policy: a New Keynesian perspective', *Journal of Economic Literature*, 37: 1661–707.

Clower, R. (1999) 'Post-Keynes monetary and finance theory', *Journal of Post Keynesian Economics*, 21: 399–414.
Coddington, A. (1976) 'Keynesian economics: the search for first principles', *Journal of Economic Literature*, 14: 1258–73.
Cohen, A.J., Harcourt, G.C. (2003) 'What happened to the Cambridge capital theory controversies?', *Journal of Economic Perspectives*, 17: 199–214.
Commendatore, P. (2005) 'Are Kaleckian models of growth and distribution relevant in the long run?', in C. Panico and N. Salvadori (eds), *Classical, Neo-classical and Keynesian Views on Growth and Distribution* (Cheltenham: Edward Elgar).
Committeri, M. (1986) 'Some comments on recent contributions on capital accumulation, income distribution and capacity utilisation', *Political Economy*, 2: 161–86.
Cottrell, A. (1994) 'Post-Keynesian monetary economics', *Cambridge Journal of Economics*, 18: 587–605.
Crotty, J. (1987) 'The role of money and finance in Marx's crisis theory', in Union for Radical Political Economics (ed.), *The Imperiled Economy: Book I. Macroeconomics from a Left Perspective* (New York: Union for Radical Political Economics).
Crotty, J.R. (1992) 'Neoclassical and Keynesian approaches to the theory of investment', *Journal of Post Keynesian Economics*, 14: 483–96.
Davidson, P. (1986/87) 'Finance, funding, saving, and investment', *Journal of Post Keynesian Economics*, 9: 101–10.
Davidson, P. (1988) 'A technical definition of uncertainty and the long-run non-neutrality of money', *Cambridge Journal of Economics*, 12: 329–37.
Davidson, P. (1994) *Post Keynesian Macroeconomic Theory* (Aldershot: Edward Elgar).
Davidson, P. (1998) 'The macroeconomics of OECD unemployment', *The Economic Journal*, 108: 817–31.
Davidson, P. (2002) *Financial Markets, Money and the Real World* (Cheltenham: Edward Elgar).
Davidson, P. (2003/4) 'Setting the record straight on "A history of Post Keynesian Economics" ', *Journal of Post Keynesian Economics*, 26: 245–72.
Davidson, P. (2005) 'Responses to Lavoie, King, and Dow on what Post Keynesianism is and who is a Post Keynesian', *Journal of Post Keynesian Economics*, 27: 393–408.
Davidson, P. (2006) 'Can, or should, a central bank target inflation', *Journal of Post Keynesian Economics*, 28: 689–703.
De Brunhoff, S. (1976) *Marx on Money* (New York: Urizen Books).
Deleplace, G., Nell, E. (1996) 'Introduction: monetary circulation and effective demand', in G. Deleplace and E. Nell (eds), *Money in Motion* (Basingstoke: Macmillan).
Dillard, D. (1984) 'Keynes and Marx. A centennial appraisal', *Journal of Post Keynesian Economics*, 6: 421–32.
Dow, S. (2005) 'Axioms and Babylonian thought: a reply', *Journal of Post Keynesian Economics*, 27: 385–91.
Dumenil, G., Levy, D. (1999) 'Being Keynesian in short term and classical in the long term: the traverse to classical long-term equilibrium', *The Manchester School*, 67: 684–716.

Dutt, A.K. (1984) 'Stagnation, income distribution and monopoly power', *Cambridge Journal of Economics*, 8: 25–40.

Dutt, A.K. (1987) 'Alternative closures again: a comment on "Growth, distribution and inflation" ', *Cambridge Journal of Economics*, 11: 75–82.

Dutt, A.K. (1989) 'Accumulation, distribution and inflation in a Marxian/post-Keynesian model with a rentier class', *Review of Radical Political Economics*, 21(3): 18–26.

Dutt, A.K. (1990) *Growth, Distribution and Uneven Development* (Cambridge: Cambridge University Press).

Dutt, A.K. (1992) 'Rentiers in post-Keynesian models', in P. Arestis and V. Chick (eds), *Recent Developments in Post-Keynesian Economics* (Aldershot, Brookfield: Edward Elgar).

Dutt, A.K. (1995) 'Internal finance and monopoly power in capitalist economies: a reformulation of Steindl's growth model', *Metroeconomica*, 46: 16–34.

Dutt, A.K. (1997) 'Equilibrium, path dependence and hysteresis in post-Keynesian models', in P. Arestis, G. Palma and M. Sawyer (eds), *Markets, Unemployment and Economic Policy: Essays in Honour of Geoff Harcourt*, vol. 2 (London, New York: Routledge).

Dutt, A.K. (2003) 'New growth theory, effective demand, and post-Keynesian dynamics', in N. Salvadori (ed.), *Old and New Growth Theories: an Assessment* (Cheltenham: Edward Elgar).

Dutt, A.K. (2006a) 'Aggregate demand, aggregate supply and economic growth', *International Review of Applied Economics*, 20: 319–36.

Dutt, A.K. (2006b) 'Maturity, stagnation and consumer debt: a Steindlian approach', *Metroeconomica*, 57: 339–64.

Dutt, A.K., Amadeo, E.J. (1993) 'A post-Keynesian theory of growth, interest and money, in M. Baranzini and G. Harcourt (eds), *The Dynamics of the Wealth of Nations* (London: Macmillan).

Dymski, G.A. (1996) 'Kalecki's monetary economics', in J.E. King (ed.), *An Alternative Macroeconomic Theory: The Kaleckian Model and Post-Keynesian Economics* (Boston: Kluiwer).

Eatwell, J. (1983a) 'The long period theory of employment', *Cambridge Journal of Economics*, 7: 269–85.

Eatwell, J. (1983b) 'Theories of value, output and employment', in J. Eatwell and M. Milgate (eds), *Keynes's Economics and the Theory of Value and Distribution* (London: Duckworth).

Eatwell, J., Milgate, M. (eds) (1983) *Keynes's Economics and the Theory of Value and Distribution* (London: Duckworth).

Ederer, S., Stockhammer, E. (2007) 'Wages and aggregate demand: an empirical investigation for France', in E. Hein and A. Truger (eds), *Money, Distribution and Economic Policy – Alternatives to Orthodox Macroeconomics* (Cheltenham: Edward Elgar).

Eichner, A.S. (1978a) 'Post-Keynesian theory: an introduction', *Challenge* 21(3): 4–10.

Eichner, A. (ed.) (1978b) *A Guide to Post-Keynesian Economics* (White Plains, NY: M.E. Sharpe).

Eichner, A.S. (1980) 'A general model of investment and pricing', in E. Nell (ed.), *Growth, Profits and Property* (Cambridge: Cambridge University Press).

Eichner, A.S., Kregel, J. (1975) 'An essay in post-Keynesian Theory: a new paradigm in Economics', *Journal of Economic Literature*, 13: 1293–314.

Epstein, G.A. (1992) 'Political economy and comparative central banking', *Review of Radical Political Economics*, 24: 1–30.

Epstein, G.A. (1994) 'A political economy model of comparative central banking', in G. Dymski and R. Pollin (eds), *New Perspectives in Monetary Macroeconomics* (Ann Arbor: University of Michigan Press).

Evans, T. (1997) 'Marxian theories of credit money and capital', *International Journal of Political Economy*, 27(1): 7–42.

Fan-Hung (1939) 'Keynes and Marx on the theory of capital accumulation, money and interest', *Review of Economic Studies*, 7: 28–41.

Fazzari, S.M., Hubbard, R.G., Petersen, B.C. (1988) 'Financing constraints and corporate investment', *Brooking Papers on Economic Activity*, 1: 141–95.

Fazzari, S.M., Mott, T. (1986/87) 'The investment theories of Kalecki and Keynes: an empirical study of firm data, 1970–1982', *Journal of Post Keynesian Economics*, 9: 171–87.

Fisher, I. (1933) 'The debt–deflation theory of great depressions', *Econometrica*, 1: 337–57.

Foley, D.K. (1983) 'On Marx's theory of money', *Social Concept*, 1: 5–19.

Foley, D.K. (1986a) 'Say's law in Marx and Keynes', *Cahiers d'Economie Politique*, 10/11: 183–94.

Foley, D.K. (1986b) *Understanding Capital. Marx's Economic Theory* (Cambridge, MA: Harvard University Press).

Foley, D.K. (1987) 'Money in economic activity', in J. Eatwell, M. Milgate, and P. Newman (eds), *The New Palgrave: A Dictionary of Economics*, vol. 3 (London, New York, Tokyo: Macmillan).

Fontana, G. (2000) 'Post Keynesians and Circuitists on money and uncertainty: an attempt at generality', *Journal of Post Keynesian Economics*, 33: 27–48.

Fontana, G. (2003) 'Post Keynesian approaches to endogenous money: a time framework explanation', *Review of Political Economy*, 15: 291–314.

Fontana, G. (2004a) 'Rethinking endogenous money: a constructive interpretation of the debates between horizontalists and structuralists', *Metroeconomica*, 55: 367–85.

Fontana, G. (2004b) 'Hicks on monetary theory and history: money as endogenous money', *Cambridge Journal of Economics*, 28: 73–88.

Fontana, G. (2005) 'A history of Post Keynesian economics since 1936: some hard (and not so hard) questions for the future', *Journal of Post Keynesian Economics*, 27: 409–21.

Fontana, G. (2006) 'The "New Consensus" view of monetary policy: a new Wicksellian connection', *Intervention: Journal of Economics*, 3: 263–78.

Fontana, G., Gerrard, B. (2002) 'The significance of the monetary context of economic behavior', *Review of Social Economy*, 60: 243–62.

Fontana, G., Gerrard, B. (2006) 'The future of Post Keynesian economics', *Banca Nazionale del Lavoro Quarterly Review*, 59: 49–80.

Fontana, G., Palacio-Vera, A. (2002) 'Monetary policy rules: what are we learning?', *Journal of Post Keynesian Economics*, 24: 547–68.

Fontana, G., Palacio-Vera, A. (2004) 'Monetary policy uncovered: theory and practice', *International Review of Applied Economics*, 18: 25–41.

Fontana, G., Palacio-Vera, A. (2005) *Are long-run price stability and short-run output stabilisation all that monetary policy can aim for?*, Working Paper No. 430 (Annandale-on-Hudson: The Levy Economic Institute of Bard College).

Fontana, G., Palacio-Vera, A. (2006) 'Is there an active role for monetary policy in the endogenous money approach?', in C. Gnos and L.-P. Rochon (eds), *Post-Keynesian Principles of Economic Policy* (Cheltenham: Edward Elgar).

Fontana, G., Realfonzo, R. (2006) *The theory of the monetary circuit: a view from the fringe*, paper presented at the 9th Post Keynesian Conference, Kansas City, 14–18 September.

Fontana, G., Realfonzo, R. (eds) (2005) *The Monetary Theory of Production. Traditions and Perspectives* (Basingstoke: Palgrave Macmillan).

Franzese, R.J. (2001a) 'Institutions and sectoral interactions in monetary policy and wage/price bargaining', in P.A. Hall and D. Soskice (eds), *Varieties of Capitalism: Institutional Foundations of Comparative Advantage* (Oxford: Oxford University Press).

Franzese, R.J. (2001b) 'Strategic interaction of monetary policymakers and wage/price bargainers: a review with implications for the European common-currency area', *Empirica*, 28: 457–86.

Freedman, C., Harcourt, G.C., Kriesler, P. (2004) 'Has the long-run Phillips Curve turned horizontal?', in G. Argyrous, M. Forstater and G. Mongiovi (eds), *Growth, Distribution, and Effective Demand: Alternatives to the Orthodoxy. Essays in Honor of Edward J. Nell* (Armonk, NY: M.E. Sharpe).

Friedman, M. (1968) 'The role of monetary policy', *American Economic Review*, 58: 1–17.

Friedman, M. (1970) 'A theoretical framework for monetary analysis', *Journal of Political Economy*, 78: 193–238.

Friedman, M. (1972) 'Comments on the critics', *Journal of Political Economy*, 80: 906–50.

Fritsch, B. (1968) *Die Geld- und Kredittheorie von Karl Marx* (Frankfurt am Main Europäische Verlagsanstalt).

Galbraith, J.K. (1997) 'Time to ditch the NAIRU', *Journal of Economic Perspectives*, 11(1): 93–108.

Garegnani, P. (1978) 'Notes on consumption, investment and effective demand, Part I', *Cambridge Journal of Economics*, 2: 335–53.

Garegnani, P. (1979) 'Notes on consumption, investment and effective demand, Part II', *Cambridge Journal of Economics*, 3: 63–82.

Gertler, M., Gilchrist, S. (1993) 'The role of credit market imperfections in the monetary transmission mechanism: arguments and evidence', *Scandinavian Journal of Economics*, 95: 43–64.

Glyn, A., Sutcliffe, B. (1972) *Capitalism in Crisis* (New York: Pantheon).

Gnos, C. (2007) 'Monetary policy from a circuitist perspective', in P. Arestis, E. Hein and E. Le Heron (eds), *Aspects of Modern Monetary and Macroeconomic Policies* (Basingstoke: Palgrave Macmillan).

Godley, W., Lavoie, M. (2006) *Monetary Economics: An Integrated Approach to Credit, Money, Income, Production and Wealth* (Basingstoke: Palgrave Macmillan).

Goodhart, C.A.E. (1998) 'The two concepts of money: implications for the analysis of optimal currency areas', *European Journal of Political Economy*, 14: 407–32.

Goodwin, R. (1967) 'A growth cycle', in C.H. Feinstein (ed.), *Capitalism and Economic Growth* (Cambridge: Cambridge University Press).

Gordon, D.M., Weisskopf, T.E., Bowles, S. (1987) 'Power, accumulation and crisis: the rise and the demise of the postwar social structure of accumulation', in Union for Radical Political Economics (ed.), *The Imperiled Economy: Book I. Macroeconomics from a Left Perspective* (New York: Union for Radical Political Economics).

Gordon, R.J. (1990) 'What is new-Keynesian economics?', *Journal of Economic Literature*, 28: 1115–71.

Grabel I. (1997) 'Savings, investment and functional efficiency: a comparative examination of national financial complexes', in R. Pollin (ed.), *The Macroeconomics of Saving, Finance, and Investment* (Ann Arbor: University of Michigan Press).

Graziani, A. (1984) 'The debate on Keynes's "finance motive" ', *Economic Notes*, 1: 5–34.

Graziani, A. (1988) 'The financement of economic activity in Keynes's thought', in H. Hagemann and O. Steiger (eds), *Keynes' General Theory nach fünfzig Jahren* (Berlin: Duncker & Humblot).

Graziani, A. (1989) 'The theory of the monetary circuit', *Thames Paper in Political Economy*, Spring.

Graziani, A. (1994) 'Monetary circuits', in P. Arestis and M. Sawyer (eds), *The Elgar Companion to Radical Political Economy* (Aldershot: Edward Elgar).

Graziani, A. (1996) 'Money as purchasing power and money as a stock of wealth in Keynesian economic thought', in G. Deleplace and E. Nell (eds), *Money in Motion* (Basingstoke: Macmillan).

Graziani, A. (1997) 'The Marxist theory of money', *International Journal of Political Economy*, 27(2): 26–50.

Graziani, A. (2003) *The Monetary Theory of Production* (Cambridge: Cambridge University Press).

Greenwald, B., Stiglitz, J.E. (1987) 'Keynesian, New Keynesian and New Classical economics', *Oxford Economic Papers*, 39: 119–32.

Greenwald, B., Stiglitz, J.E. (1993) 'New and old Keynesians', *Journal of Economic Perspectives*, 7: 23–44.

Greenwald, B., Stiglitz, J.E. (2003) *Towards a New Paradigm in Monetary Economics* (Cambridge: Cambridge University Press).

Hahn, F. (1982) *Money and Inflation* (Oxford: Basil Blackwell).

Hamouda, O.F., Harcourt, G.C. (1988) 'Post Keynesianism: from criticism to coherence?', *Bulletin of Economic Research*, 40: 1–33.

Harcourt, G.C. (1969) 'Some Cambridge controversies in the theory of capital', *Journal of Economic Literature*, 7: 369–405.

Harcourt, G.C. (1987): 'Post-Keynesian economics', in J. Eatwell, M. Milgate and P. Newman (eds), *The New Palgrave: A Dictionary of Economics*, vol. 3 (London, New York, Tokyo: Macmillan).

Harcourt, G.C. (1994) 'Capital theory controversies', in P. Arestis and M. Sawyer (eds), *The Elgar Companion to Radical Political Economy* (Aldershot: Edward Elgar).

Harcourt, G.C. (2001) 'Post-Keynesian thought', in G.C. Harcourt, *50 Years a Keynesian and Other Essays* (Basingstoke: Palgrave Macmillan).

Harcourt, G.C. (2006) *The Structure of Post-Keynesian Economics: The Core Contributions of the Pioneers* (Cambridge: Cambridge University Press).

Harrod, R.F. (1939) 'An essay in dynamic theory', *The Economic Journal*, 49: 14–33.

Harrod, R.F. (1948) *Towards a Dynamic Economics* (London: Macmillan).

Hawtrey, R.G. (1937) 'Alternative theories of the rate of interest', *The Economic Journal*, 47: 436–43.

Hein, E. (1997) *Geld, effektive Nachfrage und Kapitalakkumulation. Eine Betrachtung aus Marxscher, Keynesscher und post-keynesianischer Perspektive* (Berlin: Duncker & Humblot).

Hein, E. (1999) 'Interest rates, income shares and investment in a Kaleckian model', *Political Economy: Review of Political Economy and Social Sciences*, 5: 5–22.

Hein, E. (2002) 'Monetary policy and wage bargaining in the EMU: restrictive ECB policies, high unemployment, nominal wage restraint and inflation above the target', *Banca Nazionale del Lavoro Quarterly Review*, 55: 299–337.

Hein, E. (2004a) *Verteilung und Wachstum. Eine paradigmenorientierte Einführung unter besonderer Berücksichtigung der post-keynesianischen Theorie* (Marburg: Metropolis).

Hein, E. (2004b) 'Money, credit and the interest rate in Marx's economics. On the similarities of Marx's monetary analysis to post-Keynesian economics', *International Papers in Political Economy*, 11(2): 1–46.

Hein, E. (2004c) 'Die NAIRU – eine post-keynesianische Interpretation', *Intervention. Zeitschrift für Ökonomie*, 1: 43–66.

Hein, E. (2005) 'Löhne, Verteilung und Wachstum: Ansätze in der Tradition Michal Kaleckis', in E. Hein, A. Heise and A. Truger (eds), *Löhne, Beschäftigung, Verteilung und Wachstum. Makroökonomische Analysen* (Marburg: Metropolis).

Hein, E. (2006a) 'Money, interest and capital accumulation in Karl Marx's economics: a monetary interpretation and some similarities to post-Keynesian approaches', *European Journal of the History of Economic Thought*, 13: 113–40.

Hein, E. (2006b) 'Interest, debt and capital accumulation – a Kaleckian approach', *International Review of Applied Economics*, 20: 337–52.

Hein, E. (2006c) 'Wage bargaining and monetary policy in a Kaleckian monetary distribution and growth model: trying to make sense of the NAIRU', *Intervention: Journal of Economics*, 3: 305–29.

Hein, E. (2006d) 'On the (in-)stability and the endogeneity of the "normal" rate of capacity utilisation in a post-Keynesian/Kaleckian "monetary" distribution and growth model', *Indian Development Review*, 4: 129–50.

Hein, E. (2007) 'Interest rate, debt, distribution and capital accumulation in a post-Kaleckian model', *Metroeconomica*, 57: 310–39.

Hein, E., Krämer, H. (1997) 'Income shares and capital formation: patterns of recent developments', *Journal of Income Distribution*, 7: 5–28.

Hein, E., Ochsen C. (2003) 'Regimes of interest rates, income shares, savings, and investment: a Kaleckian model and empirical estimations for some advanced OECD-economies', *Metroeconomica*, 54: 404–33.

Hein, E., Vogel, L. (2007) *Distribution and growth reconsidered – empirical results for Austria, France, Germany, the Netherlands, the UK and the USA*, IMK Working Paper 31/2007 (Duesseldorf: Macroeconomic Policy Institute (IMK) in the Hans Boeckler Foundation).

Heine, M., Herr, H. (1999) *Volkswirtschaftslehre. Paradigmenorientierte Einführung in die Mikro- und Makroökonomie* (München, Wien: Oldenbourg).

Heinrich, M. (1991) *Die Wissenschaft vom Wert* (Hamburg: VSA).

Hellwig, M. (1993) 'The challenge of monetary theory', *European Economic Review*, 37: 215–42.

Herr, H. (1988a) 'Theorie einer monetären Produktionswirtschaft', *Ökonomie und Gesellschaft*, 6: 66–98.
Herr, H. (1988b) *Geld, Kredit und ökonomische Dynamik in marktvermittelten Ökonomien – die Vision einer Geldwirtschaft*, 2nd edn (München: Florentz).
Herr, H. (1992) *Geld, Währungswettbewerb und Währungssysteme* (Frankfurt a.M: Campus).
Herr, H. (1993) 'Makroökonomische Budgetbeschränkung und Kreditmarkt', in H.J. Stadermann and O. Steiger, (eds), *Der Stand und die nächste Zukunft der Geldforschung. Festschrift für Hajo Riese zum 60. Geburtstag* (Berlin: Duncker & Humblot).
Hewitson, G. (1995) 'Post-Keynesian monetary theory: some issues', *Journal of Economic Surveys*, 9: 285–310.
Hicks, J.R. (1937) 'Mr. Keynes and the "Classics": a suggested interpretation', *Econometrica*, 5: 147–59.
Hicks, J. (1982) 'Methods of dynamic analysis', in J. Hicks, *Money, Interest and Wages: Collected Essays on Economic Theory of John Hicks*, vol. 2 (Oxford: Clarendon Press).
Holt, R.P.F., Pressman, S. (eds) (2001) *A New Guide to Post Keynesian Economics* (London: Routledge).
Howells, P. (1995a) 'The demand for endogenous money', *Journal of Post Keynesian Economics*, 18: 89–106.
Howells, P. (1995b) 'Endogenous money', *International Papers in Political Economy*, 2(2): 1–41.
Hubbard, R.G. (1998) 'Capital-market imperfections and investment', *Journal of Economic Literature*, 36: 193–225.
Kaldor, N. (1955/56) 'Alternative theories of distribution', *The Review of Economic Studies*, 23: 83–100.
Kaldor, N. (1957) 'A model of economic growth', *The Economic Journal*, 67: 591–624.
Kaldor, N. (1958) 'Monetary policy, economic stability and growth: a memorandum submitted to the Committee on the Working of the Monetary System on June 23, 1958', in N. Kaldor (1964), *Essays on Economic Policy, vol. I* (London: Duckworth & Co.).
Kaldor, N. (1961) 'Capital accumulation and economic growth', in F.A. Lutz and D.C. Hague (eds), *The Theory of Capital* (London: Macmillan).
Kaldor, N. (1970) 'The new monetarism', *Lloyds Bank Review*, 97: 1–17.
Kaldor, N. (1982) *The Scourge of Monetarism* (Oxford: Oxford University Press).
Kaldor, N. (1985) 'How Monetarism failed', *Challenge*, 28(2): 4–13.
Kaldor, N., Mirrless, J.A. (1962) 'A new model of economic growth', *The Review of Economic Studies*, 29: 174–92.
Kalecki, M. (1932) 'The business cycle and inflation', in J. Osiatynski (ed.) (1990), *Collected Works of Michal Kalecki, vol. I* (Oxford: Clarendon Press).
Kalecki, M. (1933) 'Essay on the business cycle theory', in J. Osiatynski (ed.) (1990), *Collected Works of Michal Kalecki, vol. I* (Oxford: Clarendon Press).
Kalecki, M. (1936) 'Some remarks on Keynes's Theory', in J. Osiatynski (ed.) (1990), *Collected Works of Michal Kalecki, vol. I* (Oxford: Clarendon Press).
Kalecki, M. (1937) 'The principle of increasing risk', *Economica*, 4: 440–7.
Kalecki, M. (1954) *Theory of Economic Dynamics* (London: George Allen and Unwin).

Kalecki, M. (1968) 'The Marxian equations of reproduction and modern economics', *Social Science Information*, 7: 73–9.

Kalecki, M. (1969) *Studies in the Theory of Business Cycles, 1933–1939* (London: Basil Blackwell).

Kalecki, M. (1971) *Selected Essays on the Dynamics of the Capitalist Economy, 1933–70* (Cambridge: Cambridge University Press).

Kenway, P. (1980) 'Marx, Keynes and the possibility theory of crisis', *Cambridge Journal of Economics*, 4: 23–36.

Kenway, P. (1987) 'Realisation problem', in J. Eatwell, M. Milgate and P. Newman (eds), *The New Palgrave: A Dictionary of Economics*, vol. 4 (London, New York, Tokyo: Macmillan).

Keynes, J.M. (1930) *A Treatise on Money*, 2 vols (London: Macmillan).

Keynes, J.M. (1933) 'A monetary theory of production', in *The Collected Writings of J.M. Keynes*, vol. XIII (London, Basingstoke: Macmillan, 1987).

Keynes, J.M. (1936) *The General Theory of Employment, Interest and Money, The Collected Writings of J.M. Keynes*, vol. VII (London, Basingstoke: Macmillan, 1973).

Keynes, J.M. (1973) *The General Theory and After. Part II. Defence and Development, The Collected Writings of J.M. Keynes*, vol. XIV (London, Basingstoke: Macmillan).

Keynes, J.M. (1979) *The General Theory and After: A Supplement, The Collected Writings of J.M. Keynes*, vol. XXIX (London, Basingstoke: Macmillan).

King, J.E. (2002) *A History of Post Keynesian Economics since 1936* (Cheltenham: Edward Elgar).

King, J.E. (2005) 'Unwarping the record: a reply to Paul Davidson', *Journal of Post Keynesian Economics*, 27: 377–84.

King, J.E. (ed.) (1996) *An Alternative Macroeconomic Theory: The Kaleckian Model and Post-Keynesian Economics* (Boston: Kluiwer).

Kittel, B., Traxler, F. (2001) 'Lohnverhandlungssysteme und Geldpolitik', *Wirtschaft und Gesellschaft*, 27: 11–40.

Kregel, J. (1985) 'Hamlet without the prince: Cambridge macroeconomics without money', *American Economic Review, Papers and Proceedings*, 75: 133–9.

Kregel, J. (1986/87) 'A note on finance, liquidity, saving, and investment', *Journal of Post Keynesian Economics*, 9: 91–100.

Kurz, H.D. (1987a) 'Capital theory: debates', in J. Eatwell, M. Milgate and P. Newman (eds), *The New Palgrave: A Dictionary of Economics*, vol. 1 (London, New York, Tokyo: Macmillan).

Kurz, H.D. (1987b) 'Elastizität der industriellen Produktion, Kapitalakkumulation und Einkommensverteilung', in *Postkeynesianismus. Ökonomische Theorie in der Tradition von Keynes, Kalecki und Sraffa* (Marburg: Metropolis).

Kurz, H.D. (1994) 'Growth and distribution', *Review of Political Economy*, 6: 393–420.

Kurz, H.D., Salvadori, N. (1997) *Theory of Production: A Long-Period Analysis* (Cambridge, UK: Cambridge University Press).

Kydland, F., Prescott, H. (1982) 'Time to build and aggregate fluctuations', *Econometrica*, 50: 1345–70.

Laidler, D. (1986) 'The new-classical contribution to macroeconomics', *Banca Nazionale del Lavoro Quarterly Review*, 39: 27–55.

Laidler, D. (1988) 'Taking money seriously', *Canadian Journal of Economics*, 21: 687–713.

Lapavitsas, C. (1994) 'The banking school and the monetary thought of Karl Marx', *Cambridge Journal of Economics*, 18: 447–61.
Lapavitsas, C. (1997) 'Two approaches to the concept of interest-bearing capital', *International Journal of Political Economy*, 27(1): 85–106.
Lapavitsas, C. (1998) 'Currents of monetary theory in classical political economy', *Political Economy: Review of Political Economy and Social Science*, 2: 41–71.
Lapavitsas, C. (2000a) 'Money and the analysis of capitalism: the significance of commodity money', *Review of Radical Political Economics*, 32: 631–56.
Lapavitsas, C. (2000b) 'On Marx's analysis of money hoarding in the turnover of capital', *Review of Political Economy*, 12: 219–35.
Lapavitsas, C., Saad-Filho, A. (2000) 'The supply of credit money and capital accumulation: a critical view of post-Keynesian analysis', *Research in Political Economy*, 18: 309–34.
Lavoie, M. (1984): 'The endogenous flow of credit and the post-Keynesian theory of money', *Journal of Economic Issues*, 18: 771–97.
Lavoie, M. (1992a) *Foundations of Post-Keynesian Economic Analysis* (Aldershot: Edward Elgar).
Lavoie, M. (1992b) 'Jacques Le Bourva's theory of endogenous credit money', *Review of Political Economy*, 4: 436–46.
Lavoie, M. (1993) 'A post-classical view of money, interest, growth and distribution', in G. Mongiovi and C. Rühl (eds), *Macroeconomic Theory: Diversity and Convergence* (Cambridge: Cambridge University Press).
Lavoie, M. (1994) 'Money and credit', in P. Arestis and M. Sawyer (eds), *The Elgar Companion to Radical Political Economy* (Aldershot: Edward Elgar).
Lavoie, M. (1995a) 'Interest rates in post-Keynesian models of growth and distribution', *Metroeconomica*, 46: 146–77.
Lavoie, M. (1995b) 'The Kaleckian model of growth and distribution and its neo-Ricardian and neo-Marxian critiques', *Cambridge Journal of Economics*, 19: 789–818.
Lavoie, M. (1996a) 'Horizontalism, structuralism, liquidity preference and the principle of increasing risk', *Scottish Journal of Political Economy*, 43: 275–300.
Lavoie, M. (1996b) 'Traverse, hysteresis and normal rates of capacity utilisation in Kaleckian models of growth and distribution', *Review of Radical Political Economics*, 28: 113–47.
Lavoie, M. (1996c) 'Monetary policy in an economy with endogenous credit money', in G. Deleplace and E. Nell (eds), *Money in Motion: The Post Keynesian and Circulation Approaches* (London: Macmillan).
Lavoie, M. (1999) 'The credit-led supply of deposits and the demand for money: Kaldor's reflux mechanism as previously endorsed by Joan Robinson', *Cambridge Journal of Economics*, 23: 103–13.
Lavoie, M. (2001) 'Pricing', in R.P.F. Holt and S. Pressman (eds), *A New Guide to Post Keynesian Economics* (London, New York: Routledge).
Lavoie, M. (2002) 'The Kaleckian growth model with target return pricing and conflict inflation', in M. Setterfield (ed.), *The Economics of Demand-led Growth* (Cheltenham: Edward Elgar).
Lavoie, M. (2003a) 'A primer on endogenous credit money', in L.-P. Rochon and S. Rossi (eds), *Modern Theories of Money: The Nature and the Role of Money in Capitalist Economies* (Cheltenham: Edward Elgar).

Lavoie, M. (2003b) 'Kaleckian effective demand and Sraffian normal prices: towards a reconciliation', *Review of Political Economy*, 15: 53–74.

Lavoie, M. (2004) 'The New Consensus on monetary policy seen from a Post-Keynesian perspective', in M. Lavoie and M. Seccareccia (eds), *Central Banking in the Modern World: Alternative Perspectives* (Cheltenham: Edward Elgar).

Lavoie, M. (2005) 'Changing definitions: a comment on Davidson's critique of King's history of Post Keynesianism', *Journal of Post Keynesian Economics*, 27: 371–6.

Lavoie, M. (2006a) *Introduction to Post-Keynesian Economics* (Basingstoke: Palgrave Macmillan).

Lavoie, M. (2006b) 'Do heterodox theories have anything in common? A post-Keynesian point of view', *Intervention. Journal of Economics*, 3: 87–112.

Lavoie, M., Godley, W. (2001/2) 'Kaleckian models of growth in a coherent stock-flow monetary framework: a Kaldorian view', *Journal of Post Keynesian Economics*, 22: 277–311.

Lavoie, M., Kriesler, P. (2005) *Capacity utilisation, inflation and monetary policy: Marxian models and the New Keynesian consensus*, ROBINSON Working Paper 05-02 (Ottawa: University of Ottawa).

Lavoie, M., Rodriguez, G., Seccareccia M. (2004) 'Transformational growth, interest rates, and the golden rule', in G. Argyrous, M. Forstater and G. Mongiovi (eds), *Growth, Distribution, and Effective Demand* (Armonk, NY: M.E. Sharpe).

Layard, R., Nickell, S., Jackman, R. (1991) *Unemployment: Macroeconomic Performance and the Labour Market* (Oxford: Oxford University Press).

Le Bourva, J. (1992) 'Money creation and credit multipliers', *Review of Political Economy*, 4: 447–66.

Lee, F. (2003) 'Pricing and prices', in J.E. King (ed.), *The Elgar Companion to Post Keynesian Economics* (Cheltenham: Edward Elgar).

Leon-Ledesma, M.A., Thirlwall, A.P. (2002) 'The endogeneity of the natural rate of growth', *Cambridge Journal of Economics*, 26: 441–59.

Lima, G.T. (2000) 'Market concentration and technological innovation in a dynamic model of growth and distribution', *Banca Nazionale del Lavoro Quarterly Review*, 53: 447–75.

Lima, G.T., Meirelles, A.J.A. (2006) 'Debt, financial fragility, and economic growth: a Post Keynesian macromodel', *Journal of Post Keynesian Economics*, 29: 93–115.

Lima, G.T., Setterfield, M. (2006) *Inflation targeting and macroeconomic stability in a Post Keynesian economy*, paper presented at the 9th Post Keynesian Conference, Kansas City, 14–18 September.

Lipietz, A. (1982) 'Credit money: a condition permitting inflationary crisis', *Review of Radical Political Economics*, 14: 49–57.

Lopez, J. (2002) 'Two versions of the principle of effective demand: Kalecki and Keynes', *Journal of Post Keynesian Economics*, 24: 609–22.

Lopez, J., Mott, T. (1999) 'Kalecki versus Keynes on the determinants of investment', *Review of Political Economy*, 11: 291–301.

Lucas, R.E. (1972) 'Expectations and the neutrality of money', *Journal of Economic Theory*, 4: 103–24.

Lucas, R.E. (1976) 'Econometric policy evaluation: a critique', *Carnegie Rochester Conference Series on Public Policy*, 1: 19–46.

Lucas, R.E. (1996) 'Nobel lecture: monetary neutrality', *Journal of Political Economy*, 104: 661–82.

Mankiw, N.G. (1992) 'The reincarnation of Keynesian economics', *European Economic Review*, 36: 559–65.
Mankiw, N.G. (2001) 'The inexorable and mysterious tradeoff between inflation and unemployment', *The Economic Journal*, 111: C45–C61.
Marglin, S.A. (1984a) 'Growth, distribution and inflation: a centennial synthesis', *Cambridge Journal of Economics*, 8: 115–44.
Marglin, S.A. (1984b) *Growth, Distribution and Prices* (Cambridge, MA: Harvard University Press).
Marglin, S.A., Bhaduri, A. (1990) 'Profit squeeze and Keynesian theory', in S.A. Marglin and J.B. Schor (eds), *The Golden Age of Capitalism: Reinterpreting the Postwar Experience* (Oxford: Oxford University Press).
Marglin, S.A., Bhaduri, A. (1991) 'Profit squeeze and Keynesian theory', in E.J. Nell and W. Semmler (eds), *Nicholas Kaldor and Mainstream Economics* (Basingstoke, London: Macmillan).
Marx, K. (1861–63) *Theorien über den Mehrwert. Zweiter Teil, Marx-Engels-Werke,* Bd. 26.2 (Berlin: Dietz Verlag), 1967.
Marx, K. (1867) *Capital. A Critique of Political Economy. Volume I. The Process of Capitalist Production,* Translated from the third German edition (New York: International Publishers, 1967).
Marx, K. (1885) *Capital. A Critique of Political Economy. Volume II. The Process of Circulation of Capital,* Translated from the second German edition (New York: International Publishers, 1967).
Marx, K. (1894) *Capital. A Critique of Political Economy. Volume III. The Process of Capitalist Production as a Whole* (New York: International Publishers, 1967).
Matthews, P.H. (1996) 'The modern foundations of Marx's monetary economics', *The European Journal of the History of Economic Thought*, 3: 61–83.
McCallum, B. (2001) 'Monetary policy analysis in models without money', *Federal Reserve Bank of St. Louis Review*, 83(4): 145–60.
McCombie, J.S.L., Roberts, M. (2002) 'The role of balance of payments in economic growth', in M. Setterfield (ed.), *The Economics of Demand-led Growth* (Cheltenham: Edward Elgar).
McKenna, E.J., Zannoni, D.C. (1990) 'The relation between the rate of interest and investment in post-Keynesian and neo-Ricardian analysis', *Eastern Economic Journal*, 16: 133–43.
Meyer, J.R., Kuh, E. (1957) *The Investment Decision* (Cambridge, MA: Harvard University Press).
Meyer, L.H. (2001) 'Does money matter?', *Federal Reserve Bank of St. Louis Review*, 83(5): 1–15.
Minsky, H. (1975) *John Maynard Keynes* (London: Macmillan).
Minsky, H. (1977) 'The financial instability hypothesis', *Challenge*, 20(1): 20–7.
Minsky, H.P. (1986) *Stabilizing an Unstable Economy* (New Haven: Yale University Press).
Modigliani, F., Miller, M.H. (1958) 'The cost of capital, corporation finance and the theory of investment', *American Economic Review*, 48: 261–97.
Mollo, M.L.R. (1999) 'The endogeneity of money: post-Keynesian and Marxian concepts compared', *Research in Political Economy*, 17: 3–26.
Mongiovi, G., Rühl, C. (1993) 'Monetary theory after Sraffa', in G. Mongiovi and C. Rühl (eds), *Macroeconomic Theory: Diversity and Convergence* (Cambridge: Cambridge University Press).

Monvoisin, V., Rochon, L.-P. (2006) 'The Post-Keynesian consensus, the new consensus and endogenous money', in C. Gnos and L.-P. Rochon (eds), *Post-Keynesian Principles of Economic Policy* (Cheltenham: Edward Elgar).
Moore, B.J. (1988) *Horizontalists and Verticalists: The Macroeconomics of Credit Money* (Cambridge: Cambridge University Press).
Moore, B.J. (1989) 'The endogeneity of credit money', *Review of Political Economy*, 1: 65–93.
Mott, T., Slattery, E. (1994) 'The influence of changes in income distribution on aggregate demand in a Kaleckian model: stagnation vs exhilaration reconsidered', in P. Davidson and J. Kregel (eds), *Employment, Growth and Finance* (Aldershot: Edward Elgar).
Naastepad, C.W.M. (2006) 'Technology, demand and distribution: a cumulative growth model with an application to the Dutch productivity growth slowdown', *Cambridge Journal of Economics*, 30: 403–34.
Naastepad, C.W.M., Storm, S. (2007) 'OECD demand regimes (1960–2000)', *Journal of Post Keynesian Economics*, 29: 211–46.
Ndikumana, L. (1999) 'Debt service, financing constraints, and fixed investment: evidence from panel data', *Journal of Post Keynesian Economics*, 21: 455–78.
Nell, E. (1988) 'Does the rate of interest determine the rate of profit?', *Political Economy*, 4: 263–8.
Nell, E. (1996) 'The circuit of money in a production economy', in G. Deleplace and E. Nell (eds), *Money in Motion: The Post Keynesian and Circulation Approaches* (London: Macmillan).
Nell, E. (2002) 'On realizing profits in money', *Review of Political Economy*, 14: 519–30.
Niehans, J. (1978) *The Theory of Money* (Baltimore, London: John Hopkins University Press).
Ohlin, B. (1937a) 'Alternative theories of the rate of interest', *The Economic Journal*, 47: 423–7.
Ohlin, B. (1937b) 'Some notes on the Stockholm theory of savings and investment', *The Economic Journal*, 47: 53–69, 221–40.
Onaran, Ö., Stockhammer, E. (2004) 'Accumulation, distribution and employment: a structural VAR approach to a post-Keynesian macro model', *Structural Change and Economic Dynamics*, 15: 421–47.
Onaran, Ö., Stockhammer, E. (2005) 'Two different export-oriented growth strategies: accumulation and distribution in Turkey and in South Korea', *Emerging Markets Finance and Trade*, 41(1): 65–89.
Onaran, Ö., Stockhammer, E. (2006) 'Do profits affect investment and employment? An empirical test based on the Bhaduri–Marglin model', in E. Hein, A. Heise and A. Truger (eds), *Wages, Employment, Distribution and Growth: International Perspectives* (Basingstoke: Palgrave Macmillan).
Palacio-Vera, A. (2005) 'The "modern" view of macroeconomics: some critical reflections', *Cambridge Journal of Economics*, 29: 747–67.
Palley, T.I. (1994) 'Competing views of the money supply process: theory and evidence', *Metroeconomica*, 45: 67–88.
Palley, T.I. (1996a) *Post Keynesian Economics: Debt, Distribution and the Macro Economy* (London, Basingstoke: Macmillan).
Palley, T.I. (1996b) 'Accommodationism versus structuralism: time for an accommodation', *Journal of Post Keynesian Economics*, 18: 585–94.

Palley, T.I. (2002) 'Endogenous money: what it is and why it matters', *Metroeconomica*, 53: 152–80.
Palley, T.I. (2006) 'A Post-Keynesian framework for monetary policy: Why interest rate operating procedures are not enough', in C. Gnos and L.-P. Rochon (eds), *Post-Keynesian Principles of Economic Policy* (Cheltenham: Edward Elgar).
Panico, C. (1980) 'Marx's analysis of the relationship between the rate of interest and the rate of profit', *Cambridge Journal of Economics*, 4: 363–78.
Panico, C. (1985) 'Market forces and the relation between the rates of interest and profit', *Contributions to Political Economy*, 4: 37–60.
Panico, C. (1988) 'Marx on the banking sector and the interest rate: some notes for a discussion', *Science and Society*, 52: 310–25.
Panico, C. (1997) 'Government deficits in post-Keynesian theories of growth and distribution', *Contributions to Political Economy*, 16: 61–86.
Parguez, A. (1996) 'Beyond scarcity: a reappraisal of the theory of the monetary circuit', in G. Deleplace and E. Nell (eds), *Money in Motion* (Basingstoke: Macmillan).
Parguez, A., Seccareccia, M. (2000) 'The credit theory of money: the monetary circuit approach', in J. Smithin (ed.), *What is Money?* (London, New York: Routledge).
Park, M.S. (1997) 'Accumulation, capacity utilisation and distribution', *Contributions to Political Economy*, 16: 87–101.
Pasinetti, L.L. (1974) *Growth and Income Distribution* (Cambridge: Cambridge University Press).
Pasinetti, L.L. (2000) 'Critique of the neoclassical theory of growth and distribution', *Banca Nazionale del Lavoro Quarterly Review*, 53: 383–431.
Pasinetti, L.L., Scazzieri, R. (1987) 'Capital theory: paradoxes', in J. Eatwell, M. Milgate and P. Newman (eds), *The New Palgrave: A Dictionary of Economics, vol. 1* (London, New York, Tokyo: Macmillan).
Pivetti, M. (1985) 'On the monetary explanation of distribution', *Political Economy*, 1: 73–103.
Pivetti, M. (1987a) 'Interest and profit in Smith, Ricardo and Marx', *Political Economy*, 3: 63–74.
Pivetti, M. (1987b) 'Distribution theories: classical', in J. Eatwell, M. Milgate and P. Newman (eds), *The New Palgrave: A Dictionary of Economics. vol. 1* (London, New York, Tokyo: Macmillan).
Pivetti, M. (1991) *An Essay on Money and Distribution* (Basingstoke: Macmillan).
Pivetti, M. (2001) 'Money endogeneity and monetary non-neutrality: a Sraffian perspective', in L.-P. Rochon and M. Vernengo (eds), *Credit, Interest Rates and the Open Economy: Essays in Horizontalism* (Cheltenham: Edward Elgar).
Plosser, C.I. (1989) 'Understanding real business cycles', *Journal of Economic Perspectives*, 3: 51–77.
Pollin, R. (1991) 'Two theories of money supply endogeneity: some empirical evidence', *Journal of Post Keynesian Economics*, 13: 366–96.
Realfonzo, R. (2003) 'Circuit theory', in J.E. King (ed.), *The Elgar Companion to Post Keynesian Economics* (Cheltenham: Edward Elgar).
Renaud, J.-F. (2000) 'The problem of the monetary realisation of profits in a Post Keynesian sequential financing model: two solutions of the Kaleckian option', *Review of Political Economy*, 12: 285–303.

Reuten, G. (1988) 'The money expression of value and the credit system: a value-form theoretic outline', *Capital & Class*, 35: 121–41.

Reuten, G. (1995) 'Conceptual collapses. A note on value-form theory', *Review of Radical Political Economics*, 27: 104–10.

Richardson, D.R. (1986) 'Asimakopulos on Kalecki and Keynes on finance, investment and saving', *Cambridge Journal of Economics*, 10: 191–8.

Riese, H. (1983) 'Geldökonomie, Keynes und die Anderen. Kritik der monetären Grundlagen der Orthodoxie', *Ökonomie und Gesellschaft*, 1: 103–60.

Riese, H. (1986) *Theorie der Inflation* (Tübingen: Mohr).

Riese, H. (1987) 'Aspekte eines monetären Keynesianismus – Kritik und Gegenentwurf', in *Postkeynesianismus. Ökonomische Theorie in der Tradition von Keynes, Kalecki und Sraffa* (Marburg: Metropolis).

Robertson, D.H. (1937) 'Alternative theories of the rate of interest', *The Economic Journal*, 47: 428–36.

Robertson, D.H. (1938a) 'Mr. Keynes and finance', *The Economic Journal*, 48: 314–18.

Robertson, D.H. (1938b) 'Mr. Keynes and finance: a comment', *The Economic Journal*, 48: 555–6.

Robertson, D.H. (1940) 'Effective demand and the multiplier', in Robertson, D.H., *Essays in Monetary Theory* (London: P.S. King).

Robinson, J. (1953) 'The production function and the theory of capital', *The Review of Economic Studies*, 21: 81–106.

Robinson, J. (1956) *The Accumulation of Capital* (London: Macmillan).

Robinson, J. (1962) *Essays in the Theory of Economic Growth* (London: Macmillan).

Rochon, L.-P. (1999) *Credit, Money and Production: An Alternative Post-Keynesian Approach* (Cheltenham: Edward Elgar).

Rochon, L.-P. (2000) '1939–1958: was Kaldor an endogenist?', *Metroeconomica*, 51: 191–220.

Rochon, L.-P. (2001a) 'Horizontalism: setting the record straight', in L.-P. Rochon and M. Vernengo (ed.), *Credit, Interest Rates and the Open Economy: Essays in Horizontalism* (Cheltenham: Edward Elgar).

Rochon, L.-P. (2001b) 'Cambridge's contribution to endogenous money: Robinson and Kahn on credit and money', *Review of Political Economy*, 12: 287–307.

Rochon, L.-P. (2003) 'On money and endogenous money: Post Keynesian and circulation approaches', in L.-P. Rochon and S. Rossi (eds), *Modern Theories of Money* (Cheltenham: Edward Elgar).

Rochon, L.-P. (2005) 'The existence of monetary profits within the monetary circuit', in G. Fontana and R. Realfonzo (eds), *The Monetary Theory of Production: Tradition and Perspectives* (Basingstoke: Palgrave Macmillan).

Rochon, L.-P., Rossi, S. (2004) 'Central banking in the monetary circuit', in M. Lavoie and M. Seccareccia (eds), *Central Banking in the Modern World: Alternative Perspectives* (Cheltenham: Edward Elgar).

Rochon, L.-P., Rossi, S. (2006) 'Inflation targeting, economic performance, and income distribution: a monetary macroeconomics analysis', *Journal of Post Keynesian Economics*, 28: 615–38.

Rochon, L.-P., Setterfield, M. (2006) *Interest rates, income distribution and monetary policy dominance: Post-Keynesians and the 'fair rate' of interest*. Paper presented at the 9th Post Keynesian Conference, Kansas City, 14–18 September.

Rochon, L.-P., Vernengo, M. (2003) 'State money and the real world: or chartalism and its discontent', *Journal of Post Keynesian Economics*, 26: 57–67.
Rogers, C. (1989) *Money, Interest and Capital* (Cambridge: Cambridge University Press).
Romer, D. (1993) 'The new Keynesian synthesis', *Journal of Economic Perspectives*, 7: 5–22.
Romer, D. (2000) 'Keynesian macroeconomics without the LM curve', *Journal of Economic Perspectives*, 14(2): 149–69.
Roncaglia, A. (2005) *The Wealth of Ideas: A History of Economic Thought* (Cambridge: Cambridge University Press).
Rossi, S. (2005) 'Central banking in a monetary theory of production: the economics of payment finality from a circular-flow perspective', in G. Fontana and R. Realfonzo (eds), *The Monetary Theory of Production: Tradition and Perspectives* (Basingstoke: Palgrave Macmillan).
Rotheim, R. (1981) 'Keynes's monetary theory of value', *Journal of Post Keynesian Economics*, 3: 568–85.
Rotheim, R.J. (1991) 'Marx, Keynes and the theory of a monetary economy', in G.A. Caravale (ed.), *Marx and Modern Economic Analysis*, vol. II (Aldershot: Edward Elgar).
Rousseas, S. (1998) *Post Keynesian Monetary Economics*, 3rd edn (Basingstoke: Macmillan).
Rowthorn, R.E. (1977) 'Conflict, inflation and money', *Cambridge Journal of Economics*, 1: 215–39.
Rowthorn, R.E. (1981) 'Demand, real wages and economic growth', *Thames Papers in Political Economy*, (Autumn): 1–39.
Rowthorn, R.E. (1995) 'Capital formation and unemployment', *Oxford Review of Economic Policy*, 11(1): 26–39.
Rowthorn, R.E. (1999) 'Unemployment, wage bargaining and capital–labour substitution', *Cambridge Journal of Economics*, 23: 413–25.
Rubin, I.I. (1973) *Studien zur Marxschen Werttheorie* (Frankfurt am Main: Europäische Verlagsanstalt).
Sardoni, C. (1986) 'Marx and Keynes on effective demand and unemployment', *History of Political Economy*, 18: 419–41.
Sardoni, C. (1987) *Marx and Keynes on Economic Recession* (Brighton: Wheatsheaf Books).
Sardoni, C. (1997a) 'Marx's theory of money and interest – between Robertson and Keynes?', in R. Bellofiore (ed.), *Marxian Economics: A Reappraisal. Essays on vol. III of Capital* (London: Macmillan).
Sardoni, C. (1997b) 'Keynes and Marx', in G.C. Harcourt and P. Riach (eds), *A 'Second Edition' of the General Theory*, vol. II (London: Routledge).
Sawyer, M. (1985) *The Economics of Michal Kalecki* (Armonk, NY: M.E. Sharpe).
Sawyer, M. (1997) 'Income distribution, macroeconomic analysis and barriers to full employment', *Journal of Income Distribution*, 7: 147–60.
Sawyer, M. (2001a) 'Kalecki on money and finance', *The European Journal of the History of Economic Thought*, 8: 487–508.
Sawyer, M. (2001b) 'Kalecki on imperfect competition, inflation and money', *Cambridge Journal of Economics*, 25: 245–61.
Sawyer, M. (2001c) 'The NAIRU: a critical appraisal', in P. Arestis and M. Sawyer (eds), *Money, Finance and Capitalist Development* (Cheltenham: Edward Elgar).

Sawyer, M. (2002) 'The NAIRU, aggregate demand and investment', *Metroeconomica*, 53: 66–94.
Sawyer, M. (2006) 'A Kaleckian analysis of monetary policy', *Intervention: Journal of Economics*, 3: 331–49.
Schiantarelli, F. (1996) 'Financial constraints and investment: methodological issues and international evidence', *Oxford Review of Economic Policy*, 12: 70–89.
Schumpeter, J.A. (1954) *History of Economic Analysis* (New York: Oxford University Press).
Sebastiani, M. (1991) 'Observations on Marx's and Kalecki's approaches to the theory of effective demand', in G.A. Caravale (ed.), *Marx and Modern Economic Analysis*, vol. II (Aldershot: Edward Elgar).
Seccareccia, M. (1996) 'Post Keynesian fundism and monetary circulation', in G. Deleplace and E. Nell (eds), *Money in Motion* (London: Macmillan).
Seccareccia, M. (1998) 'Wicksellian norm, central bank real interest targeting and macroeconomic performance', in P. Arestis and M. Sawyer (eds), *The Political Economy of Central Banking* (Cheltenham: Edward Elgar).
Seccareccia, M. (2003) 'Pricing, investment and the financing of production within the framework of the monetary circuit: some preliminary evidence', in L.-P. Rochon and S. Rossi (eds), *Modern Theories of Money* (Cheltenham: Edward Elgar).
Setterfield, M. (ed.) (2002) *The Economics of Demand-led Growth: Challenging the Supply-side Vision of the Long Run* (Cheltenham: Edward Elgar).
Setterfield, M. (2004) 'Central banking, stability and macroeconomic outcomes: a comparison of New Consensus and Post-Keynesian monetary macroeconomics', in M. Lavoie and M. Seccareccia (eds), *Central Banking in the Modern World: Alternative Perspectives* (Cheltenham: Edward Elgar).
Setterfield, M. (2006a) 'Is inflation targeting compatible with Post Keynesian economics?', *Journal of Post Keynesian Economics*, 28: 653–71.
Setterfield, M. (2006b) *Macroeconomics without the LM curve: an alternative view*, paper presented at the 9th Post Keynesian Conference, Kansas City, 14–18 September.
Shaikh, A. (1978a) 'An introduction to the history of crisis theories', in Union for Radical Political Economics (ed.), *US Capitalism in Crisis* (New York: Union for Radical Political Economics).
Shaikh, A. (1978b) 'Political economy and capitalism: notes on Dobb's theory of crisis', *Cambridge Journal of Economics*, 2: 233–51.
Shaikh, A. (1983a) 'Economic crises', in T. Bottomore (ed.), *A Dictionary of Marxist Thought* (Cambridge, MA: Harvard University Press).
Shaikh, A. (1983b) 'Falling rate of profit', in T. Bottomore (ed.), *A Dictionary of Marxist Thought* (Cambridge, MA: Harvard University Press).
Shaikh, A. (1987) 'The falling rate of profit and the economic crisis in the US', in Union for Radical Political Economics (ed.), *The Imperiled Economy: Book I. Macroeconomics from a Left Perspective* (New York: Union for Radical Political Economics).
Smith, A. (1776) *An Inquiry into the Nature and Causes of the Wealth of Nations*, R.H. Campbell and A.S. Skinner (eds), The Glasgow Edition of the Works and Correspondence of Adam Smith, vol. I and II, (Oxford: Clarendon Press, 1976).
Smithin, J. (1997) 'An alternative monetary model of inflation and growth', *Review of Political Economy*, 9: 395–409.

Smithin, J. (2003a) *Controversies in Monetary Economics,* revised edition (Cheltenham: Edward Elgar).

Smithin, J. (2003b) 'Interest rates, profits and economic growth', in E. Nell and M. Forstater (eds), *Reinventing Functional Finance: Transformational Growth and Full Employment* (Cheltenham: Edward Elgar).

Smithin, J. (2004) 'Interest rate operating procedures and income distribution', in M. Lavoie and M. Seccareccia (eds.), *Central Banking in the Modern World: Alternative Perspectives* (Aldershot: Edward Elgar).

Snippe, J. (1985) 'Finance, savings and investment in Keynes's economics', *Cambridge Journal of Economics,* 9: 257–69.

Snowdon, B., Vane, H. (2005) *Modern Macroeconomics: Its Origins, Development and Current State* (Cheltenham: Edward Elgar).

Sowell, T. (1972) *Say's Law: An Historical Analysis* (Princeton: Princeton University Press).

Sraffa, P. (1960) *Production of Commodities by Means of Commodities* (Cambridge: Cambridge University Press).

Steindl, J. (1952) *Maturity and Stagnation in American Capitalism,* 2nd edn (New York: Monthly Review Press, 1976).

Steindl, J. (1981) 'Some comments on the three versions of Kalecki's theory of the trade cycle', in J. Lois (ed.), *Studies in Economic Theory and Practice* (Amsterdam: Elsevier).

Stiglitz, J. (1997) 'Reflections on the natural rate hypothesis', *Journal of Economic Perspectives,* 11: 3–10.

Stiglitz, J., Weiss, A. (1981) 'Credit rationing in markets with imperfect information', *American Economic Review,* 71: 393–410.

Stockhammer, E. (2004a) 'Is there an equilibrium rate of unemployment in the long run?', *Review of Political Economy,* 16: 59–77.

Stockhammer, E. (2004b) *The Rise of Unemployment in Europe: A Keynesian Approach* (Cheltenham: Edward Elgar).

Stockhammer, E. (2004c) 'Financialisation and the slowdown of accumulation', *Cambridge Journal of Economics,* 28: 719–41.

Stockhammer, E. (2005/6) 'Shareholder value orientation and the investment–profit puzzle', *Journal of Post Keynesian Economics,* 28: 193–215.

Stockhammer, E. (2006) *Is the NAIRU a Monetarist, New Keynesian, Post Keynesian or Marxist theory?,* Working Paper, No. 96, March (Vienna: Vienna University of Economics & B.A.).

Sweezy, P.M. (1942) *Theory of Capitalist Development* (New York: Monthly Review Press).

Sylos-Labini, P. (1969) *Oligopoly and Technical Progress,* 2nd edn (Cambridge: Cambridge University Press).

Sylos-Labini, P. (1979) 'Prices and income distribution in manufacturing industry', *Journal of Post Keynesian Economics,* 11: 3–25.

Taylor, J.B. (2000) 'Teaching modern macroeconomics at the principles level', *American Economic Review,* 90 (2): 90–4.

Taylor, L. (1985) 'A stagnationist model of economic growth', *Cambridge Journal of Economics,* 9: 383–403.

Taylor, L. (1991) *Income Distribution, Inflation, and Growth: Lectures on Structuralist Macroeconomic Theory* (Cambridge, MA: MIT Press).

Taylor, L. (2004) *Reconstructing Macroeconomics: Structuralists' Proposals and Critiques of the Mainstream* (Cambridge, MA. London: Harvard University Press).

Terzi, A. (1986) 'Finance, investment and saving: a comment on Asimakopulos', *Cambridge Journal of Economics*, 10: 77–80.

Terzi, A. (1986/87) 'The independence of finance from saving: a flow-of-funds interpretation', *Journal of Post Keynesian Economics*, 9: 188–97.

Thirlwall, A. (1979) 'The balance of payments constraint as an explanation of international growth rate differences', *Banca Nazionale del Lavoro Quarterly Review*, 22: 45–53.

Tobin, J. (1993) 'Price flexibility and output stability: an old Keynesian view', *Journal of Economic Perspectives*, 7: 45–65.

Trautwein, H.-M. (2000) 'The credit view, old and new', *Journal of Economic Surveys*, 14: 155–89.

Trigg, A.B. (2006) *Marxian Reproduction Schema: Money and Aggregate Demand in a Capitalist Economy* (Abingdon: Routledge).

Van Parijs, P. (1980) 'The falling-rate-of-profit theory of crisis: a rational reconstruction by way of obituary', *Review of Radical Political Economics*, 12: 1–16.

Van Treeck, T. (2007) *Reconsidering the investment–profit nexus in finance-led economies: an ARDL-based approach*, IMK Working Paper, 1/2007 (Duesseldorf: Macroeconomic Policy Institute (IMK) in the Hans Boeckler Foundation).

Vernengo, M., Rochon, L.-P. (2001) 'Kaldor and Robinson on money and growth', *The European Journal of the History of Economic Thought*, 8: 75–103.

Walsh, C.E. (2002) 'Teaching inflation targeting: an analysis for intermediate macro', *Journal of Economic Education*, 33: 333–46.

Weeks, J. (1981) *Capital and Exploitation* (Princeton: Princeton University Press).

Wicksell, K. (1898) *Geldzins und Güterpreise. Eine Studie über die den Tauschwert des Geldes bestimmenden Ursachen* (Jena: Fischer).

Williams, M. (1992) 'Marxists on money, value and labour-power: a response to Cartelier', *Cambridge Journal of Economics*, 16: 439–45.

Williams, M. (2000) 'Why Marx neither has nor needs a commodity theory of money', *Review of Political Economy*, 12: 435–51.

Wolfson, M.H. (1996) 'A post Keynesian theory of credit rationing', *Journal of Post Keynesian Economics*, 18: 443–70.

Wray, L.R. (1988a) 'The monetary theory of distribution – a critique of Pivetti', *Political Economy*, 4: 269–74.

Wray, L.R. (1988b) 'Profit expectations and the investment–saving relation', *Journal of Post Keynesian Economics*, 11: 131–47.

Wray, L.R. (1990) *Money and Credit in Capitalist Economies: The Endogenous Money Approach* (Aldershot: Edward Elgar).

Wray, L.R. (1992a) 'Alternative approaches to money and interest rates', *Journal of Economic Issues*, 26: 1–33.

Wray, L.R. (1992b) 'Alternative theories of the rate of interest', *Cambridge Journal of Economics*, 16: 69–89.

Wray, L.R. (1995) 'Keynesian monetary theory: liquidity preference or black box horizontalism', *Journal of Economic Issues*, 29: 273–82.

Wray, L.R. (1998) *Understanding Modern Money: The Key to Full Employment and Price Stability* (Cheltenham: Edward Elgar).

Index